A POCKET HISTORY OF SEX

in the

TWENTIETH CENTURY

A POCKET HISTORY OF SEX

in the

TWENTIETH CENTURY

[*a memoir*]

Jane Vandenburgh

COUNTERPOINT
BERKELEY

The author is grateful for the encouragement of the editors of the following
publications, in which some of this book's materials appeared in earlier forms:
Nimrod, the *Los Angeles Times Magazine*, *Image Magazine*,
and San Francisco's *Focus Magazine*.

The author's understanding of the physical ordeal undertaken by those who
walked two thousand miles from Independence, Missouri, to settle the West
is indebted to Keith Heyer Meldahl's magnificent *Hard Road West:
History and Geology Along the Gold Rush Trail*.

Library of Congress Cataloging-in-Publication Data

VANDENBURGH, JANE.
A pocket history of sex in the twentieth century : a memoir / Jane Vandenburgh.
p. cm.
ISBN 978-1-58243-459-9
1. Vandenburgh, Jane. I. Title.

PS3572.A65 Z46
813'.54—dc22

2008035702

Cover design by Natalya Balnova
Interior design by Megan Cooney
Printed in the United States of America

COUNTERPOINT
2117 Fourth Street
Suite D
Berkeley, CA 94710

www.counterpointpress.com

Distributed by Publishers Group West

10 9 8 7 6 5 4 3 2 1

THIS IS A WORK of nonfiction whose events happened in the real world. I have, however, employed some of the techniques of fiction in order to tell the story that exists most vividly in my recollections. I have also changed the names of some of the participants in order to protect their identities.

For my aunt, Janet Vandenburgh Godfrey,
who didn't get the starring role in this production, but is nevertheless its hero.

CONTENTS

it seems they were all cheated of some marvellous experience
which is not going to go wasted on me which is why I'm telling you about it

—FRANK O'HARA

A POCKET HISTORY OF SEX

in the

TWENTIETH CENTURY

1

THE PULL OF GRAVITY

1
Normalcy

THE LAST HOUSE I will live in with both my parents and my two brothers is one built on a sandy lot in Redondo, a development in a beach town near Los Angeles. Our house is distinguished only by the pepper tree our father planted out in front, where other, more normal dads would dump topsoil and then scatter lawn seed. The house is new, but there isn't any hope for it. It smells of wet cement, as if something is wrong with its foundation. Cold leaks upward through the floorboards, drawing body heat down and out of our bare feet, back to the lot's damp sand.

My brothers and I are blond, tan, tousle-haired beach rats, seriously unkempt. Will and Geo and I know, because one of our more elegant San Marino relatives told us, that we are being raised "by Gawd." "By Gawd, quite obviously, since John and Maggie cannot be bawwthured." Our parents' parenting is described by our Aunt Nan as *benign neglect*.

My brothers and I know no discipline. We wander for miles, going off to the beach or to the pier to fish. We ride our bikes on the esplanade and come home late, idly poking sticks into the already rotting stucco on the outside of the houses to get at the scraps of tar paper, which we pull out and chew like gum.

It is the 1950s, and both of our parents—who come from privileged backgrounds—believe they've ended up in this dump because their money and their luck ran out. Luck is no longer John and Maggie's specialty. They can still count on one or the other set of grandparents, however, to swoop in to fix things when they mess up. My grandparents say it's always trouble whenever the phone rings and it concerns Maggie and Johnny. That's when they have to make phone calls to The Powers That Be, or help my parents out financially. Buying them this house at the beach in Redondo may be one of their last-ditch attempts, getting a starter home for people no longer starting out.

Redondo is an object lesson: How Normal People Are Content to Live.

Other families seem less ambiguous about what you're supposed to do. You get this job. You buy that house. You raise your children. You build a foursquare life, you go forever to live in it.

On Avenue B in Redondo, our parents are losing any wish they've ever had to fit in. Folks believe in America as a Melting Pot, in which everyone urgently needs to learn to conform. The Melting Pot reminds me of Little Black Sambo, who is chased by a tiger around a tree every Saturday morning on cartoons: They go round and round until they melt together into butter.

Redondo is *I Love Lucy*, which I hate for its noisy domestic chaos, and *My Little Margie*, which I like because Gale Storm has a good haircut and a job she keeps from week to week. The name Gale Storm also contains the one grown-up joke I understand.

There is little about being an adult that is clear to me. What I do know is that the foursquare life doesn't impress my parents. Homeownership does nothing for them, either. Homeownership involves housekeeping, home maintenance, staying in one place. And awwwctually? our mother remarks as she swooshes her paintbrush around in the bright dyes she uses to paint on Bristol board. Truuuthfully? I'd *much* prefer to move.

Homeownership is a family tradition; real estate is what amounts to almost a family religion, everything being predicated on growth, on the ever-skyward direction of California land values. Everyone in our family has always owned houses, plural—the main one in town and also the ratty dream shack in the mountains or up the coast in Cambria, or at the beach for the summertime, when—like all real Californians—you hike and fish and swim. You very vehemently *picnic*, as my mother says, or you *are forced* to camp out in those gawd-awful sleeping bags on the wretched sleeping porch that is never heated, in order to simulate being in the tyrannical Out of Doors.

My god how I hate *na-chur*, our mother likes to say, how it's all red in tooth and claw.

She says these things to any and all who listen as she works at the kitchen table, where she is painting the storyboards she makes for Disney. Homeownership doesn't make you *a good person*, she says. The Vandenburgh Seniors *awwwwnd* the Whites *awwwwnd* the Ainsworth-Rutherford-Rolands all own *houses, plural,* she goes on, and did we imagine this was anything that got them immediately into their version of heaven? Honestly?

She glances up from what she is doing, one eye winked shut against the upward bloom of her cigarette smoke. She then flicks her gaze over the four corners of her work.

Honestly? she asks again. Just look how crappily *they* turned out.

She inhales smoke, changes brushes in the water jar. Shitheels, she pronounces, whispering to herself.

〇〇〇

Ours is a blue-collar neighborhood where the kids are tough and the fathers—cops, plumbers, workers in tool-and-die—will beat up a son who seems to be turning out to be a pansy. No one aside from our father—who is an architect—drives off to work on Wilshire Boulevard on the Miracle Mile wearing a dark suit, white dress shirt, and bowtie. No one aside from our artist mother acts like she does, sitting at the kitchen table, drinking beer and smoking cigarettes, as she first inks in and then colors the Donald Duck comics that will be printed over Walt Disney's famous signature. There is no one else playing Bartôk, as our father does late into the evening, on the baby grand that takes up too much of the tiny living room.

There is bingo in our neighborhood and there is bowling, but my parents don't go.

My parents can neither abide the normal world—the house, the marriage, the children—nor exit it entirely. They aren't rich enough to afford their privacy. They won't live long enough to find the more tolerant cultural atmosphere my brothers and I will someday enjoy (and even that tolerance will sometimes seem like a window only, one that is opened to let in light and air, but that can easily be slammed down and shuttered again).

Our little beach house is full of big, heavy, old-fashioned furniture that our parents inherited from Various Dead Rich Relatives Who Never Gave a Damn About Us When They Were Alive, as our mother will explain to anyone even vaguely interested. These dead relatives include enfeebled grammas and great-aunts and uncles who tend to live across the Los Angeles Basin in the leafier, more prosperous suburbs. Our parents don't actually *want* this furniture, which arrives unbidden by truck from Pasadena or Santa Monica, as these are artifacts of the fancy Vandenburghs, the Ainsworth-Rutherford-Rolands, the Moseses, the Whites, all that is *ritzy fitz,* she says, very high up, dontcha know, in all the la-dee-da crap. They were wellborn, while we are Class Damage.

My parents' bedroom furniture, which is huge, mahogany, and ornately carved, came to them from our father's Grandmama Nell. It is so massive that it needed to be taken apart and then rebuilt in their bedroom. There is also a bureau and a dresser and night tables. The solid headboard is so tall it reaches almost to the ceiling, so wide it has to be pushed diagonally back against the bedroom's corner windows.

Oh Jesus Fucking Christ, our mother said when the truck showed up to deliver all this. Our father stood, hands on his hips, gazing into the truck's back, helplessly bewildered by the burden of what was their history.

What the Jesus fucking goddamn *hell*? she asked him, as if this were a form of existential question.

Our father, an elegant man who doesn't use profanity, gazed into the dark guts of the moving truck and shook his head. He was evidently baffled as to what he was supposed to make of this. He'd been depressed recently. *This* was supposed to cheer him up?

000

Our father has bright blue eyes and a space between his two front teeth. He is charming, winning, cultivated. That he is also promiscuous will come to me years later from his sister, my aunt, the woman who—aside from my mother—knew and loved my father best. According to Aunt Nan, my father wasn't particularly well equipped for the life he led. He roamed, yet suffered for it. Suffered, then roamed again.

He is so devotedly atheistic that he can find no spiritual avenue, not the road that would bring him home to us, not the one that will take him away for good. The religion practiced in our household is Freudian psychoanalysis, in which confession is offered on a daily basis without either resolution or absolution at the end.

Our parents met at UC Berkeley during the Second World War, when the only men left on campus were those who had enough wrong with them to have been classified 4-F. There was nothing physically wrong with our father. He was tall, dark-haired, blue-eyed, tan from sailing. He was handsome and he was charming. Where my mother was loud and strident, he was soft-spoken, often offering a wry comment half-humorously and sotto voce.

Your father was always *highly* attractive, my mother will say, and always adds, to *both* women and men. She says this as she says most things, in a tone laden with irony, but I know she admires his beauty. It is as if our father's being good looking is just another of her life's own amazing miracles, like their shared artistic talent or the physical beauty of their own three children.

Our grandparents tell my brothers and me over and over again that what is wrong with our parents is that they've always indulged their *artistic* natures, that they chose the wrong friends at Cal, friends who were funny looking and leftist. That my parents imagine they can live outside the rules, as *bohemians*. That my parents have little regard for consequence. We were very small when the chorus began speaking to us like this, in a tone of diagnosis, the ominous shadow of penalty hanging over our uncombed heads.

We endure a double dose of what is wrong with each of them: their promise, their brilliance, their high IQs, their complete lack of common sense. They are intellectually arrogant, the two of them positively convinced they are the two most interesting people either has ever met.

They harbor antisocial attitudes.

And we are their inheritors, our more conventional relatives tell us; they warn us that we are going to have to keep a sharp lookout for our own wayward tendencies. This is also told to us by our grandparents, who are educated and collect art, who love books, music. This confuses me—aren't books and music *artistic*? I eventually figure out that the problem isn't that our parents are *artistic*. It is that they get caught being that.

Others in the family present as more upright, normal: bankers, teachers, the prosperous owner of a building supply company, a consular officer posted to various oil-producing countries. One uncle shocked the family a few years ago by going beneath his *class* in marrying the woman who had been his secretary; she was pregnant when they married. Marriages in our family aren't normally made like this. You don't marry people randomly, and the women are always educated. A woman might even work, as long as it is agreed that it is economically unnecessary.

Our mother's working is not only necessary, it is being practiced with an ever more thinly veiled desperation. *Where is all their money going?* I wonder. Our parents are both *highly neurotic,* as is openly said. I've known words like *neurotic, psychotic, Miltown,* and *breakdown* since before I learned to read. Each is in psychoanalysis, which means driving to West Los Angeles and lying on a psychiatrist's couch four or five times a week, then giving him every cent they ever hoped to make, plus more from their parents, something their parents are not going to ever allow them to ever forget. This huge expenditure is thought to be the fee to purchase what the 1950s promises to people like my parents: happiness, prosperity, normalcy. Our parents' two analysts are discussed so much and so intimately, they seem to me to be invisible members of our own nuclear family.

000

My parents look out of the plate-glass window of what will be their final Slumgullion Dream Shack and drink. They drink, they smoke, they say wry things to each other, talking back and forth in code or shorthand, a volley no one else is in on, their words, half joking, only partly said, as one will leave off at what the other is left to finish. They say, We started out with such high hopes, only to find ourselves living next door to Tony and Sylvia Castanzo—Tony, whose job is *itinerate knife sharpening*; Sylvia, who is *always pregnant*. They call the Castanzos *The Dynamic Duo. Big She, Little He. The Psychopathologies of Everyday Life.*

My parents write and paint, each with little to show for it. Each is in *conflict* about what my mother ironically refers to in the singular as their *identity*, as if their twin identities were something they share spiritually. They do seem intimate in a way that transcends language.

It is a terrible time and place for a family like ours. HUAC is in its heyday. In the infant suburbs of postwar Los Angeles everyone is actively afraid of differences. You can See Spot Run. My brothers and I are sometimes taunted at school because we are smart and because our last name, which has a *burgh* at the end, apparently proves that we are Jewish. We are teased because our father wears a suit and tie to work, because that shows we think we are better'n everybody else on our street.

We don't, do we? I ask my mother. We don't think we're better than everybody else.

On Avenue B? my mother says. Oh, yes, we most certainly do.

000

My mother hates Huey, Dewey, and Louie, so she quits Disney and takes other awful jobs. For a while she goes door-to-door in high heels and her outdated suits from San Francisco, surveying housewives on the contents of their kitchen cabinets. She can be charming and persuasive when she wants to be. She talks her way inside housewives' front doors, gets them to let her open their refrigerators and their cupboards to do a tabulated inventory. Then they get busy together to mix up little test packets of what will become the first salad dressings and sauces to be marketed as *convenience* foods. She teaches French at a private school, hired on the basis of her fake French accent. Finally she becomes so desperate that she goes back to Disney. She spends even longer hours at the kitchen table, spilling beer and coffee on the Bristol board, flipping her cigarette ashes into empty cans of Pabst Blue Ribbon, talking to Sylvia Castanzo, to me, to anyone who'll listen about how she's noticed that these *ducks* have whole elaborate outfits, shirts and shoes and hats, but *none of them owns any underpants!*

She is drinking heavily by now, and our father has been arrested again. He is arrested for being in *certain bars*. One is called The Lighthouse; it is on the water in Hermosa Beach, where jazz is played. *Certain people* go there—black men, white men, men who might not yet have begun to refer to themselves as "gay." Going to these bars is against the law. I don't yet know why.

He gets arrested even though he is a man incapable of committing a real crime.

Whenever my father is arrested, his psychiatrist, her psychiatrist, his parents, and her parents all talk on the phone, or else meet to confer: Whatever to do about Johnny *this time*?

Call it crime or call it disease—these are the two answers to the question that shouldn't have actually been asked in the first place. But it is finally decided that he needs treatment, so he's sent off to a sanitarium. The logic goes like this: He is married and he has three children, so he can't be a *real* homosexual—perhaps it is something adolescent, something he hasn't outgrown?

So he'll be gone to the hospital that is out in the desert near Palm Springs, or he'll be gone to Mexico, which has a different attitude toward men and masculinity. It was to Mexico his family had always gone on summer holidays, where he was free to be himself, my mother says, where he lived with La Señora, where he practiced his Spanish, admired the new architecture, despised the old neoclassical colonial buildings. Where he wasn't persecuted for being the man he was born to be.

Then he'll come home again, rehabilitated. He'll go back to work, and then he'll be gone again, flying on business out of Los Angeles Airport on a prop plane to Texas or Chicago.

One postcard he sends us from a business trip shows the exterior of the Palmer House in Chicago, an X etched in ink on the high window of the room in which he is staying, maybe measuring the drop.

He is tall, broad faced, freckled, lean, always smiling. He stands at his drafting table, which is shoved into one corner of the already crowded bedroom, smiling hard, as if it hurts his face somewhat to do so. He is working on a house that he says our family will go live in and be happy in. He is a disciple of Wright, of Lescaze, of Neutra, and this ultramodern structure he is drawing looks to me like the shape of a box kite laid on its side on the ground. It is the sort of thing about which my mother will invariably remark, Oh, how *très* ultra-ultra!

One wing is for the adults; the other is designed for the three of us, my brothers and me—they call us *the poor, the huddled, the great unwashed*—to go be unruly in. The connecting struts—the long sides of the box—are solid and walled on the outside, then tiled in waxed flagstone so our wet feet won't mark them. The long halls, with sliding glass that opens onto the interior patio, will be hung with artwork done by our parents and their abnormal Berkeley friends. The outdoor pool in the open center of the house is enclosed on all sides. This, our father says, is so our mother will be able to sunbathe naked. Oh, my darling baby, she tells him when she hears this, arching an eyebrow to say it's he who'd be the one more likely to lay his lanky body out on a chaise, naked in the sunshine, facedown, his dark head cradled on his folded arms, while she stands in the doorway, eyeing him wryly. She'd be turbaned, wearing stylish sunglasses, covered from neck to toe in some smart wrap made of turquoise terry cloth.

He is a better cook than our mother is, but she is a better painter. She recently painted our mailbox in oils, in an abstract expressionist design unappreciated by the neighbors. There are gem cubes that resemble blobs of Jell-O, a huge anti-Disney eye or two, curves and squiggles, black-bordered areas of oceanic blues and greens. The block letters, each stranger and more cubist than the last, spell out THE VANDENBURGHS, which you can read only if you already know what it says. The whole of the mailbox is painted, each inch, and small clay objects have been placed inside to activate its magic, my mother says. The galvanized steel box is covered in paint, and so is the wooden post it sits upon curbside, and even the used-to-be-red sweep-up flag.

That! our grandfather Virgil thunders when he sees it, *no longer conforms to postal regulations.*

2
The Pull of Gravity

IT'S THE WINTER they put Sputnik up. I am nine years old. Our father is gone. He is supposed to be traveling for business in Philadelphia, but he is actually in the desert in a private sanitarium, which is what they call the kinds of mental hospitals that cost a lot of money.

He is there because of LAPD Vice, because of his being arrested again, because of his *acting up*, because of the bribes my grandfather paid to keep him out of jail, because he's cracked up again, as my mother says. When our father is arrested, the captain in Vice calls my paternal grandfather in Glendale. Grandfather John is prominent in building and construction. He goes down to the jail and pays what amounts to a bribe so my father won't go on to be booked and have a record, which would cost him his job.

My grandfather pays the bribe and my father is diverted into the Mental Health side of things. He has to take a leave of absence from work and he's sent out into the desert for months on end, to rest.

That's not what they tell people, though. My mother lies easily; she says he is in Philadelphia, or Dallas, *Texas*, or Houston, *Texas*.

Houston and Dallas are only now being invented, but our mother already despises them, hates Texas, hates anywhere Becket, who is our father's boss, wants to send him to make another city. It is Welton Becket *and Associates*, our mother says, who is responsible for building the same ugly place Los Angeles is turning out to be. Like Mr. Disney's Tomorrowland, it is crappy, tinny, junky.

Becket's offices are on the Miracle Mile, right next to the La Brea Tar Pits. When we drive down Wilshire to take our dad to work, he shudders as we pass beneath the shadows of the new glass-faced office buildings—it's his half-fake shudder, at once real and not real. These are skyscrapers walled with mirrors that mirror nothing. "I will work there until I die," he said one day, which he then very literally did.

But now he's away, so our mother dresses up. She's taking us to dinner at a fish place on the Rainbow Pier. This pier is where my brothers and I hang out on weekends, on school days too. We're now so conspicuous in our truancy that Mr. Loss, the truant officer, knows where to come to look for us. He finds us fishing for bonita, eating saltwater taffy. Mr. Loss piles us in his car and brings us not to school, since we're barefoot and in our bathing suits, but home to our mom. He drives us to our house because, as our mother says, Mr. Loss is a sad, sad little man. Still, she will sometimes ask him in for a breakfast beer. She'll be painting in oils, using one of our dad's white dress shirts as a smock, sleeves rolled up, turned around and buttoned backward.

Her hair is curly, light brown streaked with gold. She doesn't go to the beauty shop to get it *done*, like the other mothers do. Instead, she wears it any way she wants to, long and down in defiance of the fashion or piled up on top of her head, kept there with pencils, paintbrushes, chopsticks, whatever's around for her to stick in it.

Will says Mr. Loss has a *thing* for her. I have no idea what this thing might be.

The place she takes us to is what our mother calls one dump of a jukey joint—the lobster and crab are local; everything is cheap. She sashays in, leading the three of us, orders the first of what she calls her Plural Martinis. Men come around, try to talk to her. Will's seething, challenging, snarling. She very elaborately brushes these men off, saying, I am *married*, but even if I were not, my dear . . . You? *You?* You very obviously do not 'ave enough money for me . . . "

She says the last piece in her fake French accent and turns away.

Never apologize, never explain, she whispers to herself.

Then, to the three of us, she instructs, When a stranger speaks to you, you simply look at him directly and speak slowly and distinctly. You must enunciate clearly. This is what you're to say: I'm-sorry-but-I-do-not-speak-English.

Whatever person was hanging around us until this moment now skulks away; she watches with withering scorn. Then she arches her ironic eyebrow at the hardened starfish twisted into the fishnet that drapes the ceiling, flicks her ash into the abalone shell that's set out for this purpose, and says, only a little too loudly, You'll note, my special darlings, Jukey Joe's clever use of the *seasick* theme?

She's tall, and thin to the point of being bony. She's lately losing interest in what she calls The More Mundane—that we get to school on time, that we go to school at all, that any of us eat. But her attitude toward what she calls *all that* is to remain upbeat, comic, jokey. She's thin, she says, because she's lost her appetite, and *who wouldn't*, she asks, *what with . . . ?*

She gestures around with her cigarette, as if pointing out what's wrong with the tip of her strangely glowing object in the dimness of what is really a cocktail lounge, pointing out *This* and *That* and *That Too.*

Her suits, already out of date, are now too big. These are silk or woolen, tweedy, used-to-be stylish. They were bought in San Francisco, which is a more formal city than L.A., she tells us, where she always wore a hat and gloves when they took the train over the bridge from Berkeley to go for dinner and drinks in downtown San Francisco. San Francisco *suited me*, she says. It *suited* your father, too. You don't call it *S.F.*, she adds, as if this is something we three might do.

She looks pointedly and directly at *me*, as if she has discovered that I am the disloyal one and have actually been thinking I somehow know *better* than she, thinking that I will dare to say *S.F.* even though she has told us not to. It is a piece of my mother's craziness that she can read minds.

This is a dinner Geo, who has just turned five, will not eat because it is lobster, which isn't a hamburger and a chocolate milkshake, and is therefore *upchucky, sickening, icky*, or, as our father says, *enough to makes one's bilge rise*. I know Geo has decided not to eat, because he is resting his forehead on the edge of the table and staring down into his upcurled hands that lie open in his lap. When he does this, my parents call it Geo's *praying*, or *keening*, or *acting tragic*.

Ah, well, old boy, our father would say with faux hardiness, all the more for the rest of us. And he'd reach over with his own fork to take what he wanted from Geo's plate.

After dinner we go to the arcade at the foot of the pier, where my mother, my brothers, and I all cram into the photo booth to have our pictures taken, four shots for a quarter. Will wins a plush purple animal, grabbed out of the glass box by the mechanical claw he calls the Sky Hook. This stuffed dog is so inspired in its ugliness, it moves our mother, now being hilarious, to take us to another booth, where we sing into the mic to cut a scratchy record that the machine presses out of bright red plastic and delivers within minutes.

In the playback booth, my mother and I hear ourselves sing in our high, hurt voices that only hover next to notes, while Will self-confidently booms louder so his voice stands in front of ours, as if he's our leader now and is marching us up and down this song's hills and valleys.

Will is thirteen, now taller than our mother, and his voice is lowering gracefully. I hear him singing around the house when he thinks no one's listening. "But no 'tis not a boy at all," he sings, "'tis Axle's castle's spires so tall . . . " This is a song he's learning for glee club. Will is good at singing and at school and at sports, girls like him, he's good at everything. I worry about this because being good at things is both good and bad, because each time we succeed it takes us further from our parents.

Geo's real name is George Charles. They call him Geo, short for Georgio, because—they say—he was conceived in an Italian villa, a beautiful house with terraced gardens and a water course, someplace my parents were house-sitting for rich friends of my father's rich parents. Villa Vino Santo Multo Vino Vino Santo, they call it, a place of vineyards, olive trees, abundance. God knows why they really named him this. I was alive when Geo was born, and I can remember where we lived, and this was a certain apartment in Verdugo Woodlands. It had nothing to do with Italy, which is on the continent of Europe, somewhere I happen to know my mother has never been.

Geo's voice is beautiful, too, as warbling and ethereal, our father says, as one of God's more neutral angels'. Our father often says this kind of dreamy, inscrutable thing. He says Geo sings to the birds in their own language, which is why they follow him home. Geo resembles a certain saint in this, our father says, the one who was too crazy for people to listen to, so he spoke his wisdoms to the birds.

Geo accumulates living things; they accrete to him by magnetism. He has recently brought home a damaged parakeet with only one good leg. He found it wounded in the dirt of the alleyway behind our house. This bird hopped to him, then rode home perched on Geo's finger.

Another time he found a baby finch and took it home wrapped and cradled in the hem of his T-shirt, a bird so small we had to feed it with an eyedropper. Once it was a litter of mongrel pups that arrived in somebody else's wicker laundry basket, meaning Geo probably stole them.

Can we keep them? we begged our father anyway. There were three puppies, one for each of us. And our father was always great about pets; we always got to keep them. He'd get us a puppy or a kitten as a consolation prize anytime anything went wrong—we had countless pets because of it. We got Ziggy because L.A. County outlawed fireworks. Ziggy is short, black, and fattish, and our favorite dog. Anytime we'd get a new pet we'd take it to Olivera Street for the Blessing of the Animals on the Feast Day of Saint Francis of Assisi.

And now we want these puppies. He always says yes, but this time he's different. Not this week, he says. You won't be here this weekend to take care of them. I'm out of town and you're going to the Whites'.

The Whites are my mother's parents. The Whites are *a piece of work*, our mother says, *scary business, hell on wheels*. The Whites *lower the boom* when they're around. The Whites show up and *there's hell to pay*.

Can't we take them to Lina and Virgil's? Please? Please let us have them, please! we beg.

We think he's going to say yes. He always says yes. But this time our father says, I wouldn't take them to the flea circus.

I don't know what a flea circus is, or if a flea circus in fact exists. Does he mean that while he wouldn't take these other people's dogs to a flea circus, he might take them someplace else?

Frankly, our mother says, you show up with a new batch of puppies for my mother to housebreak, and she will *kill herself*. Geo, you need to show Daddy exactly where you got those dogs. She's saying this just as the family with the mother dog arrives on our front porch.

Geo sings out from the speakers in the playback booth, where we're playing the bright red record. "How much is that doggie in the window? The one with the waggedy taaa-aaa-aaail?" Geo is singing with so much feeling and sincerity, it would make the sentimental weep, except that no one in our family is the least bit sentimental. Life has a way of beating sentiment right out of you, our mother says, what *with* . . . ? As we listen to the scratchy record playing back this part of the song, we can also hear the other three of us in the background, laughing softly at Geo's innocence.

The record is part of a gift we're accumulating for our father, for our mother to take to him for us. So far we have a bag of saltwater taffy, the photo strip, the scary purple dog–ish thing, and now this record that we've just made for him. We'll send this package off to him in the desert, then wait for him to come back to us. He will always come back to us, our mother says, because we are irresistible. *Nothing*, no one, has ever come between them, she says, and *nothing* ever will.

We all walk along the beach at the waterline, watching the waves for the shadowy shapes of grunion, the sand for hermit crabs and blobs of jellyfish. We search the sky for Sputnik, which is easily spotted as it blinks across like a dot-dot-dotting star. It resembles an ellipsis, the mark you put on the page to show something's been left out. Our father is an ellipsis, now here, now here, now not. The satellite is beautiful. The only thing wrong with Sputnik is that our enemies put it up.

On the map of the world in my brothers' bedroom, my mother has painted half the countries various shades of red and named them The Domino Effect. Whatever this means, we don't believe in it.

All the *good* relatives—that's what our mother calls her parents, the Whites, also the Ainsworth-Roland-Rutherfords, the Moseses-Vandenburghs-Snowdens—are Republicans, which is why they're afraid of the communists.

If you're a Republican, she says, you talk about how you like Ike and how the commies want to bomb us. If you're a Democrat, you prefer to speak of how the Russian language has written this great literature. It could do this because it has a hundred words for *vodka*, another hundred for *potato*, and a hundred more for *dirt*. Russia is somehow the reason Jewish people in Hollywood have lost their jobs, and our parents know people like this, those said to be *commies, pinkos, reds.*

My mother is wearing a pair of her good high heels, though we're walking on the sand. She takes them off to walk along the waterline. She wears hose, almost never goes barefoot. She wears shoes because she hates na-chur—she is, she says, an admirer of the Great Indoors. She also wears shoes because her father, who was a banker, believes people's character can be judged by the quality of their shoe leather. This is a value her father, whom she calls Virgil *Elmo* White—as if to differentiate him from all the other Virgil Whites who were rattling around in our family—has instilled in her, though this life lesson, she says, is perfect and utter crap.

Listen to me! she'll say in her I'm Giving Instructions voice. Sometimes she'll wake us up in order to Give Instructions. Listen! she'll say to our heavy bodies, struggling to climb out of sleep. This is what your parents do to you! They make you believe all sorts of idiotic stuff, lousy shitty useless things that are in no way true—do you understand me?

We stir and nod and nod, though this makes no sense to us.

Other wisdom she needs to impart is that you do not, for instance, get sick from sitting on a toilet seat. Urine is sterile, she says, which is why soldiers in battle are told to pee on their wounds.

Her banker-giving-loans-on-the-basis-of-your-shoe-leather father is the reason my brothers and I are hardly ever told to put on shoes. We go barefoot because we pretend we're Indians, being raised by these ghostly ancestors who are just so much better than our own. We are Ishi, the last Yahi, and we hide from Mr. Loss in the crumbling sandstone caves that are wave carved and wind carved into the hillside above the beach, where the air is cold and wet and ancient. Ishi is the story our father tells us; he took anthropology at Cal from Kroeber, who was the white man Ishi lived with. Ishi was the last of his people, a real Indian who came down out of the hills near Oroville and walked out of the Stone Age and into the twentieth century.

It is the miracle of our century, our father says, that it started with prehistory and now has Sputnik in it.

More Life Instructions from my mother: You do not get pneumonia from going out with a wet head. If you sneeze three times, a letter will not come, and if you swear—*I swear to God*—God does not fucking launch fucking lightning bolts to strike you dead. If there is a G-a-w-d, which she sincerely doubts, he'd have *much more* important things to worry about than striking people dead over that kind of crappy shit.

We wear bathing suits in all weather; we pull on shorts and sweatshirts over them. And we wear flip-flops that we call zoris, which our father buys in Chinatown—it's where he gets me tabi socks. Our mother would never wear anything like this. Even in the house, she clomps down the hallway in her high heels to the bathroom in the middle of the night, where there is sometimes blood in the toilet if she forgets to flush it.

〇〇〇

What holds it up? Geo asks. He's looking at the wavering dot-dot-dot blinking across the whole huge dome of lesser stars. *Sputnik*, in Russian, means *traveling companion*.

Gravity, Will says shortly, as if Geo's a fool for asking. My older brother tests as a genius in math, science, and language, but being as geniusy as he is, my mother says, is *its own special problem*. It makes a kid impatient, she says. She knows all about this because she was that kind of genius, too. They kept skipping her through the grades, so she graduated from high school when she was barely sixteen and had to stay out for a year before they'd let her into Cal. Her skipping grades accounts, she says, for at least *hawwwwwf* of her social maladaption. The other half being that everything cutesy and girlsie has always bored her to fucking tears.

What's gravity? my little brother asks.

Will breathes out a withering little blast and stares off without answering.

It has to do with forces, I tell Geo. We'll look it up in *Compton's* when we get home, I say. I know gravity has something to do with pull, that it lies in the same realm of whatever force makes iron filings come out of the sand and attach themselves to the ends of magnets so they look drippy and wet.

Forces are what things have that make other things come to them.

Words like *force*, like *vice*, like *S-E-X*, like *badminton* and *shuttlecock*, are simply beyond me. I am an ordinary child, and it's too hard to understand or even think about these things without the illustrations that will explain them. This is why I am reading *Compton's Pictured Encyclopedia,* or if not reading then at least looking at it book by book, looking at the pictures, imagining that all this knowledge, when taken together, might yield a better map than the one of the world my mother is doing on the wall of my brothers' bedroom, where many of the countries are painted in strange, un-maplike colors and aren't even named.

History and science are what my family has, because we don't go to church. We don't go to church because we're the branch of the family who are what our father calls *card-carrying atheists*. The California Indians had no maps and only the bare rudiments of a written language, as our father has explained—pictures on rocks and things. Something happens to the mind when you write things down, when you can begin to see the world as an orb observed from above. He thinks about things from above because of his work as an architect.

Geo isn't happy with my answer, so Will relents and bends down, and is now drawing a chart of our solar system with a stick in the hard sand, showing Geo that Sputnik is traveling, like our own moon, in orbit around the earth, and that the stars are farther off.

Then what holds the stars up? Geo asks our mom. Through that pure night air, the stars seem to jiggle and dance, this jitter caused by *atmosphere*.

Why, sweetie-honey-baby, she sighs, I honestly have *no idea*. Then she smirks. She smirks as if she's sharing this joke with our dad, the now-here, now-here, now-not-here, who is what she sometimes calls Your Faw-thur Which Aren't in Heaven. This is how I know she's drunk.

Geo begins to cry.

Wrong answer, Mom, I say. Wrong answer for a five-year-old.

Geo's crying harder now, so our mother kneels on the hard sand and takes him in her lap, singing in her broken voice, Ground-round version, mother and child, holy infant so tender and mild, sleep in heavenly peeeep, sleep in heavenly peep. She sings this though it is February.

There, *there*, there, *there*, she tells Geo, holding him to her, grimacing over his head to go, See! From this Will and I are supposed to get how hilarious it is that our mother is being expected to act like a mother, instead of what she really is, which is this rare thing, this wonderfully gifted and spectacular being, the Radiant Child she has always been.

We carefully pack up each part of my father's present, and on the weekend we go to stay at the Whites' while my mother drives the present out to him, to where he's staying in the desert. She drives in her new car, which is blue and white two-tone, which her father has recently bought. She is supposed to use this car to go back to work at Disney in Burbank, but our mother despises Mr. Disney and plans to go nowhere near the man.

Her car has slanted *OOO*s all along its sides, and when she comes home from the hospital this time, she has my father with her, and he's pale and seems afraid. He stays in bed with a pillow over his face, or gets up in his PJs and moves to the couch. He spends weeks without speaking. He's too fearful to drive a car; he believes the police are following him. When he does drive, it's to go to Blackie's to buy a six-pack of beer; then he stops on the side of the road so he can hide the beer somewhere in the trunk.

We go to the beach with our aunt and uncle and our four cousins, and we're going to play cribbage and put up the badminton net, and we have inner tubes that my dad and my uncle got us from the service station, and it starts out being fun, like in the Olden Days, when things used to be easy and even ordinary, back when my mom and dad and my aunt and uncle were the best of friends.

My aunt has brought my father's favorite kind of sandwich, which is avocado with cut-up green onions and mayonnaise on a kind of bread they call Dutch crunch. I can see how her eyes watch him behind her sunglasses, because my father is her big brother and they've always been the favorite persons of each other, and he's lying on his side in the sand, trying to smile the wide hard smile he's always been able to smile with the gap between his two front teeth, but now he no longer can.

And suddenly he's lying facedown on his towel and my mother's bending over him, and my uncle orders us all to walk down the beach with him and pick up litter, which he calls policing the area, and when we get back my mother and father are gone and my aunt's face is pale behind her tan.

We go home that afternoon with Nan and Ned in their station wagon, seven kids lying in the back, sunburned and sandy. We stay with them in the Valley at least through the weekend, and my cousin Graham and I sleep in the same bed, with our heads on pillows at opposite ends, but we kick each other and fight, so my aunt moves me into Lizzie's room.

My mother tells us later our father had a sunstroke. I've begun to dream that he is drowning and that I'm on the cliff above the sea where the caves are carved below and I cannot get down to him and I know I cannot save him. This dream makes no sense, since he's an expert swimmer who grew up sailing his own little skiff from the pier at Hermosa near his parents' beach house, and it is he who has taught me to swim in the ocean. I dream I see the shape of his body in the waves as they rise up, the sun gleaming through so it shows in silhouette, then see the shape dissolving as it twists and swirls and comes apart as grains of sand.

My parents call their psychiatrists Dr. Maudlin and Dr. Moody. We sometimes wait in the car, reading comic books and chewing Black Jack gum, while our mother's seeing her psychiatrist.

My father sees his psychiatrist every day of the week on his lunch hour. This is Dr. Mailin, whose office is up the street from Becket, near Bullock's Wilshire. An accident of history has placed my father, a couple of days a week, riding up or riding down in the same elevator as Marilyn Monroe, whose own psychiatrist, Dr. Ralph Greenson, has an office down the hall from Mailin's. She wears no makeup, keeps a scarf over her hair, and wears huge sunglasses, and she and my father very carefully ignore each other, each recognizing the other as fragile and distraught.

Dr. Mailin approves of my father's flirtations with good-looking women—and my father does flirt with women, and sometimes even goes off with them—because this is a "boysie" thing to do. What LAPD Vice does not approve of is my dad's flirting with good-looking men.

One of the more important pieces of advice my parents' psychiatrists have given them is that my father must begin to act more "boysie" and my mother must start to act more "girlsie." Toward the aim of my father's acting boysie, his psychiatrist orders him to start doing more typically fatherly things, to work on being the kind of man any father would like his boys to grow up to be—less of a hanging-out-in-bars father, more of a hunting-and-fishing one. He is to take my brothers camping, and only the boys can go. Fathers Camping with Sons is evidently the way people act in other, more normal families.

I am shocked when I hear this plan, too hurt and astonished to even cry. Instead, I take the kitchen scissors into the bathroom and cut off all my hair. My hair is blond and curly, it is Shirley Temple hair, it is one of the major things Will makes fun of me for. Now it's gone. With my hair cropped close, I dress in his jeans, put on his Keds and ball cap, and shove myself into the backseat of my father's car, hold on to the armrest, and scream that they will never get me out of the car, that they will never never never make me stay home.

They pull me out and drive to Lake Piru, which my father tells me later is just this *hole in the wall*.

I am left alone in the house with my mother for the weekend, and while it's my father who has been sent camping for his mental health, it's my mother who is insane, as I have always known.

Meanwhile, my father's life on Earth is ending, and though we don't know this, we still sense time going faster in the way it will when a story is winding itself up, when all the events begin to crowd in and collide, in order that each has a chance to decree itself, and they compete in getting themselves told.

And now my parents are being ordered by their psychiatrists to take us to Disneyland, though they both hate this kind of thing, though he is too depressed to speak, to lift his head. Inside the park he sits on a bench, holding his arms as if they ache, waits as we joylessly stand in line. I refuse to have fun out of loyalty to him. The only ride I will go on is Peter Pan, which is beautiful, which shows the lights of London far below, and I think about being able to fly one day out a window and far above the lights of Earth, and that I'd be certain to take my brothers and our dog and leave nobody behind. Wendy and her Lost Boys.

But time has now become foreshortened and oppressed, and my brothers and I finally become so inoculated by the sodden hopelessness that we, too, turn quiet and no longer beg for anything. We've become such good children, it is as if we've learned to behave. We are the ones who sit in the backseat on the drive home with our empty hands up-turned in our laps. We ride along in silence, and maybe it is this new quiet of ours that speaks to the quiet in our father, because when we pass a carnival alongside the highway, he pulls over, stops the car, and takes us on the Ferris wheel, that one last time.

3

Thirty-Six Miles

IT'S A WEDNESDAY in February. Our mom keeps us home from school and makes Will and me stay in, though she lets Geo out to play. The phone rings, then rings again. We have only one phone, which is in the hallway between the living room and the kitchen. We can hear it ring and the murmuring of her voice, but not any of the words she's saying.

Will and I are playing chess in my mother and father's bedroom. I play with Will, also with my Grandfather Virgil, though I'm never allowed to win. My family is harsh like this—you don't get to win because you're younger or don't know how to play, and especially not because you are a girl.

We are sitting on the huge mahogany bed our dad got from his grandmother. This kind of furniture came Round the Horn, our mother says. Your faw-thur's family, she says, came to California by ship and train, while the little girls in her family, like Perseus Bartholomew and America Orchard, got behind the ox cart and walked. This is to make some point I have never understood, about the difference in class between their two very similar families. I hate thinking about these things.

The Oregon Trail, the people who did or didn't come west by walking two thousand miles, bores me in a particularly headachy way. It's the same as having to watch some educational movie in school or a stupid filmstrip on a hot day with the blinds down, the motes being all I can concentrate on. I hate cowboy-and-Indian movies for this same reason, for the long shots of dry, dusty landscapes in which there is no town as far as you can see, and the whole thing is done to show the puny plume of smoke that is the dust cloud blooming up behind the tiny horse and even tinier rider.

I already get the insignificance of Man Against the Elements. The thought of these things fills me with the kind of terrifying loneliness and existential dread I imagine my father feels.

My mother comes into the bedroom and stands framed in the doorway, holding one arm to her side in the rigid way she has. Children, she says, your father committed suicide this morning.

I cry out, I scream, I am doubled over weeping. My mother flinches. My brother is embarrassed by my reaction—they both hate it when anyone is being what they call *emotional*. Neither of them cries; neither says much of anything, except to say I need to calm down, that we need to plan and put this plan into action.

She tries to hold me in her arms, but I shrug her off and climb through my parents' oversize and crowded-together bedroom furniture to stand in the window behind the headboard, sobbing into my own hands.

My mother hands me one of my father's handkerchiefs. I bring it to my face and begin to sob harder because it smells like him.

The morning is whitening. The sky carries the particular yellowish color of the light reflected off the sandy soil of our back lot, which has never been planted. My mother and brother are asking me to come out, saying I have to stop crying, that we have to go find Geo. We need to pack our animals and drive across the L.A. Basin to the Whites'.

Why? I ask. *I'm not going with her*, I think. *I'm staying here to wait for my father to get home.*

In that moment, I hate my mother as intensely as I did on the weekend I was left home with her while the boys went camping at Lake Piru. We were *supposed* to do girlsie things while they were away, which—to my mother—meant we *would not clean house, would not shop, would not wear an apron.* She dressed up, put on makeup, took her daughter, and went to the Rainbow Pier, where I sat next to her on a barstool, drinking ginger ale with cherries in it while she drank martoonies and ranted about how the psychiatrists of the state of California were engaged in this conspiracy that involved the Vice Squad of the Los Angeles Police Department.

I don't ask her how he died, because I don't actually believe that he has. I am reframing the events linguistically, telling myself he attempted suicide but failed, as my parents have so determinedly failed at everything else they've tried.

He attempted suicide, I keep saying to myself.

You're going to have to stop crying, my brother says. It's upsetting Mom.

But I will not. *I will never stop crying*, I think. *The two of them can't make me. They have no way of understanding what I've lost. They're not crying because they still have each other, but it was my father who approved of me. Now I have no one but Geo and my dog.*

⫘

The manner of my father's death is nothing anyone wants to discuss, so I don't find out how he died until several days after. I imagine ways he's died—driving our mom's car off a cliff into the sea, for instance. I imagine. I don't ask.

But later that week, my mother and I drive home from Glendale to pack up some things we need—the house will be sold, we'll never live in Redondo again. When we get there there are newspapers collected all around the front porch. I open them until I get to the one that was published the morning after my father's death, and I begin to read.

It says he jumped off the roof of his office building into the parking lot.

⚶

It is years later, after I become an adult, when I finally talk to my father's friend Peter DiFrenzi, who walked with him that morning at the La Brea Tar Pits. My father was gloomy and markedly anxious. He'd tried calling his doctor time and time again, but the psychiatrist had yet to call back, as Peter told my mother when he phoned her on the morning of my father's death. Peter'd also called my grandmother and my father's sister, whose husband phoned the doctor and threatened him with bodily injury.

You're a quack, my uncle said.

Though he and Peter had already gone out walking earlier that morning, my father gathered up his coat from the hanger where he kept it, saying he guessed he needed to get some air.

My father worked standing at his drafting table, which faced that of Peter. They both worked in their shirtsleeves. On that day, my father rolled down his sleeves and buttoned the cuffs, then put on his coat, saying he was going on a coffee break.

Some coffee break, my mother liked to say.

⚶

The day our father dies, we have to gather up our animals to take them in the car to go to our grandparents' house. When we get there, things will be better because Dr. Greenly is coming to give our mother a sedative, but first she has to drive us there, so she can't crack up quite *yet*.

She has decided that Will and I can know, but that Geo, who doesn't know what the word *suicide* means, is too young to understand, so we aren't to discuss this with him, which also keeps us from saying anything about what has happened. We tell Geo our father has gone away on a business trip, so we're going to Lina and Virgil's for a while. This makes him happy because he's Lina's favorite person.

Ziggy is riding shotgun. He has short legs but no sense at all that he's small. He's my favorite dog because he's happy and self-confident. We always get mutts from the pound because our father says they're more well adjusted.

My brothers and I ride in the backseat, holding our other pets. Will and I are at either window; Geo is in the middle, with his hermit crabs' terrarium on his lap.

Will has these friends named Norman and Yvonne Fisher who live across the street and down the block. They are a brother and sister about a year apart in age. Norman and Yvonne miss as much school as we do, so Mr. Loss knows them, too. It's because their parents are separated and their mother works. The only other woman who works a steady job in our neighborhood is Ann, of Bud and Ann next door. Because they don't have children, it's whispered that Ann has something wrong with her *parts*.

The Fishers are worse kids than even the Vandenburghs, so wild and truant that Maxine Woodman calls them Bad-Uns. Will told me it was at the house of Norman and Yvonne Fisher that the neighborhood kids a little older than I am established a sex club. This is like, I'm guessing, the pigeon club we've had as a semi-organized activity, with parental support, that Will has recently outgrown.

I've read *Where Babies Come From*, so I know what sex is and am not surprised that Norman Fisher's involved, as he's already famous for his proto-perversions, his bragging that he can suck his own balls or his peeing into a milk bottle that's half filled with water, his demanding that little kids drink a sip of it before they're allowed into the Fishers' house, which is something I don't do, because that place is somewhere I don't actually want to go.

Norman and Yvonne are lurking in their side yard as we go back and forth to pack our car. They're stooping to pick up some green fruit that lies around a tree, throwing it hard against the stucco wall of their house, but also watching us. As we close the car doors and begin to take off, they start toward the street, peering in to make sure Will's in here with us. Our mom hasn't really accelerated yet and is only letting the car roll downhill in neutral, as if she can't quite remember how to drive.

She brakes as she pulls over on the wrong side of the road, stopping next to the Fishers' mailbox, which sits on a post by the curb. Yvonne wanders out, moving hips-first in a sultry way that is already knowing and seductive.

Can Will come over and play, Mrs. Vandenburgh? she asks. She is leaning over to peer into our car, curious about why we're traveling with all our animals.

Our mother is smoking, her left arm dangling out the window. She catches my eye in the rearview mirror and arches an eyebrow ironically, as if to say, See? Even on an extraordinary day such as today, you can count on Yvonne to act so totally *Yvonne*.

Not today, dear, my mother says.

She waits and purses her lips in a certain way she has, as if she's thinking about trying the punch line out on Yvonne. It will become, over the years, our most riotous and cosmic joke. It becomes our tagline, our appositive, that without which we are no longer ourselves, as it defines us away from the world in which we did once live.

Will can't play today, our mother says. His father has *committed suicide.*

And later I'll understand that she'll have to say it over and over again in order to believe it, because we still could not believe it, would never really quite believe it, so we say this to people, then watch their faces for shock or horror or pity, as if—if it did turn out to be true—their expressions might give us a hint of what we are supposed to feel.

Yvonne lets out a little yelp, like she's been stung by a bee, and her eyes immediately fill, which bothers my mom. Crying always bothers my mother because she never cries herself.

Oh, there, *there*, dear, she says to Yvonne, though she is no longer paying very close attention. Buck up, dear, we all must buck up now, mustn't we? she says, but she isn't looking at Yvonne. Instead, she is fiddling with the rearview mirror. We're in the Nash, so everything needs adjustment, as she is only that moment noticing.

Everything needs adjustment because our father, who was so tall, was the last one to drive this car. This day he's evidently driven our mother's new blue and white one to the office.

Our mother sighs hugely, theatrically, at the arduousness of everything, *what with* . . . ? She examines the expression on her face in the mirror on the sun visor, sucks her cheeks in, then flips the visor up. Her face is focused and plain as she presses her foot to the accelerator.

She is steering carefully, concentrating on driving us safely down the road. She drives us from Redondo Beach north, along the Harbor

Freeway and through downtown, then up into the foothills that stand between Glendale and Flintridge, then up Montecito, then down over the culvert and onto Vista del Mar to our grandparents' house. It is thirty-six miles. It is the hardest thing she will ever do.

They are outside waiting for us. She gets out of the car and falls down in the middle of the street.

4
The Salisbury Court Reporter

AFTER MY FATHER steps forward, falls six stories, and disappears, my mother finishes going crazy. She buys a new house with a bomb shelter, a gold Naugahyde sofa bed, a black-and-white kidney-shaped coffee table, Johnny Mercer albums. She calls everyone she knows long-distance and talks for hours.

We move to a new house that has a pomegranate tree, on a street called Salisbury Court. We have two birds: a parakeet named Perky and a finch named Pickering, after the colonel on the *My Fair Lady* album, where the record sticks, going, Pickering, Pickering, Pickering. Our mother is crazy now, so we all need to attend to this kind of magical underscore, certain patterns and repetitions that here and there emerge. There is algebraic significance to these sets of threes and sevens—also to the appearances of dogs and birds and various saints.

Perky is a broken yellow parakeet with one lame foot that is curled into an unnatural shape, some imperfect mark of punctuation. He is flawed, so Perky is, of course, our favorite. Geo is the one who found him. Geo, who has always been silent, is witchy now; like St. Francis, he speaks only to the animals now, so that's how they find him. Perky dies, or flies away, after a few weeks in the new house.

The finch flies freely in the house until it drowns in the dishwater in the kitchen sink. My brothers and I fish the wet bird out, then bury him in a shoebox under the dirt floor of the bomb shelter, this cold, damp, concrete-smelling alcove. We have a bomb shelter because this is the 1950s and everyone is afraid of communists. Our mother believes in a conspiracy that has to do with how our parents had been Leftists in college, but not, evidently, Leftist enough. You could never be the right kind of Leftist, our mother says, and this is the reason, evidently, that now the commies are after us.

The conspiracy accounts for the absence of our father, who either is or isn't dead, according to the degree of her craziness, which is in perpetual flux. The conspiracy is intricate. It involves Russia, electronic surveillance, each and every psychiatrist either of our parents has ever seen, including a psychiatric social worker whose name is Marge le Farge or, variously, Marge the Barge de Farge, and also the operators at the telephone company at Ninth and Hope in downtown Los Angeles, who have now begun to listen in on our mother's phone conversations.

She knows about the conspiracy because her French professor laid it all out for her in drabs of dusty chalk on the blackboard when she was at Cal. It took the form of a mathematical equation involving an Unknown Quantity. Our father was an Unknown Quantity, she said— neither This-nor-That, but rather Both-And, and so, she said, were we. We three were also Other.

If we were filling out a form, she instructed us, we were to write down *Other* when we were asked to say what we were.

Our father was better at math than she was, but she is the better writer. But she understands the arithmetic of the conspiracy—the French professor had explained it to her because he'd been in love with her. And he wasn't the only one, she reminds us. Seven men asked her to marry them, though her underwear was dirty. Do we understand her? she asks. Do we understand exactly what she is alluding to?

We nod, but we have no idea what she is talking about, except that it probably has something to do with what she calls *S-E-X*.

She has proof of the plot against her in that there are cars driving past our house in sets of threes. Her psychiatrist is the one in the red-orange VW, see? And it is being driven by his right-hand man, Marge the Barge de Farge, and when our mother calls her his right-hand *man*, she says, she is using the term advisedly.

I never see this car, but still I nod with my brothers and act as if I get her jokes, the one about Marge being his right-hand man and so forth. I know this is a joke the way our new house is a joke: She chose it because Salisbury Court was a dead-end street.

Dead. End. Street. Words like these now come freighted with all kinds of important meaning. *Dead-end street* now rhymes, in our mother's musical, comedic mind, with *sets of threes* and with *Pickering.*

000

Without my mother's aid or governance, my brothers and I make up schedules for ourselves that we then struggle to follow. We have a meeting every Sunday, when the program guide comes out, to vote on television programs for the week. Will calls this meeting to order. He also instructs Geo on various matters of etiquette and propriety, telling him, for instance, that he has to finish his carrots and his peas.

Why? Geo asks.

Because you have to.

Why? Geo asks again. Daddy says I don't have to. Daddy says, All the more for the rest of us.

Said, Will tells him. *Daddy said*, but Geo just stares away. Geo's face is tanned, sunburned, freckled all at once, the individual hairs so blond they look glassy and transparent, eyes so blue they are like turquoise marbles in the mahogany game Grandmother Delia has on her coffee table that her father brought from China, marbles that are speckled and swirled with layers of golden iridescence.

Just eat them, Will says.

Will also tries to help our mother budget her money, which seems to have descended upon us in an incomprehensible blizzard. He once looked up from the mess that was her big-as-a-photo-album checkbook—this was a checkbook out of Dickens, really, and it had elaborate ledgers on which to do complicated double-entry accounting. Her father, who was a banker, was the person responsible for her having this ridiculous account, with its black and pebbled self-important cover and its checks set up three to a page that you needed to tear out carefully along their rigorous lines of microperforations. These were huge, like comic-book checks, and Will was now regularly signing our mother's name.

He glanced up and asked, Hey, Mom, why can't you be a more regular mom, like the one on *Leave It to Beaver*?

A *Leave It to Beaver* mother? our mother asked. As opposed to the kind I *really* am, which is the Queen of the Fucking May?

She loves Will particularly well, so he is permitted to say this kind of thing to her, which coming from me might sound like less of an observation and more of a criticism.

The huge, official-looking checkbook is a joke and the telephone is a joke and the bill that the telephone company sends us is another of the jokes in this portion of our lives, which—to our mother—have begun to resemble some grimly comedic light opera in which our father flew from the roof of a building and won't reappear until a later act.

Will opens the telephone bill. He says that it is more than $300.

She talks on the phone all night, every night, while Geo has now stopped speaking almost entirely. It is nearly summer, so Will has arranged to have Geo go to the Talako Club, which is for all the rich little boys and girls. Will is doing these things now, as our mother seems unable to. But she says Geo needs to learn to swim and ride horseback like all of the other rich little boys and girls of La-Dee-Da La Cañada-Flintridge. We are in disguise now, our mother says, as rich little boys and girls. She's hidden us among the rich because the rich are almost always safer.

Will keeps getting into fights at school. When he gets caught, the principal calls my mother to come and get him. I am home one day when this happens. I stay home because I don't want to go to school, where I have no friends, or sometimes I have friends but I don't like them because they aren't the friends I used to have when we lived in Redondo. I stay home because my mother wants me with her, as if we're in this together, and she talks to me like I'm her confidante.

I watch her ready herself in the bathroom mirror. It's always theatrical, as if she's getting herself into costume for her role in some play. She splashes her face with baby oil, pouts, draws on lips. She is wearing huge dark glasses and, in the fashion of the times, has her hair wrapped in a terry-cloth turban. She is tall and is now thinner than she's ever been. She's stopped eating, preferring, she says, to get most of her vitamins and essential nutrients from the hops and grains and barley in Pabst Blue Ribbon, which is—as everybody knows—one of Nature's Most Perfect Foods.

When the principal calls again, our mother sighs hugely and then goes to meet him. She has a new motto now, which is Public Opinion No Longer Worries Me, which she got from a *New Yorker* cartoon that she's taped to the wall. It has a Gahan Wilson monster: warty, three-eyed, hugely deformed, surrounded by beautiful people at a cocktail party. The monster is sipping a drink. "Public opinion," he is saying urbanely, "no longer worries me." This is why she drives the car dead drunk, wearing what she is wearing, which is high heels and her bathing suit, her hips draped with a bright red floral sarong.

I am in the fifth grade, but I don't go to school very often, and I have no friends there. One time a girl, whose last name is really normal—something Normal! Normal! Normal! as my mother says, flashing her fingers open and shut like her hands are a warning signal—invites me to spend the night. This girl's father is a minister, and the entire family sits around the table after dinner—guided by the Reverend Smith or Jones—to talk to me about sins on my soul. They keep a Bible sitting diagonally on a table in the corner; I try not to look at it, but its gilt edges shine out in a manner that feels inevitable. I understand that a Bible is a perfectly ordinary, everyday object in the lives of other people, but it is completely terrifying to me—that or anything else that seems to reek of any kind of religiosity, any kind of potent relic. I think this Bible might burst into flames if you hold it, or that if you open its cover you'll find it to be a literal portal to a literal hell from which live snakes might begin to writhe and crawl.

I fall asleep that night with bubble gum in my mouth and wake the next morning with my face stuck to the pillowcase. I know they will never ask me back. It doesn't matter. My father was an atheist and I am an atheist. My mother was an atheist, too, until she started hearing voices.

My favorite show is *I Led Three Lives*. My favorite singer is Harry Belafonte. Someone has given me a miniature printing press with rubber letters, so I start a newspaper called *The Salisbury Court Reporter*. I watch, I listen. I begin to practice the plain dumb blank face that is the pretend neutralness of journalism. I begin to write in an infinitely neat and exacting manner, forming block letters that are tiny, miraculously precise. *It is an architect's hand*, I think, *one that I've never learned, but here is my father's own printing that has been magically bequeathed to me.*

I write down the *pointedly average,* the usual, the friendly, the news that everyone wants to hear. I have a specialty that is the human-interest story that shows some mild ironic twist. What I don't put in is anything about what is going on at our house, where the four or six or even eight of us—if you count birds and dogs and ghosts—exist in this hypertheatrical manner that our mother now seems to believe is being stage-directed by some perversely unfunny god.

What I don't put in is that our mother has buried her new car in the garage, beneath hundreds and hundreds of beer cans. She is hiding her beer cans in the garage. She is hiding her cans from the neighbors, the communists, the psychiatrists, and our grandparents.

Her fear is new. In Redondo she'd been afraid of no one. She'd been a porch drinker, who refused, on goddamned principle, to pour her beer into a civilized glass. She drank from the can on purpose, in defiance of the etiquette of the time, of being all nicey-nice or Too Goddamnned Girlsie for Words.

In Redondo, my mother would not be nice, she would not be girlsie. She'd sit on the concrete of our house at the beach with her long arms wrapped around herself against the chill of the late afternoon, drinking a beer, smoking a cigarette. Maxine Woodman, who was hugely fat, was the boss of our neighborhood, but our mother wasn't afraid of her. Maxine would trundle herself uphill from where she'd been, which was down the street meddling. She puffed as she walked, scuffed in her slippers and housecoat out in the middle of the street. She walked in the street because she was from the country, our mother said, which made her an Oakie or Arkie.

Been drinking, Margaret? she'd ask as she puffed uphill.

Been eating, Maxine? our mother would say right back.

000

I don't put in my paper the perhaps newsworthy item that both toilets in our house are broken and none of us seemingly has the wit or guile to call the plumber. We either can't or won't, but anyway we haven't, and the toilet will not fix itself. Things do not get better by themselves. Instead, we simply come to a new low in this new Slumgullion, to which we've been perplexingly assigned and to which we are becoming adjusted.

My brothers and I have been raised as half savages anyway, running barefoot on the beach, so we just stake off one corner of the yard, at the back near the concrete block fence beyond the overarch of the pomegranate tree, where we go quietly in the moonlight to the place where we keep the shovel so we can bury it.

I keep having a dream that we are all in the car, that our mother is driving. We're driving along the Pacific Coast Highway near our old house, and we round a bend in the road and see my father standing off to the side. He is in darkness, his face half-erased by shadows. It is so dark that I don't recognize him until we pass him by. His face is ash-white and hurt, as if he is disappointed that we aren't stopping for him. It occurs to me that we have failed him, that we are still continually failing him in imperceptible ways. There is, for instance, no place to go put flowers on his grave, which might be a normal thing to do. We don't do any of the normal things. There was no ceremony when he died, because he'd committed suicide and his family was ashamed of him.

The reason for burial is that it helps the dead stay dead, as the dead intended. Without a funeral, none of us can remember from day to day that he has actually died. Geo and our mother especially seem to struggle with the concept. Our mother keeps waking up from her naps on the gold Naugahyde sofa bed and asking us, Isn't your father home yet? Where's your father?

It is his mother—Grandmother Delia—who is particularly ashamed, as it is against the rules of her religion to kill yourself, so a person who commits suicide cannot be buried in consecrated ground. I think it might be argued, though I don't, that a person as tormented as he was is exactly the kind of soul most in need of whatever solace a religion like hers ought to offer.

His mother is ashamed, while everyone else in our family—which is large and old—is embarrassed that he'd got his name plastered all over the front page of the *L.A. Times*, instead of in some small, laudatory article on its realty or business page, the way his own father always did. And that our father left this embarrassing widow and these three motley urchins, all of whom talk like guttersnipes.

And then there is a final humiliation: that since our father is the only son of an only son, we, these guttersnipe-ish orphaned urchins, will actually be the ones to carry on Our Important Family Name, one that is registered with the Holland Society, since Vandenburghs first washed up on these shores in 1644.

Suicide is rude, unmannerly; it is not very *Holland Society*, it is not very 1644. It is shameful and embarrasses everyone, which is why people never know what to say. It is actually impolite to even mention it, as we are told, which is why we begin to mention it all the time.

Suicide. Suicide. Suicide. Suicide. My brothers and I say it constantly. Our saying it makes people uncomfortable, we notice, so we say it more. We are actually told to knock it off, at some point, to stop it, and if we don't, then we are told to go away. We are supposed to either learn to be quiet or else make up a better story, such as the version that is called The Accident. The Accident goes like this. "He'd been taking medication, he got dizzy, and he went to the roof for air." That version is the one preferred by the more genteel of our grandparents' generation, such as our father's great-aunt Bertha Hopkins, who is somehow related to us, but how exactly I'm never interested in enough to remember.

Our mother has other versions that are elaborated over time. They go way back and back, to what's always been wrong with everything, and this has to do with Calvinism and what it says about the human body, which is that we are born in iniquity, which is another word for Vice, which is another word for the LAPD, which has special problems of its own.

Our mother's versions are infinitely various, as if she's making them up as she's going along, and they always have this little piece of discernable truth in them, which is how she tricks you, so you never know which piece of the story to believe and which piece is complete and utter bullshit. She tells these stories in an ulterior way, that lets you feel like she's letting you in on something that must remain our little secret, but this too has a piece of what I'm beginning to identify as irony, which means this is something you both do and do not believe, in equal parts and completely simultaneously.

We're not ever to go by certain versions, however, to go by any story that contains the word *polio,* for instance, or *TB,* as we don't go by that. We also do not go by Dallas, *Texas,* or Houston, *Texas.* And we're never to believe any story that contains any of the crap about how any of the men in our family have *died in the war.* Men in our family, frankly, do not die in *their* crappy war, she says, because it's rare that they even participate in *their* crappy war.

She talks about all wars as if they are the one same thing. Our father, for instance, did not die in their war because he wasn't actually boysie enough for those assholes to let him go anywhere near their crappy army.

Which assholes? Will asks.

The Higher-Up ones, she says. The Higher-Up in the Uppity-Up assholes who take it upon themselves to decide these kinds of things.

Those Shitheels, she says, to be more definitive.

000

Now it is Geo who is getting in trouble. He is brought home one day by the scruff of his T-shirt, which is clutched at the back of his throat by the huge fist of a uniformed cop who will let him off this time—next time, juvie for sure. Geo and his friend, this cop says, broke into the house of a neighbor and tore the place apart, dumping food out of the refrigerator, smearing the walls with mustard and ketchup. Will and I can't believe it is our little brother who's done what they say he's done, which was flushing the living goldfish down the toilet, one by one.

No one can understand this, as Geo and his friend didn't steal anything and it was the house of the leader of the Talako Club, who has always been kind to them. Geo is in the second grade. He can't read and he can't write, and no one can any longer remember when he last said more than two or three consecutive words.

Will just keeps punching people. He fails Latin, punches his Latin teacher. I am ordered by my mother not to set *that* in boldface and put it on the first page of my newspaper.[+]

But my mother needn't worry, as I write only the nicey-nice, I write the girlsie, I write that my father was six-foot-three and handsome, that it is his *prestigious* architectural firm that was building Century City, and I brag about it, though this is a project my father referred to as The

---

[+]But I've anyway misunderstood as my brother's Latin teacher is a shapely woman, as I'll find out later, who wears soft, tight sweaters, and my brother, of course, hasn't *hit* her but may have said something odd to her, as all of us (aside from Geo who doesn't talk) are *always* saying the odd or inappropriate thing.

Heat Death of the Universe. I write that my mother is back working for Walt Disney, that when it looks like she is talking to herself, she is actually working on the songs for a musical comedy set in an animated heaven where all dead animals get to go. It is my grandmother's asshole church's version of heaven that says animals are excluded, as—according to church doctrine—animals do not have souls.

I write a story called "Will's Incredible Will," about my big brother's fabulous fastball. I don't mention that he quit Little League the year before. I report on Geo's unusual gifts, his obvious ESP, his specific birdsongs, that he is St. Francis reincarnate, particularly expert on hermit crabs.

〰

My mother's madness now consists of her getting wildly drunk, of her wearing her bathing suit, wrapped in a sarong, down to the store on the corner of the main street of La Cañada-Flintridge, where she buys more beer and cigarettes, where she'll mention to anyone who will listen that my father died under the *most suspicious circumstances.*

When she is very deeply crazy, she calls it Your Father's Supposed Suicide. When she is more together, she answers the question What does your husband do? by saying, He was an architect but he committed suicide, as if this were one of the world's best jokes. Or she'll say, He was murdered by homosexuals who were angered because he wouldn't leave us and altogether *join up.*

She doesn't believe it anymore, anyway, at least not most of the time. Someone killed him, she now knows—when she is well enough to remember he is dead—and he'd been surrounded by malignant forces.

Becket had wanted him to go to Texas, where they were building Dallas and Houston, but Johnny had refused, so maybe Becket murdered him. Or he was murdered by psychiatrists who were trying out drugs on him—drugs that, she said, made him really, really sick but that he believed kept him going.

Our mother's being insane makes her take the three of us out of school and move us, by taxi, to a hotel in downtown L.A., where she shops for new and glamorous clothes to befit her new status as a wealthy widow, gets us a babysitter from the front desk, then sits smoking in the darkened bar, where she runs a tab and talks to whomsoever is there and will listen.

When she is more crazy, Marilyn Monroe figures even more prominently in the tale of my father's last year, a story that becomes more elaborate over time to include the involvement of both John and Robert Kennedy, and the Mafia, and the heads of the Roman Catholic Church.

My mother also likes to concentrate on who is secretly gay in the LAPD, and wants to know why—if they are not gay—these men are hanging out in the bathrooms of beachside jazz clubs in Manhattan and Hermosa, getting ready to beat on people as innocent as Johnny.

❀

My mother has money from an insurance settlement, much reduced in amount because his death was ruled a suicide. She is flagrant; her money is running out. She needs to get her hands on what she calls Her Estate. Will tries to reason with her: More properly, this is our Grandfather John's estate—he died suddenly while off in Illinois, visiting other Vandenburghs. At the time of his death, he and my father were estranged. This was because my father, in taking his psychiatrists' advice, had stopped speaking to his mother, his father, and even his sister Nan, who was three years younger than he was and was nothing in the family constellation if not blameless.

My mother begins phoning her friends from Cal long-distance to try to get them to help her with Her Estate—the phone bill from our house on Salisbury Court grows higher and higher. She is given one of the first credit cards, which is a Diners Club—her being issued this card makes her believe she is somehow *meant* to go live in another hotel, where our grandparents can't find us.

She, for all her artistic sophistication, is like a primitive person in her relationship with money. Money, she seems to believe, is like a substance that is issued always from somewhere On High and intermittently, like rain. It comes from her parents, or her husband, or her husband's parents, or the insurance company, or else you find out you have this other little inheritance that has been tucked away for you on your mother's grandfather's side, and that these funds are now finally going to be released, but only if you manage to begin to behave yourself. Her mother's family—the Ainsworths—were founders of the town of Orange.

She begins hallucinating voices, and she is actively paranoid about the LAPD. The LAPD, my mother says, is still vitally interested in us, which is why she parks her new car in the garage and then hides it beneath hundreds and hundreds of beer cans.

After our father died and they lost that conduit to what she said was All Our Money, the psychiatrists who had the rent on their fancy offices on the Miracle Mile began, quite naturally, to take gradually less of an interest in us. She tells me they were driving by our house in *sets of threes*, that anyone could see this, that all you had to do was look.

This is when I begin to understand that it will turn out to be fairly important to my psyche to take what my mother says not particularly literally, in that it usually lies near the truth in the way art will, and will often shine with art's particular valence.

The people are at first interested and concerned, then they aren't. Her psychiatrist calls a couple dozen times, then—when my mother hangs up on him over and over again—he abruptly stops.

The ladies from the Welcome Wagon show up on our stoop. They see the mess this house cannot begin to contain and smile hard at us with their plastered-on fake-ish 1950s smiles. They put their basket down amid the beer cans and ashtrays on the kidney-shaped coffee table, and—as our mother begins to tell them about the angels and communists who are listening in on our party line—they smile harder and back out the door.

҉

One morning, Will, Geo, and I line up along the front-room windows to watch through the blinds as our grandfather finally arrives to take us away from our mother. We are going to live at our Aunt Nan's. We're watching, we've been waiting for this, as we've somehow known this would finally happen. My mother will end up spending years and years in the State Hospital at Camarillo. Our grandfather will come to get us and we will end up at Aunt Nan and Uncle Ned's when our mother loses custody. We will never again be allowed to live with her as her minor children.

Our mother is hiding from him behind the pomegranate tree at the back of the lot, but my grandfather doesn't know this and we will not tell on her, so he looks for her in the garage. He raises its door on its hinge, then stands back as a wave of beer cans, the thousands of beer cans she's been hiding there, begins to spill out around his ankles, this bright metallic river of red and silver and gold.

When we see the shock on his face—on everybody's faces—my brothers and I are glad.

We are our parents' children. We are *embarrassing*, we are *like* them, we are like those who arrive at a party where nothing's wrong and set about wrecking everything, unable to help ourselves from telling and retelling this terrible story, to the hilarity of no one but the three of us.

5

Arsenic Hour

JORDAN! MY AUNT SCREAMS. You knock that off! I want you to stop acting like you've been invaded. And you! She whips around to glare at me.
You're to stop provoking him with your pronouncements.

My cousin and I stopped fighting when we heard her coming, but
we're still breathing hard, sweating. My aunt is smart, at least as smart
as I am—she was in medical school when my uncle made her quit to
marry him—and there's no real way to hide things from her. My mother
calls her the brains of the outfit.

I am fifteen, Jordy's one year younger. My aunt had four children of
her own, then got my brothers and me.

Jordy is—I know—her favorite child, just as I'm the one she likes
least.

The skin of my aunt's face and neck and arms is deeply tanned
year-round because she's a lap swimmer. It's so thoroughly freckled
that looking down into her skin, you can see the flecks of color in all
the layers. My father, her brother, had skin like that. He's been dead
five years.

My own brothers and I haven't been in this family long enough to know what's meant by the things these people say. I'm not sure, for instance, what a *pronouncement* is.

My Aunt Nan and Delia, our San Marino grandmother, address children formally, using their real names—they're trying to appeal to what is civilized in our natures, so my brother Geo is called George Charles. Grandmother Delia likes to say children are the Limbs of Satan. She's usually drunk when she says this; then she and whoever's in the room with her will laugh.

Aunt Nan is furious, but I am madder still. I've just discovered this mute ability, that of watching her, or anyone, longer and harder than they can watch me. I watch her until her eyes glitter and she has to look away. She knows something, I understand, and whatever she knows is purpling the depths of the skin of her neck and face. Under my scrutiny, her tan is turning gaudy.

Aunt Nan's dark hair is sticking up from the way she combs it back to dry after swimming. She has a cowlick at her hairline that makes her bangs pop up—they come up and sway, like a wave on the verge of crashing. My father's hair was dark like hers, but his, like mine, was curly. They were the only dark-haired ones in a family that is mostly blond. My aunt's hair is stick straight, as she says. I can hardly get it to bend around the rollers when she has me set it for her cocktail parties. She's rich but hates for anyone to know this. She's rich but, as my mother says, cheap-cheap-cheap, so she won't waste money on a beauty parlor. Instead, she goes to a regular barber, who whacks it off into this sleek cap.

Jordy and I fight all the time, but this one's bad. My scalp aches from how he yanked me up by my hair. We're the same size but he's suddenly stronger than I am—this is absolutely new, as is his no longer being the one pudgy boy of my aunt's three. He's stronger than I am, but I'm still faster and smarter, and I know more words. I aim these words at him. I choose them carefully.

∭

These are performances, my aunt is saying, in which we demonstrate our complete lack of gratitude. It's four-thirty in the afternoon, the time right before dinner when all hell usually breaks loose, the time my aunt and uncle call the Arsenic Hour. We're fighting and Geo and Thomas aren't to be found and my uncle's just phoned to say he's not coming home, that Visiting Firemen are in town so he's taking them to dinner. He's with Lockheed. He's often out with Visiting Firemen or traveling out of town.

These are performances and we need to knock it off immediately, my aunt is saying.

I don't know what she's talking about. Jordy and I fight for a simpler reason: We hate each other.

It's during the Arsenic Hour that my aunt and her friends sit in the shade by the side of one or another's pool with their long, brown, Coppertoned legs stretched out into the still-hot sun of the late afternoon. They smoke and drink their tinkling drinks and talk about their husbands, who are out with Visiting Firemen or traveling out of town. It's the San Fernando Valley in the middle of the sixties, and the kids stay in the water until our eyes are red and squinty, swimming until our lungs ache. My blond hair has turned mint green from the chlorine.

The mothers wear the tennis dresses they drove home in from the club, or after swimming, they wear wraps, like terry-cloth turbans and caftans. They talk about their husbands as *him*, as if they were all married to the same one man.

My aunt, however, doesn't talk about my uncle. This is because she is a devout Episcopalian, as is Grandmother Delia. Religiousness is strange to me—though I am now baptized and confirmed at St. Nicholas Parish, I don't think my aunt's faith has much of anything to do with me. She doesn't gossip but enjoys listening to the husband stories. I lie flat out, my wet front pressed to the hot cement, face to one side. With my arms by my sides, my eyes squinted, they can't tell I'm listening.

Aunt Nan takes a deep drag from her cigarette, makes some low wry comment. She is droll, my mother says. Then her tilted face, in the shade of her hat brim, lights up with the white of her smile. She keeps her face in shadow, smiling as the others laugh.

She's tall, thin, handsome as a model, but she keeps her face bowed over her embroidery. She's working on vestments for the altar guild of St. Nicholas in Encino. My aunt is from the High Church part of my father's family, as my mother says—she and my father weren't Low Church as much as they were No Church Whatsoever. The threads my aunt is using are wound with filaments of real gold and actual silver. My aunt and uncle are too High Church to divorce—our father's mother's family has been in the country since the Moseses landed in Plymouth Colony in 1633, and there has never been a divorce. They're too High Church to kill themselves or to get themselves committed, as my own parents have done.

Still, I'm watching because something is wrong.

Something is wrong, though my aunt and uncle never argue, being too High Church to ever openly disagree. Instead, they'll have drinks and a discussion, the ironic tone of which I can hear through the wall of the living room. This wall has been made so the living room *communicates*—this is the word that's used—with the dining room, which is also the family room, and it's here that we are very rarely allowed to watch TV, though never on a school night. The things in this wall—fireplace, hi-fi, television—all work from either side, the TV being on a track that lets it slide through and swivel around. My aunt designed the wall one of the three or four times she was redoing this house, which is one of her ongoing and seemingly endless projects.

Is she still adding-on? my mother asks. This is one of the times my grandfather has driven us up to see her at Camarillo, where she gets a day pass and comes out with us to a restaurant for lunch. She says *adding-on* and then smiles knowingly at me, as if we both know this is truly aberrant behavior. One of the times my aunt was adding-on, she added a slide-out cupboard in the kitchen that holds nothing aside from the empty drum and rattle of the hung-up lids to pans.

I hear my aunt and uncle, lean over to look through the open fire-place, made of fieldstone. Her head is down; she's smiling hard at her bright embroidery. The silver of the needles leads the shining gold she's jabbing through. Oh, you talk a good fight, she says.

My uncle's done something for which he will not act sorry. He is teasing, playful. My uncle is very good looking. She takes a deep breath, smokes, presses her lips together. He hates her smoking, so she does it ever more defiantly. They met at Pomona College, he made her quit med school, and now she's stuck at home with all these kids. He's just bought a new Mustang convertible, and he's always out now with Visiting Firemen.

He's done something, and try as she might, she can't forgive him though she positions herself each Sunday in her own pew at the front of the church on the dark burgundy leather of the kneeler, her long tan fingers covering the darkness of her tan face, and prays fervently to God for the ability to do so.

〇〇〇

Though lacking in the virtue of forgiveness, my aunt is the most sainted woman in the neighborhood. She's famous for her good works, for her service to the altar guild and for Girls' Friendly Society and for having her own four kids, and for her then taking in her brother's three when *all that* went completely to hell.

She's so good that she at first took our dog, Ziggy—people said it might help my brother Geo adjust. My little brother's in the fourth grade, and he still can't read or write. He's been held back though he's tested as intelligent. We are all three much too intelligent, our Grandmother Delia says, which is at least *hawwwwlf* our problem. Now my brother Geo's getting so big, he doesn't look like he belongs in elementary school.

Aunt Nan got rid of Ziggy because he fought with my cousins' dalmatian. Murphy's valuable, unlike Ziggy, who was a mutt. Anyway, as my uncle put it, Murphy was here first. Murphy's stupid, which is fine because there's a certain admiration for the dumb in this portion of our family. This is a dog bred for looks, bred without leaving room behind his eyes for brains. Murphy is actually so completely stupid that he once loped, as we all watched, right across the way back of the backyard, behind the swimming pool, and ran right into a spurting Rain Bird. From that he got ten black Frankenstein stitches across his forehead; he looked like someone had finally broken down and paid for a brain transplant.

That's not funny, my aunt says.

Is so, I say back, but quietly, because I'm not allowed to sass her.

Murphy was show quality until he got the stitches. Ziggy was short, black, fattish. They fought because they were both males. Ziggy, like my brothers and I, was poorly disciplined. Aunt Nan took him to the pound, where he was placed in the E Room and *put to sleep*—the E stands for *euthanasia*. Then, to be fair, she had Murphy castrated. Because of med school, she uses the Latinate terms: *euthanized* or *castrated* instead of *altered, fixed, neutered,* or *put to sleep.* Because I'm furious, I say *killed* or *murdered.*

Our dog was killed, then my brother Will was sent to a military academy in San Rafael. One of his roommates is the son of Dear Abby. Another is the son of a prominent psychiatrist and they're both, Will says, at least as screwed up as we are.

Or maybe worse, Will says. He tells me stuff like this when he calls from Union Station. He calls at least once a month, when he runs away from the military academy and comes down to L.A. by train. Last time, he just walked away from drills, still wearing his dress uniform. He's so tall now, people on the train believed he was in the regular Army.

Do you remember the time Mom forgot us at that nursery school? he asks this month when he phones. When she was so late coming they had to leave, so they locked us outside the school and left us on the porch, sitting in the rain?

I have no recollection of this event and am imagining it must have happened when I was very little, before Geo was even born. I'm holding my breath. I can't even breathe out any kind of reply.

They could have been arrested, he says. What they did was against the law.

Who? I ask him. *Our mother and our father?* I'm suddenly yelling at him because I'm so startled. The memory of our parents is fragile, like woodsmoke on a windy day—never do Will or I say a word against them. Never, really, do we even think it. Will and I don't speak ill of them, and Geo hardly ever says a word at all.

Not them, my older brother says. The ones who had the nursery school. Put Geo on; let me ask him.

Geo holds the receiver to his ear, staring at the floor. His nose is huge and extravagantly freckled, shiny red where it's peeled and peeled. The nose itself is big, but the nostrils are absolutely tiny. Through these small holes, my brother has the enormous task of first breathing in, then breathing out. Sometimes, when I sneak out of the house at night, I go around to the boys' wing and stand at the window next to my brother's bed. He always sleeps with the light on, so I'm able to watch him. He lies flat on his back without ever moving, breathing noisily in, then noisily out. I am fifteen years old, and I've learned a couple of things. One thing I know?

This is not the sleep of a child.

∭

When Will runs away and comes down to L.A. by train, he spends one night with elegant Grandmother Delia before they put him back on the train going to San Rafael. This grandmother has just left her big house, where she was—as it's said—rattling around, to stay all year in the beach house at Manhattan. We see her every weekend day when we go to the beach from late spring through the fall—it's so my aunt can check on her.

I've stopped belonging to the kind of family I used to have, which was artists, writers, and intellectuals, and have come to live here in this house of surfers.

My big brother's shown me a picture of a bird he says resembles our Grandmother Delia. It's a brightly plumed bird of prey called the harpy eagle. *Cchchcchchhhhh* . . . Will breathes loudly from deep in his throat, imitating her. Lips drawn wide, he's wagging his tongue in the back of his wide-open mouth, just as our grandmother does when she's drunk and comes bumping down the hall of the beach house to tuck us in again.

When we sleep at her house, she stays up late to play the piano. She has a grand piano in her living room at the beach that was moved from her old house—also an upright, also an antique organ you pump with your feet that we're not supposed to mess with.

As she plays, she drinks vermouth from a tall crystal water goblet. I listen to her ice tinkle.

After a while of playing, she starts weeping on the keys. She drinks, plays, weeps, then comes down the long hall in the pitch black night to tuck us in again, though we're already deeply asleep. In this way, breathing her rasping alcoholic breath, she once came to Geo's bed to lean over the place where he was too laboriously sleeping and woke him up, scaring him so much he threw up apple juice and cashews all over her French-laundered sheets.

〇〇〇

My aunt and uncle's house sits on almost an acre of land in a tract that was recently walnut groves. They bought it new, then started adding wings to it—the boys' wing was first. My aunt does the design herself. In this way she's copying my father, her older brother, who was an architect.

She copies him just as I copy my brother Will by being a smartass.

I lie in bed at night and try to imagine seeing this house from above, as an architect might, the wings reaching out and away from one another around the patio that sits in front of the lap pool. I can't imagine my father in heaven, spying on the things I do. Will says he killed himself over the ugliness of buildings, over his having to design the same gross thing over and over again all down the Miracle Mile, like Tishman One, Two, Three.

I want to believe our dad died of the ugliness of buildings, but I remember the look on his face one night, the night when the three of us tricked him.

It was winter; we were living at the beach. When my father came in from work, his face felt freezing to the touch of my lips. His homecoming had a ritual aspect to it. How was your day, dear? he'd always ask my mother, to which she'd say sardonically, Oh, ginger peachy keen. By then they both hated almost everything.

How was my day, Daddy? I'd say, at which my parents both laughed.

This night we called out to him: Daddy! Can we get you *anything*? Your paper? Your slippers? Can we bring you *a beer*?

Our father's face, which was gray with cold and weariness, opened like the quick shutter of a working camera. We brought him the *L.A. Mirror*, which was the afternoon paper, and handed him his beer. We watched him drink, then sputter, then gasp and gag, then spit the beer out. He looked at us, hurt, aghast. April Fool's! we yelled, jumping around. We were all clean and bathed and dressed in our pajamas. We'd splurted the can open using the opener called a church key, poured some beer out, and funneled a big handful of salt into it.

Not funny, I think now, sounding like my aunt. *I'm lying in the dark in another one of these other people's houses, and it's years too late to tell him I am so, so sorry.*

∭

Our parents were the way they were, Will says, because they were bohemian. The others in our family are all upper middle class, or petite bourgeois, as Will says. He says this the way our parents did, in order to laugh at them: *pet-IT ber-goys*. He calls our aunt's house *ber-goys*, her furnishings *ber-goys*. One main reason he's been sent to the military academy in San Rafael is for him to learn to comport himself.

Our tiny, exquisite grandmother is fluent in Spanish. *Comporté bien,* she tells us when she's asking us to behave ourselves.

Aunt Nan's color scheme is marine: all sea blues, sea greens, and the beige she calls *sand*. Her furniture is teak and modern. With six kids at home, she does all her own housework with help only from a once-a-week cleaning lady and Eunice, who's the laundress. My aunt and Eunice work together to wash the sheets and hang them out in the laundry yard by the side of the garage. Our grandmother has her sheets washed and starched and pressed at the laundry, but my aunt believes in the healthy properties of linens dried in the air and the sun.

She doesn't allow us to eat sugar. She swims a mile of laps every morning, then gets out, dries off, and starts smoking cigarettes. She and my mother and our Grandmother Delia all smoke cigarettes—the women smoke because they went to college, because they think it will keep them from becoming fat. My uncle says smoking is a filthy habit. My aunt says cigarettes are cheaper than tranquilizers. My grandmother owns stock in R. J. Reynolds, so she smokes with small, patriotic puffs.

My aunt swims laps and makes us do so, too. The biggest boys—my cousin Jordy and his big brother Graham—swim competitively, and so will Geo and Thomas soon. Lizzie and I are exempted from swim team by virtue of being girls—the girls' team trains at the swim club at different times, so my aunt can't really get us there.

Girls in this family do other, more home-based, more pioneer-seeming things. My aunt's taught me to sew my own clothes from Simplicity patterns, and we save money by shopping at the Samples and Seconds store in Reseda, where the dresses are already ripped from being tried on by girls too big to fit into them. My aunt takes me to her barber for a haircut. My hair is matted and dirty. I almost never comb it, so it clumps at my neck in tangles and knots. My going around like I don't care what I look like drives my aunt nuts. She says I look *unkempt*, but I know what she really means, which is, You look like your mother, who is—as we well remember—*a mental patient!* In a *locked ward* at Camarillo!

So? I think. So what? So I'm supposed to be *ashamed* of that . . . ?

She saves money on the boys' haircuts by doing them herself with her own clippers. She accomplishes this task on the screened-in porch, where she has them sit on newspaper on the picnic table. Her face becomes small and mean when she concentrates, as if she did become a surgeon.

The boys first laugh at one another, at how—with their hair suddenly short—their freckled noses look bigger and more sunburned and their ears stick out from their scalps. Then it comes to be their turn. Jordy and Lizzie have my aunt's dark hair, while Graham, Thomas, Geo, and I are all blond, so the four of us look more closely related. She leaves each boy with only the slightest fringe in front, which he can comb upward with Dixie Peach Pomade. Everybody laughs at everybody else and somebody always cries.

I'm spared homemade haircuts and swim team and Poopy Patrol, which is the cute name given to picking up after Murphy in the yard, because I am a girl. Lizzie and I never have to do yardwork, as that's what boys do while girls work inside.

And because I'm a girl, I'm prohibited from setting foot in the boys' wing, which is exactly where I go if I ever find myself home alone, something that almost never happens. My aunt designed the wing as one long room divided by built-in bunks and closets, one desk per alcove, one alcove per boy. The ceiling is papered with the eerie see-through blue of sunlight breaking into a thousand pieces in the waves in dozens of surfing posters. I study them as I lie on the top bunk, right next to a closet wall, breathing in and out like my little brother does. I dream of drowning, of being dead, which would be like being extinguished; dream, too, of the weight of various boys I know from school lying on top of me.

My aunt's calling me from the kitchen, but I cannot be found.

She wants me to help look for Lizzie's kitten, which has been gone all day. My aunt calls one more time, then takes the little kids—Geo, Thomas, and Lizzie—out through the laundry yard.

As soon as they're gone, I go into the boys' bathroom to smell their things. They have different products than girls do: powder for athlete's foot, a tube of Clearasil, acid for Graham's plantar warts. Graham's a year ahead of me in school. When we pass in the hall—though we look alike—we ignore each other by tacit agreement. I put his gunked-up safety razor to the side of my own face and watch myself in the mirror. It would be easier on my aunt, I know, if I were not a girl—she knows what to do about boys, at least: drive them here and there, drop them off for sports, ship them off to San Rafael to learn to behave themselves.

I go out to walk through the lines of still-damp sheets in the laundry yard—the smell of bleach and wet and cleanliness is better than any perfume, and I feel it on my face and arms. I climb up onto the half fence, then onto the roof of the bike shed, from which I can boost myself onto the redwood shakes of the garage. I climb the slope to the top of the garage roof, where I can lie on my stomach and peek over while well hidden by the leaves of a huge walnut tree.

I'm watching them: the way my aunt is so sure of what she's doing. This confidence comes, I believe, from her faith in God. I'm watching her shepherding the kids as they go door to door, the little boys taking every other house, my aunt and my cousin Lizzie going up to the ones the little boys are skipping, she having organized them to hopscotch efficiently.

It's Lizzie's face I'm watching. She's eight years old; her face is pure and innocent. Nothing bad has happened to her yet, so she doesn't even know to resent us. According to Jordy's version, when we came it wrecked everything—we remind my uncle of tragedy, so he started staying away. Jordy calls us The Invasion. It's Lizzie's kitten that's missing, but she doesn't think it's dead. Instead this is exciting, it's new, so she looks eager, interested.

〇〇〇

My uncle says I'm his favorite niece, that he's my favorite uncle. This is a joke because I'm his only niece and, since my mother was an only child, he's my only uncle. I'm his only niece because boys run in our family. My uncle wanted a daughter but had to wait through three boys to finally get to her. Lizzie is like my aunt: the baby girl, the youngest. My aunt was my father's favorite person.

Thomas prefers not to be called Tom, or Tommy; he wants his serious and formal name to be used. It's because he's the youngest of my aunt and uncle's boys and he wants to distinguish himself somehow, something my brothers and I will never have to worry about, having been distinguished forever by our parents' actions.

I'm lying on my bed, watching Thomas out my window. He's talking seriously to some grown-ups at my aunt and uncle's cocktail party. He says something to someone not the slightest bit interested, then pushes his glasses back up his nose. He's saying something about how his middle initial is actually NMI, meaning No Middle Initial; that by the time my aunt and uncle got to Thomas, they'd run out of good boys' names.

That's nice, honey, some big-busted, hairsprayed, Hollywood-type woman is saying to my little cousin, as she's reaching past him to get at what she really wants to do, which is pluck some fancy toothpicked food chunk from the ornamental pineapple on the buffet table. Many of the people in our neighborhood are modestly famous because they work in what people here call The Industry.

Thomas! I'm trying to caution my cousin through my powerful powers of mental telepathy: *Movie Lady doesn't give a shit about your No Middle Initial, doesn't care about dinos, either . . .*

This decorated pineapple, also some of its jolly pineapple friends, are all bristling gaily with chunks of orange cheese, big pink shrimp, and cubes of ham, all of which have been stuck into them with bright and frilly cocktail toothpicks. The idea came from a women's magazine. I am one of those responsible for the way these pineapples are now sitting there, completely armored with snacks. While we were doing it together this afternoon, I told my aunt, You know, this is *exactly* the kind of fun-type item—and I showed my aunt a pretty party toothpick—that makes me want to kill myself.

That's not funny, Jane, she said.

Is so, I said back, but quietly, at which she fluttered her eyelashes involuntarily, which meant she was furious with me.

No, *really*, I went on, at least seven Americans die annually of tooth-pick death. I added, Goes in, gets swallowed, gets lodged sideways.

They do not, she told me.

Do so, I said. And they die from choking on party balloons, which is completely easy to understand, the way little kids will get a balloon and put it in their mouth and bite it until it pops, and a piece of rubber snaps back into their throats and completely seals their airways.

Where do you get all this? my aunt asked.

I shrugged. Here and there, I said.

Why do you imagine we need to know these things?

Be prepared? I asked. Or maybe it's only depression, I add, which is really truly epidemic in our family, do you realize this?

What I do about depression, my aunt said, is either swim or pray, or if that doesn't work, I do both.

I was thinking, *You!* Even *you* are depressed sometimes? But I didn't ask her this. Instead I went on saying what I was saying, which I was saying in order to be what one of my grandmothers calls Negative and the other calls always being *anti*-this and *anti*-that. I like to concentrate on the grim details, on the way kids die every day from aspirated balloons or choke on a chunk of sucked-down hotdog that really effectively plugs the airways, or of accidental woundings from a lead pencil, which is poison, which is why they're switching to graphite, or from flukeily falling out a window or having a tree fall over on you or getting hit by a car as you cross the street in the crosswalk, completely minding your own business.

◌◌◌

It's later that same night. I'm in my room with the light out, looking back into the lit-up portion of the house, where her party is going on. I can't see my uncle, which means he's probably in the family room. I'm no longer talking to my aunt and I'm no longer helping.

Before the screened porch was added, my windows opened to the outside of the house. It's hot—the sliding glass doors to the living room and dining room are all standing open so air and guests can circulate, and my own windows are open so I can overhear.

Lizzie's kitten, which I've been keeping in the record cabinet of my mother's hi-fi, is meowing. I go and get it out. There are clots of shit in there on my mother's albums. My mother loves musical comedy but I don't, but I keep her albums anyway, not to listen to but to gaze at as I remember her. She has *South Pacific, Oklahoma!, Annie Get Your Gun,* and *My Fair Lady.*

The kitten's fluffy and purring. It weighs so little that my hand holding it feels only the slightest heft, a tiny piece of fur and its vibration. I cradle this purring bit of pale gray fluff to hold it to my face, but then, as I feel myself beginning to love it, this gets in the way of what I feel for my own things, my own mother and father, my own brothers, and especially Ziggy, who was my own dog. I miss my mother, so I open the top of the console, where the record changer is, and breathe in deeply the air that stays in there because I never leave it open. By keeping the lid down all the time, I'm saving the air she breathed and that still belongs to her, as it contains her smell.

I open the door to the hall and push the kitten out. It moves off on a diagonal. I close the door and go back to my window.

My aunt's wearing a sleek, black, beaded evening dress with spaghetti straps. Her back is tan and lean. She has a red flower in her hair because of this party's hula theme. Her dress is one that has arrived unbidden, sent by Grandmother Delia, who bought it for her at some chic, expensive shop on Wilshire Boulevard in Beverly Hills. Our grandmother likes to shop by phone, to arrange to have a package brought round by messenger, using the unexpected delivery as a form of wordless criticism. She's recently had a vanity table and chair delivered to me. I sometimes look at them, about the least likely objects I would ever own. *Exquisite*, I can hear her saying as she ordered the fancy mirror, the delicate wrought-iron legs that hold the glass tabletop, the sweet chair that's covered with the most darling pink plush fur.

The card that came with the furniture wasn't signed. It read: "Stand up straight and get your clothes on right."

I look at the card over and over and think, *What the hell?*

The three shiny bumps on top of my aunt's head show the crimp of the roller pins where I put her hair up for this party—she makes me do

71

it, though I totally lack hair skills, just as she does. She doesn't believe I can't do it, because, like my mother, I am artistic, and my mother, very famously, could cut hair. My aunt thinks I can make her hair look good and even stylish if only I put my mind to it, when this is completely outside the realm of any possibility. Besides, she doesn't take time to pamper herself.

Father Robert Gerhardt of St. Nicholas Parish is one of my aunt and uncle's party guests. My aunt looks young and shy around him, like she knows Father Gerhardt is watching. We call him Father Bob. Because we're Episcopalians, our priests can marry and have families, but Father Bob isn't married and lives in the rectory with his mother, who is English.

Because he's a priest and is dressed in black with his white collar, he makes people nervous. I watch them talking to him for a moment, smiling too warmly, then moving away so they can snarl and swear and think bad things. He is actually a pretty cool guy who talks to us in youth group on Sunday evenings about our fucked-up families.

He is sitting on a dark green and blue plaid chair that goes with the theme of sea and sky and hula-ness.

You know, I told my aunt as we were pinning the crap on the pineapples, even the sound of the word *Hawaii* somehow makes me want to kill myself. That was when she told me to go to my room and not come out, saying *that* would be about enough of *that*.

Father Gerhardt is holding his drink in one hand and has a toothpicked shrimp on a fancy napkin balanced on his knee; this shrimp is covered by his tented fingers. My cousin Thomas is bothering him— Thomas and Geo are both in training to be acolytes, so Thomas is trying to get him to pay attention by talking to him about a thousand thousand years ago when the dinosaurs roamed the earth.

Father Gerhardt is also listening to an angry lady who's still mad at him for when he spoke from the pulpit in favor of the Rumford Fair

Housing Act. We are all in favor of desegregation in our family, of de-segregating schools and neighborhoods and workplaces. We're in favor of desegregation since it in no way affects us, since no one in our family has ever known someone who was anything but completely white, except the help, and except when traveling to far-off countries. When Father Gerhardt spoke in favor of Rumford Fair Housing, more than half of the congregation got up and walked out.

Now he's keeping his shrimp resting on his knee because the lady's too angry to have a priest eat food in front of her, and he doesn't want to mix up the mess of eating with what he's supposed to be doing as a priest, which is listening carefully.

He's paying patient and courteous attention to what she's saying, even as his eyes track my aunt as she moves around the room. He puts his drink down, swipes his palm down the length of one thigh, and puts the shrimp down on the side table on top of its napkin, where it will stay, uneaten. He's a man, I see, who's virtually overwhelmed by what it takes to be at a party, and he looks over at my aunt longingly, as if he is there only because of her and only she can save him. Then he crosses his leg the wide way, to show he's not a fairy, and this is exactly when Lizzie comes into the living room to show her mom the kitten and all happy hell breaks loose.

I've just learned that in the San Fernando Valley at this hula-themed party, a screened-in porch goes by the name *lanai*.

※

I'm lying flat out on the shake roof of the garage, hidden by the bending branches of the heavily laden black walnut tree, whose nuts hang in their bright green sheaths like an odd kind of fruit, slightly smaller than tennis balls and good for walnut wars.

I can hear Jordy climbing up the bike shed behind me—he's no doubt mad at me over something I said or did and I can't even remember any longer.

I'm eating a bag of Corn Nuts while I watch for Father Gerhardt's Karmann Ghia, which will pull onto our street and drive two blocks north before it pulls into our driveway. He comes to visit at least once a week, always during Arsenic Hour. If it's four-ish, he and my aunt have tea; if it's more like five, they have drinks my aunt makes at the two-way bar.

Corn Nuts give you horse breath, my cousin has, evidently, climbed all the way up here to tell me.

Oh, go to hell, I say, but mildly. He's as annoying as a constantly droning insect, so I'm trying a new tactic, which is ignoring him. I'm watching my aunt as she suddenly opens the front door and looks out, imagining the entry as a guest might see it: bright flowers on either side of the door in blue enamel pots her mother brought her from Mexico. The entry's new, added on in the last round of addings-on, when the master suite was built out into the front yard.

The floor of the entry is greenish-black polished slate and hard to maintain, so she works away at it. Her perfume, a fragrance called Replique, seems to pool right there at knee height when she's subtly dressed up for Father Gerhardt's visit and can't keep herself from buffing.

You can't swear at me, my cousin says. This isn't your house. You don't even live here.

Oh, go to fucking hell, I say. I sound bored, unimpressed by the way stupid fucking Jordy is now standing over me and straddling my body. He is upright on the shakes, which are slippery with moss and lichen, so he's holding on to one of the larger branches of the walnut tree. He's wearing moccasins but no socks, and there are calcified knots on the tops of his feet from kneeling on his surfboard. The skin along the top of his feet and as far up his ankles as I can see is deeply brown and as hairless as a girl's. He has hair now in other places, which I know because he's been moved to Lizzie's and my wing and we now have to share our bathroom with him, where I find evidence of his recent puberty.

With one set of toes gripping through the mocs, he lifts the other foot and takes a little kick at my side. I said, he says, you *may not* swear at me.

Oh, up yours, I say. Up yours, actually, with a ten-foot pole. I'm watching Father Gerhardt's little burnt-orange sports car turn onto our street and start toward our driveway. He drives carefully, like a priest, with his hands on the steering wheel at ten and two o'clock. I am watching him so intently that it's a surprise that Jordy has started huffing, kicking his lame little ineffectual, one-footed kicks at me.

Know what, Jordy? I ask him. You kick like a fucking girl.

Which is when he actually goes a little bit nuts. He falls on me right there on the roof of the garage and is sitting on my hips and weeping down upon my shirt as he slugs me. I turn to look at him.

Jordy's eyes don't match—he has a brown one and a pale green one that's more or less the color of the sheathed walnuts. His eyes put me in mind of the word *diabolic*, and of how our grandmother always uses a foreign language to correct us, saying, ¡*Callate!* to us in Spanish.

Your mother's *crazy*, Jordy's saying, even as he weeps down on me. You don't even *live here* and you can't even *say* the stuff you say. Your father threw himself off a roof, just like you're going to do. He starts prying at my fingers, trying to get me to loosen my grasp.

Jordy is one of Father Gerhardt's favorites—he serves as an acolyte behind the rail, helping with communion. He's at church all the time for this or that and is easily the most devout of my aunt's children. Still, he doesn't want to grow up and have a peaceful profession. Instead, he says, he wants to be a sheriff, though this is the kind of wish most boys outgrow by the time they're six. Everyone knows it's so Jordy can enforce the rules. Jordy is, has always been, rulebound, and very interested in everybody else's going by the rules as well, though the rules, in the part of the family I come from, aren't anything about which anyone really gives a shit.

Well, I say imperiously, in my best imitation of Grandmother Delia, my mother *may indeed be* crazy, and my father *may have* committed suicide, but at least *they* didn't have *a thing* for the parish priest.

I'm lying on my stomach and cannot fight back. He smashes his fist into the center of my back as hard as he can. He's saying things that even he can't really understand, as he tries to pry my fingers up. Then he abruptly stops, stands up, and slides back down the slope on the slick soles of his mocs—the shakes are mossy and stained with the rounded shapes of exploding walnut husks that pelt down in wind or rain.

He hops off the bike shed, then runs across the side yard by the boys' wing with Murphy rocking along next to him. Murphy's so stupid he thinks Jordy's romping alongside him, that they're both having a little impromptu fun, though my cousin has his fists clenched tightly at his sides and is sobbing so loudly I can still hear him.

Jordan! my aunt calls from the back of the house. What in God's name is going on?

Nothing! he shouts out angrily, but my aunt knows, I know, because my aunt knows everything.

I'm silent, dry-eyed, still holding my bag of Corn Nuts. He's weeping from frustration, I understand, that I'm nothing but a girl who doesn't even live here and he still can't make me cry. He doesn't get it; he thinks he has this strange cousin who never cries, when what I really am is someone who once did cry, then suddenly didn't.

◍

It's because Jordy's been so mean to Geo and Thomas in trying to get them to behave that he's been moved from the boys' wing to the oldest part of the house, which is the hallway along which Lizzie's and my bedrooms are. This is why we three all need to share a bathroom now.

Every night Jordy waits behind his closed door to hear when I start down the darkness of the carpeted hallway, always being as quiet as I possibly can. Every night I almost get there, but his bedroom is at the corner right next to the bathroom and across from it, so all he needs to do is open his door, take two steps, go in, and shut the bathroom door behind him, which is what he does every night after he listens patiently to hear me coming.

It's been going on now for days, for weeks. Jordy never gets tired of doing it—I can tell it's what he's thinking about when he looks at me at dinner and smiles his triumphant, weird-eyed I-was-here-first smile.

Graham and I usually have almost nothing to do with each other but recently have started speaking really softly to each other about Jordy. We speak of him in the third person because it bothers him.

Left-handed, Graham says. It's the origin of *gauche*, also *sinister*. They used to burn them as witches.

What do you imagine someone like that would put on his driver's license in the place for eye color? I ask. Answer D: all of the above?

And there's a breed of dog like that, Graham tells me quietly, as my aunt gets up from the table to go get something.

Jordy sits right across from us, on the left-handed side of the dining table. My family is almost all boys, and more than half, counting Will, are left-handed, which is statistically anomalous. The left-handed kids—Lizzie, Jordan, Thomas—all sit opposite Graham, Geo, and me, who are right-handed, blond, and currently looking angelic.

Jordy, I notice, is trying to ignore the new alliance between Graham and me. He's gazing off into later that same evening, when, he imagines, he'll experience yet another bathtime victory.

He always wins and he doesn't get tired of doing this, though it's boring and repetitive and I've begun to notice he's not as quick out his door as he once was, which means he's overconfident and getting a little bit lazy.

I never win; then one night, I do. I'm wearing the shoes Graham and Jordy tease me about—these are dark brown clunky oxfords. I wear these shoes on purpose, even though dressing like this is a chop. I wear them though Jordan and Graham call them my Little Man Shoes. I wear them because they remind me of my father. My father wore dress shoes made in Italy. He had them professionally shined.

This night, the night I win, I am wearing my leather shoes, nothing a normal girl would wear, and I get one foot into the doorjamb before my cousin can manage to lock it.

We're whispering hard words at each other through the crack in the door so my aunt won't hear us. She's off in her wing of the house, sewing vestments and listening to *La Bohème* as she bends over her embroidery. She goes off by herself to listen to opera because my uncle can't really stand it. He calls it *caterwauling* and plays his own music loudly in the living room. His favorite singer right then is Nancy Sinatra; his favorite song of hers is "These Boots Are Made for Walking."

My turn, Jordy guy, I tell him. My voice is sweet and persuasive. Fair's fair, I say. I'm taking my turn tonight, Jordy-Pordy-Lordy. I'm going first this time.

No you aren't, Nikita, he says from the other side of the door he's trying to close. You don't even live here, Fidel.

If I don't live here, I ask, why do I keep turning up like this, day after day after day?

Jordy thinks my parents are communists because they were the first people in our family to stop voting Republican.

You kick like a girl, I say. Know that, Jordy. Plus, you're weak willed. You're just a stupid surfer acolyte and you cry and cry. You didn't think that you, in the whole huge scheme of things, were actually going to win, did you?

I am more determined—this is what I have, it's my secret, it is what will always save me, I can wait and wait. I can outwait him, I can out-wait anyone. I sense him inside wavering. I use this wavering in his resolve to shove the door back so it rides up over his toes. He yelps and starts hopping around on one foot, like he's severely wounded, which he quite frankly is not. He's doing all this silently, so my aunt won't hear him. Fighting is now completely prohibited since we got in trouble last time. The next time we're caught fighting, Jordy and I will both be grounded for most of the rest of our lives.

I walk in calmly, lean over, turn on my bathwater. I am acting like he's invisible. He's still hopping; leftover tears still fly off inadvertently from his mismatched eyes. His face is so twisted with pain of various kinds, I practically feel sorry for him.

Get out, I say, or I'm telling her you busted in here while I had my clothes off in order to spy on me, and in saying this into the air, I make it real and so begin to unbutton my shirt, which begins to show my bra, which is when Jordan begins to understand the many and profound ways in which he has so totally and forever lost this war, the wrong one, the one he never knew he was fighting.

But he doesn't want to give it up, which is how we all are when it's our childhood and we're suddenly so terrified of losing the only thing we've ever known. So he comes flying like it's still before, back in the Olden Days, and we fall to the floor and are wrestling around in the same old way, though the charge of it is completely different, and my aunt, who has always known everything, is suddenly there at the door, pounding on it with the flat of her hand and yelling.

We freeze. We watch each other's faces, we are intent on the frozen look on the other one's face. Jordan, she says, turn the water off! Leave some hot water for others.

All right, my cousin says. He and I stare at one another and his eyes have suddenly opened and he is startled by what he's thinking. It's as if we've just stumbled into this strange new place, like the pioneers did when they walked west across the entire country and crossed into a desert of Deep Geologic Time that had landforms in it that were simply beyond their understanding.

My cousin is afraid, but this is because he's a boy and he is younger than I am and he hasn't lived through all I've lived through, which has made me eerily confident. I am confident and determined to make myself at home in this new place and he senses this in me so now he'll mind me, I know, no matter what I tell him to do.

Turn the water off, I mouth. I am moving my lips, making no sound at all.

Water off, I tell him. *Then go, and lock the door.*

6
Some Boy

I AM TURNING SIXTEEN, and I'm being raised by relatives, which means I have to learn to adapt to the rules of what feels like a different country. I try, therefore, to assimilate, all the while keeping my most true self— this is the child who is my own mother's daughter and my own father's daughter—hidden away from them. I am as odd, as strange as my parents were but I am better at hiding it. What I am hiding is myself, and it's like I've shoplifted something valuable that does in fact belong to me, but I have to keep it safely out of sight, grasped in the palm of my hand that I then keep shoved deep into the front pocket of my jeans.

My aunt says I'm not to slouch. She says it; I glare at her. I'm as tough as the boys but I can't win physical fights with them so now I have to boss and trick them. I must become better at being a girl, an identity that's vague to me, inexact, and hard to fathom.

My cousins and my little brother keep reptiles and amphibians: salamanders, snakes, also a chameleon that changes colors not only in different surroundings but also according to its moods. I'm like this— learning to dress in a new bright way, a chameleon turning all her happiest colors. I am tan. My hair is now long and blonde and straight. I live in a household full of surfers so I've become a surfer. Jordy and I have become friends. He minds me and we share effortlessly, as if we're brother and sister. We have a board we have to share with the littler kids, which is a Hobie and wrecked, both dinged and waterlogged, but I don't care because I don't really care about surfing. The board is long and old fashioned and heavy. It's so ugly it's a chop, but I only own my part in it so I'll be asked along by Graham when he and his friends head out early, even before dawn, so early the day comes alive in the east with the morning light as we drive north toward Trestles or south toward Orange County, where we surf Doheny Point or Rincon. I go with them so I get to be with boys.

Graham is an amazing surfer and is turning out to be a friend of mine. The girls sit on towels and sunbathe and talk. At home we put lemon juice on our hair to bleach streaks into it as we lie out by the pool, then we set it and iron it straight and go to the beach, and we don't swim because getting wet would wreck all the work we've just put into it. All the boys surf except for Robert Burlingham, who's thuggish and hangs around us like a shadow. Robert's a friend of Graham's, not mine.

Robert's the oldest of the Burlinghams—his parents, Sarah and Michael, are from England and are close friends of my aunt and uncle's. Together they play bridge, go out to dinner, drink. The mothers sometimes take all the kids on joint camping trips.

Robert's the oldest of four children: three boys, then a girl. The youngest is Katrina, who's the same age as my cousin Lizzie. Robert is Graham's age or maybe older, but he's been held back, so sometimes we have classes together.

Robert's the only one of the Burlingham boys who's dumb. Not only is he dumb, he also isn't that good-looking, as his face comes forward hawkishly and his forehead looks Neanderthal—my eyes see and my mind notes this, while my body has meanwhile begun to pay attention to his.

I see what Robert Burlingham looks like, I note that he isn't that good looking, but what my mind knows my body doesn't seem to care about, as it's my body that reacts to him, so it becomes alert and even nervous when he's around.

Now it's complicated: If my body decides it likes the body or maybe the look of the lips or the neck of a boy, it moves through the house toward the boys' wing where this boy might be. Robert Burlingham is sometimes over, visiting my cousin. But my mind and mouth disparage him, insulting his bad grades in algebra, and Robert, who doesn't like me either, insults me back, saying my being a freshman of the most lowly sort—this is called being a B-9 to his A-9—is the biggest chop of all. It's a symptom of how dumb he is that all Robert can come up with is to criticize my being a half grade behind him.

And no one would ever accuse Robert Burlingham of being clever, but my body is oblivious to his stupidity. He does have command in the social world and wears a letterman's sweater for swim team, as does Graham.

Michael and Sarah are wry and sophisticated. Michael went to boarding school in Austria and skied with my father, and he's somehow related to Louis Comfort Tiffany, as people often mention, and I'll nod though I have no idea who this is.

So Robert is anyway always around, hanging out with Graham, watching TV in the boys' wing, and he's someone I run into not only in the halls at school but in the kitchen of my own house, in which case he and I each make faces and say, *Ewwww, gross.* Robert doesn't like me any more than I like him but his body is aware of mine, too, so when his real girlfriend breaks up with him, he asks me out.

We're supposed to be going to some event—maybe this is a dance that's sponsored by a church or maybe it's Cotillion—but instead we go to the drive-in, where we make out throughout the entire movie called *Soldier in the Rain,* starring Steve McQueen. This is the first time I understand what sex is and why a person might get caught up in it, even though you don't basically even very much like this boy or very much respect him, in that your body doesn't actually care that he isn't as smart as you are and he isn't even consistently nice to you, sometimes saying hello in the halls, other times ignoring you because he's walking along surrounded by all these bitchen girls from his own grade.

It's that you like the way he smells and the way his mouth tastes and that the soft insistence of his tongue seems like exactly the right kind of tongue to you and his lips are shaped just so and have a softness and a firmness, but it is honestly mostly his weight on you, the actual physical weight of this boy lying on top of you in the back seat of his mom's station wagon, as he's trying to shove your shirt up to get at what you know he calls your tits, though you won't let him because he's basically a clod who isn't even your boyfriend, so you shove his hand away whenever he moves it toward you, and you'd probably let him feel you up if it were not for the fact that your underclothes are, as usual, wrecked, what your grandmother calls *disgraceful*, in that they're all old and you refuse to sew your bra back together so it's just this ruined thing held together with safety pins.

My aunt and his mother belong to the daytime bridge club in the neighborhood, and our families vacation together in San Clemente during the month of August, where my aunt and Sarah Burlingham rent side-by-side houses to hold their ten kids and all these dogs and even grandparents. Grandmother Delia, who hates being left out of anything, comes along—though she's a redhead and won't go in the sun, so she stays in the house away from the beach, cooking magnificent French meals with dainty vegetables she gets at Jurgenson's, like white asparagus that comes in cans, and meat whose sauce so reeks of wine that us kids won't eat it—and there's Robert all the time, looking at me cross-eyed or sourly or in a smartass way, with him and Graham talking loudly about which girls they *really* like, which has to do with their having tits or not.

It's nothing but boys at the beach in August. Because Lizzie and Katrina, who's called Missie, are so much younger than I am, I sometimes hang out with Jordy. My cousin and I barely even remember how much we hated each other when I first came to live there; now he and I are the closest friends.

"Familiarity breeds contempt" was one of our Grandfather Vandenburgh's sayings, or so my mother tells me (I can hardly remember him), but Jordy and I are like an old married couple who have mutual interests. We talk, bodysurf, fish, watch the same TV shows, have a shell-and-rock collection. We beat each other at chess and cribbage, at which we're pretty evenly matched.

But at the beach one late afternoon during those last sad days of summer, when the shadows in the sand elongate and suddenly become so dark they look like holes that drill down into the middle of the earth, and the light changes in such a dramatic way it's as if it's meant to illuminate everything's emptiness, Robert Burlingham lets it slip that he and I, in those days of yore, didn't go to Cotillion and ended up instead at the drive-in movie, not watching *Soldier in the Rain*. Everyone stops what they're doing—eating mixed nuts, reading comic books, doing crosswords, or playing the game of War—and turns to stare at me.

I am usually in hiding in this family, which is like a foreign country, in which I try to dress as much like a boy as I can and come and go as if I were a boy, so everyone turns to look at me, as if I've been an imposter or a spy and am suddenly being revealed as the girl I am. Now everyone's eyes seem to see me differently, as if I'm new to them and they now see that I'm dangerous.

My face becomes instantly hot and it makes no difference that I deny it, saying, In your dreams, Burlingham; my aunt knows it's true in the way my aunt always already knows everything.

So she asks to speak to me privately, and I get up and follow her out of the living room and see Robert Burlingham, the smug idiotic shit, grinning and wagging his too-thick one-brow at me up and down like he's Groucho Marx.

My aunt says that when we get home from the beach I am grounded for the first three weekends of the school year. I say it isn't fair, that Robert's not going to be in any way punished, and she says that's up to Sarah and Michael, and I say but it's his fault, that he's the boy, that he's older than me, that it was his idea, that he only asked me out and took me to the drive-in to make his real girlfriend jealous.

No one, my aunt says, ever said anything about any part of this being fair, and she gestures around at not only the dumpy little vacation house where we've all been stashed away for the entire month of August, but also the entire circumstance of what it is to be the woman my aunt is or my mother is, one who's educated and sophisticated yet finds herself perched here on the very edge of the civilized world, far away from everything she once imagined she might care about.

And of course it isn't fair, I realize, that my aunt—who was once in medical school—is now stuck in a crowded vacation house that smells of wet towels and mold, with dogs and mostly boys, the one saving grace being that at least Sarah Burlingham, who's witty, is along to hate it with her. And there's our drunken Grandmother Delia, as well as assorted female relatives, such as Great Aunt Hoppy, or a loopy cousin of my dad's named Jocelyn, who've been imported to make a fourth for bridge, while the husbands—who come down only on weekends—are back in town, drinking delicious alcoholic beverages while eating out at expensive restaurants with who knows, and making money hand over fist.

Because this was the West, where women grew up knowing it was never fair, that fairness played no part in it. This was ingrained in Our People, as my mother calls girls and women, and it was never Our People who wanted to come west, as their journals make abundantly clear. They believed this place to be their soul's death, that they were doing this out of self-sacrifice, in which they were trained from their earliest moments; that it was for the sake of their husbands and their children and a more prosperous future that they'd leave everything they cherished—hometown, parents, flower garden, friends. Leave everything, even the only landscape their eyes recognized, the cloud shapes that comforted them, weather they might anticipate. There were colors of green that they'd never see again, birdsongs their ears would never again hear.

And no women actively wanted to make the trek, as they were medically at risk and taking their lives in their hands. There was also nothing for them in the West, aside from a preponderance of men to feed and clothe and in all ways nurture, and—if they survived the trek—physical labor to perform in farming or mining their new claim or maybe, if they were lucky, merchanting. The trek took from late April or May, when the spring mud dried enough that the wagon wheels didn't sink, until the first snows of late October, by which time they'd made it through the coast range, if they were lucky.

They walked behind the oxcart into Deep Geologic Time, through mountain passes, over Basin and Range, into a fold-and-thrust terrain so bizarre it was unlike anything they'd even heard described. They forded rivers of mud that snaked back and forth across a broad and otherwise naked plain, and their wagon wheels stuck in quicksand, so they began to unload anything that was extraneous or decorative or girl-like, anything that let them believe they were bringing civilization with them: any book that was not a Bible, all pictures, musical instruments, art.

They departed Freshwater and trudged out into the Forty-Mile Desert, strewn with the carcasses of livestock and the homely items some other woman had cherished. Nearly four hundred thousand people made the trek by the mid-1800s; between twenty and thirty thousand of those pioneers died. The oxcart emigrants, like those in my family's background, were almost always young families. Many of the women were in some stage of pregnancy or had just given birth, and they bled and were anemic and medically at risk, and their babies died in infancy or under the wheels of the oxcart. They came unaccompanied by their sisters and had no one else to help them with the arduousness of this very terrible life, so some of them came west wearing wedding dresses they'd dyed black to symbolize that even if they made it to Oregon or California, they knew they'd never see their own mothers again, so their lives were essentially over.

And once there, they had to acclimate to what life would have been in the Middle Ages, to live in villages that lacked schools, streetlights, sidewalks, libraries. They'd look forward the whole trek to a place called Nevada City or Oregon City, but, arriving there, would find only a tiny settlement made up of the homesteads of a few families.

Emigrants wrote home words such as these: *I wish California had sunk into the ocean before I had heard of it.*

۞

The only reason I was ever even allowed to go out with Robert Burlingham in the first place was that my aunt and uncle *know him*, know his parents, know that he—with all that Louis Comfort Tiffany whoever-he-was stuff—is from a good family.

This is a strict rule of my dating life: Any boy who invites me out on the weekend must, by Wednesday, have made arrangements to come to my house to be introduced to my aunt, which means this boy's having to sit stiffly upright, trying to think of something to say to my aunt in her sand-sea-and-sky-colored living room, as she smokes cigarettes and fastens her eagle eye on him. This is her most direct and confrontational stare, which seems to say, I have *boys*, I know what *boys* are, I know *exactly* what boys like you are up to.

And I find that almost no boy is interested enough in me to actually show up to this introductory meeting, as my aunt is actually notorious for being strict and even severe. She'll become perfectly silent, which makes you think she can literally read your mind, in which case you're pretty sure you're about to be arrested.

So I have mostly avoided dating, which is fine with me because I basically hate being in a car alone with some boy I barely know, which is awkward, which usually involves my babbling on in a cute fake way, talking all excitedly with my hands, and going out to someplace I have no actual interest in being.

Instead of dating, I go out with Reggie and Steve, who are football players and friends of mine, nice boys—even my aunt likes them. Steve, who is regular, is the quarterback and Reggie, who is Mexican, and a wide receiver. My aunt knows Reggie and Steve because they hang out at our house. We drive around in Steve's red truck to parties or dances, where we go as friends, as each of the three of us is always interested in people who aren't interested in us, which somehow suits us perfectly.

But my being away all of August, then being grounded for the parties at the beginning of the school year, is a complete stone drag, as this is when all the intricacies of the year's friendships and romances are being laid down along a complex social grid of nuance and association. We get new clothes for the start of school, then come as versions of new people, better and more exact copies of the people we're hoping to become. I am adept at *becoming*.

I've always loved September. The school year starts and every class is potentially interesting and my notebook is still neatly organized behind its dividers by subject and I haven't yet messed up and it's a good time to see who's changed over the summer and so become less what they were, which is always because we're teenagers, somehow moist, inexact, and larval—and more the clean dry upstanding people we hope to one day be when we go out to own the world.

But all this is going on without me, which wouldn't have bothered me before I'd lived in my aunt and uncle's house long enough to became better adjusted. To become better adjusted, I've had to very willfully abandon certain allegiances I've had toward my mother—who (and usually for good reason) hates almost everyone and everything, the why of which she can also always perfectly articulate—and become more like my father, who had friends because he, like my aunt, was both attractive and vivacious. Inside the house, I'm still known for who I am, which is my parents' daughter, which means I'm dark and somehow twisted. Outside the house I'm this other more radiant being. My hair's long and blonde and straight. My skin's okay. I'm funny and I have friends.

Besides, I have Graham and Jordy, who arrive at school with me, and my aunt's bought us our own car, even if only Graham has his license, even if it's only this shitty little Renault, the ownership of which is actually a chop. My aunt got it for us so she won't have to lend us her car, the reasons for her not wanting us to borrow it becoming immediately obvious.

So my boy cousins and I arrive at school like this completely bitchen phalanx, a self-possessed cadre of good-lookingness and popularity. And we're suddenly all friends of one another's and our friends are friends of theirs and our friends are suddenly everything to us, as it's a relief to escape finally from who we are within the messy network of our okay-on-the-surface but secretly really messed-up family.

∭

It's the second weekend of my grounding when Reggie and Steve stop by on a Friday afternoon to tell me there's a party that night. They've come to ask Aunt Nan if I can't go out with them. They tell her they'll keep track of me, and she's charmed by them because they're brotherly and kind and they stand up straight and look her in the eye, like they're not ashamed of what they've just been in the bathroom doing.

Reggie and Steve are what she calls Good Kids. This means they know how to show up on time and behave in a mannerly way. They also dress appropriately, wearing what is almost a uniform of chinos, pressed shirts, and their maroon letterman's sweaters with white stripes on the sleeve for each of their sports.

And I can see my aunt being even tempted, as this would give her the night off from watching me, but even as she wavers she remembers she isn't one to change her mind about rules and punishments.

My aunt doesn't believe in being flexible; she can easily imagine—I imagine—based on my parents' example, where *all that* might lead.

And she's still basically this scientist who didn't finish med school because my uncle made her quit but who still believes things to be logical—that is, set out in a certain way. Fish or cut bait, she tells us, then demonstrates by chopping the chunk of air that's balanced on her up-turned palm with the axlike movement of the side of her left hand (doing this left-handedly, of course), saying, *Bomp, bomp, bomp.* Everything as it is and ever shall be, my aunt believes, as is droned each Sunday in church, world without end, amen, and so on and so forth.

She calls the imagined order of the world its Thus And So.

Steve and Reggie are so well known to my aunt that they're invited to stop calling her Mrs. Snowden and call her Aunt Nan instead, but they're too shy to call a person as formidable as my aunt much of anything. Charmed by them, she wavers but doesn't change her mind, because it has no doubt occurred to her that, aside from the episode with Robert Burlingham at the drive-in movie, there's just *so much* other stuff I've done to get in trouble: the inappropriate clothes I've shown up in on a Sunday morning just as she, by herself, is trying to get everyone in the car for church, while my uncle, who is an atheist for reasons analogous to mine, is still in bed because he's recently announced he will no longer go to church with us.

And there was the episode of my driving my grandmother's car one weekend when us kids were all staying there, though I don't have a license and haven't actually even taken drivers' training, so I don't know how to drive and was so panicked I shifted from park while flooring it, thereby doing what my cousin Graham calls grinding a pound of gears.

Plus, there's all the other stuff she's more than right about, even if she's only guessing.

Robert Burlingham still hangs around our house but I don't speak to him, since he got me in trouble and he—of course, since life isn't fair—has never been punished in the slightest way. Even the girlfriend he was trying to make jealous when he took me out went back to him immediately.

So Reggie and Steve can't get Aunt Nan to change her mind; then a ton of people come over to hang out before going off to the party, so I go to my room, as I can't actually stand it, since I will not be going, and one of these friends is, of course, Robert Burlingham, that shit fuck asshole, whom I still secretly like.

And I'll try to get the stories of what went on out of Reggie and Steve and my boy cousins, although they are all such boys that they're mostly looking only at who has, and I am not kidding, *tits* or not, and *tits* is the word they honest-to-god use when they don't know I'm listening.

And I'll ask them if So-and-So was there and they'll be like, Huh? What? I dunno, no really, I actually have *no idea*, and I'm wondering, *How can you have no idea*? And, feeling pressured, Reggie'll say yes and Steve'll say no, and they'll stare at each other in that blank way that reads as *nnnnnnnnnnn* or boy-mind drone—that is to say, *totally* noncommittal.

And it absolutely baffles me that boys, in general, will let such important details go by without their even noticing.

So I'm sulking and miserable and it's later that evening when the phone rings and my cousin Thomas goes and gets it because he likes to answer the phone, which gives him a chance to say, Snowden residence, Thomas speaking, which always makes me want to get up, go over to him, and strike him really hard in the muscle of his upper arm. But then he holds the handset out to me, saying, It's for you, and I silently mouth, *Who is it?* and Thomas says completely loudly so whoever's there can hear, I dunno, some boy.

And we of course have no privacy in our phone calls, as the only phone we're allowed to use is the kitchen phone that hangs right next to the red Naugahyde booth where we all must crowd in to eat a hot breakfast, as my aunt believes in hot breakfast the way she believes in the Nicene Creed, so we shove in there disorganized by our handedness, showing up by who's ready first. My aunt makes the plates all at once and keeps them warm in the oven, so breakfast's this heat-hardened thing that's accompanied by the chaos of left- and right-handed kids all shoving and elbowing.

I go to the phone and hear this voice I don't know saying it's John Philip Hudsmith.

Who? I ask, though I vaguely know this person from some classes we may have sometime had.

John Philip Hudsmith, who somehow knows I'm grounded, says he's going to be in the neighborhood later if I want to sneak out. If I want to sneak out he can wait in his car under the streetlight over on Oak Park, which is the street behind our street; he'll be there by eleven or so, and he'll wait if I want him to take me to the party.

He names friends who are already at this party, which he says he's already been to and is going back to later, and I'm so eager to get there it doesn't actually bother me that, for someone I hardly know, he knows much too much about me. I figure he's a friend of Graham's or Jordy's, that he's been to our house in one of these pre-party crowds of twelve or twenty that congregate in the boys' wing, talking about who has tits or not and getting ready to go out. These gatherings are always impromptu, as Jordy and Graham and I have never been allowed to have a party ourselves, which is fine with us since my aunt's so strict that she would no doubt die if she knew how we act when she is not around to watch us.

⚇

It's ten thirty or so and I'm waiting up, watching television in the family room, hoping my aunt will finally go to bed or at least to the front part of the house to work on the vestments she's embroidering for altar guild, but she's still puttering in the kitchen, which means she is basically hiding food. She puts food Geo and Thomas might sneak, like the cookies she buys in bulk in white paper bags at a certain grocery's bakery, really high on the highest shelf, out of everybody's reach.

She puts all the individual bakery sacks in a big Tupperware tub that's supposedly hidden above the actual cupboards, but Thomas, who is small and agile, has perfected this certain silent stealthy crouch whereby—even with my aunt listening to music in the living room—he can get to that part of the big room that is the kitchen/dining/family room unnoticed and hide behind the cooking island, then use the drawers she's designed to glide out silently to climb to the counter, where he stands up and uses a wooden spoon to quietly lift the tub down. We all watch neutrally, uninvolved, so that if he gets caught it's only Thomas who's screwed. Still, we're all completely rooting for him to get away with it, and we watch as he lifts the cookie tub down and sneaks it over so he can share its contents with the rest of us, so we won't tell.

My uncle's out, as usual. She's finally finished unloading the dishwasher that runs at least twice a day, folding the last dishtowel, turning out the lights.

All set? she asks me.

I nod. I'm barely speaking to her, so I don't take my eyes off the TV screen.

Night, she says.

Night, I answer, still not looking at her.

She turns in the doorway. Well, after this, she says, you only have one more weekend. Then you can be out and about and up to your old tricks.

For my aunt, this is an astonishingly fond and friendly thing to say. My ears hear this and my mind takes it in, but I'm so burrowed into my fury, which is the true dark core of who I am, that I'm far beyond caring about this tiny pinprick of loving kindness.

Right, I say, and I turn to look up at her so I can fix her with my coldest stare.

Geo and Thomas and Lizzie are all in bed. Jordy and Graham are gone in the Renault, which is a rickety foreign car we kids would never have. We've been told its name is said *Rey-NO*, but everyone at school calls it a *Run-ALT*. My aunt needs only a single teenaged driver to help her with kid pickup and incidental errands, which is Graham.

Besides, Jordy's not yet old enough to drive and I am in no way trustworthy, as she and I both know, which was confirmed amply in the incident in the liquor store parking lot, when my grinding a pound of our grandmother's Studebaker's gears totaled its transmission, which then cost, as Aunt Nan said, *the earth*.

000

My aunt is so concerned about the harm that might come to me and Graham and Jordy now that we're teenagers and driving and going to parties where there may be drinking that she herself has almost entirely stopped going out in the evenings, so she can be here to smell our breath and otherwise monitor our temptation to self-destruct, which— as she and I both know—is intricately woven into the spiral helix of the very DNA of us, about which I've just studied in Anatomy and Physiology.

Our grandmother is, very famously, a drunken driver who will drive her seven grandchildren while, as my mother says, *plotzed, smashed, swacked, plowed, blasted, blitzed,* or *stink-o*. She will do this even arrogantly when some version of the whole troop of us is staying overnight with her. She'll order us all into the Studebaker, even if Graham or Will is there, who'd be better at driving than she is, and she'll set out in the early evening to go drink with her friend Alice Herbert, though it's abundantly clear the moment we arrive that Alice Herbert has no wish whatsoever to entertain this herd of Delia's bored and errant grandchildren, so the women will just knock back a few quick ones before we're sent on our way. We pile back into the Studebaker, which doesn't have seatbelts or even a back on the bench in the second seat—it's more of a fabric drape that lets us crawl into the trunk, where whatever group of us it is huddles, white-faced and scared, as our little grandmother, who's so short she nearly has to look through the steering wheel and is *snockered, ripped, bombed, tanked-up, wasted*, drives us away from wherever Alice Herbert lives and back through El Segundo toward the ocean, into the more and more dense fog we find on the Pacific Coast Highway, all while accelerating and braking at exactly the same time so, the whole way home to Manhattan Beach, the car lurches and shudders and halts.

Our grandmother is a tiny person, the only woman in our family who might be described as delicate. Her hair's done up in a hair-salon chignon and dyed a color called Champagne; her fingernails are always impeccably manicured and painted to match her hair. She has always competed with my mother and my aunt over any man's attention. This is because she grew up being accustomed to being the most beautiful girl in the room.

She's used to being beautiful and the center of everything. She isn't yet used to having become old and a widow and the mother of a dead son—this would be my father—who wasn't even talking to her when he committed suicide. The deaths of her husband and her son took place within a year of each other and have happened recently enough that she's still being forgiven for the way she's not yet adjusting. People still feel sorry for Delia, my mother says, which is why she gets to act the way she does.

But don't be fooled by my mother-in-law, my mother says. Delia doesn't have a grief-stricken bone in her entire body and she's always been *exactly* like that, which is to say, not only a completely hopeless dipso but also totally, narcissistically self-involved. And she's just so plain nasty, my mother adds, that what she felt when your father died was largely embarrassment.

∭

My aunt knows about her mother's driving the car drunk, though we've never told on her, and she knows about Delia's sending me to the liquor store with a note saying I'm authorized to buy her cigarettes, which is when I ground the pound of gears. I had no idea what I thought I was doing getting behind the wheel of the Studebaker—only that she ordered me to do it, as neither Graham nor Will was there.

My grandmother has never had much use for girls, who either are baby darlings and therefore exactly like she is or—like my aunt and me—exist mainly to do her errands.

My aunt knows because her mother will require certain things of us, swear us to secrecy, then call to tell my aunt *herself* to tell her daughter *herself* exactly what we aren't telling her, as if to demonstrate her theory about how children really *are* the Limbs of Satan and utterly disloyal, so my aunt should never trust us.

So my aunt is understandably afraid of being driven around by drunks, since she probably grew up with that. My parents never drove drunk, though each was almost always completely *blotto* or at least *well oiled*. Instead, when they were *soused, pickled, snockered, juiced,* or *trashed,* they'd famously take taxis at unbelievable expense all around the Los Angeles Basin, and this wasn't just for safety's sake but mainly because it was such a *Not* Middle Class thing to do.

Besides, my mother sniffs, taking cabs made us feel like F. Scott and Zelda.

∞

My aunt has ordered Graham and Jordy and me to never drive a car if we've been drinking, to never get into the car with anyone who's been drinking, that we're not to worry that we'll get in trouble, that being in trouble in this case is suspended, that all we need to do is call—even if we're at her mother's house at the beach—and no matter what the circumstances, she'll drop whatever she's doing and come directly there and get us.

This was after Graham got drunk and threw up all over the front seat of the new Rey-No, which then had to be sent to some specialized car-cleaning shop where everything in the dashboard was taken apart, which is what it evidently takes to get the vomit out of a car's heating ducts.

The night of the party I go into my room and put music on, then begin to get clothes out of my closet. As I do this I play records on my hi-fi, which once belonged to my mother. Hers were albums, mine are 45s, which I stack on a thick spool that adapts the record changer. If you leave the arm out, the same record will play over and over, which is what I do with a song like "Duke of Earl," which anyway sounds like it's playing over and over, as it is and ever shall be, burrowing down through the scales of the earth's rock-hard mantle, downward toward the molten flux, or magma, that—as we've just been taught in Geology—exists at the heart of everything.

I build a body in my bed, and this isn't just some clumsy pillow thing—rather, it is positively sculpted, a girl's body on her side with her back to the door, knees drawn up, face turned away. The body is in proportion and has shoulders, hips, and a waist, and the head, which is made of a tiny pink baby pillow I've probably stolen from Lizzie, is wearing a cloth cap that's filled with my own outsize hair rollers.

I turn off my own overhead light in order to witness what I've made. I view it in the light that falls through the doorway: Girl Innocently Sleeping, which is what my aunt will see if she comes to check up on me, as—and I know this to be so—she sometimes does.

I set two final 45s on the hi-fi and move the arm so the equipment will turn off as soon as the second song has finished. I play "To Know, Know, Know Him Is to Love, Love, Love Him" and Roy Orbison's "Pretty Woman," because they're both sweet songs but muscular enough in tone to hide the movement of bodies in the house, and not so loud that they'll bring Aunt Nan from the wing in the front of the house to tell me to turn my music off.

I haven't really dressed for this party, but I have a bag with clothes and shoes I can change into. For what I'm doing I need to be barefoot, as that's how I'm most surefooted.

Most of the windows in the house have screens on them, which are impossible to climb through, but Graham and Jordy and I have figured out the exits. One of my windows opens onto the screened porch, as does the opposite window in the boys' wing, and these have no screens. Going through the screened porch, you are, however, momentarily exposed through the sliding glass doors to whatever's going on in the living room and kitchen, so this works only when that part of the house is dark. Murphy also needs to be stashed somewhere else than his dog bed so he won't try to come along with you.

You need to go through the dog door because the metal door it's in has no key and locks from the inside and is flimsy and the noisiest one to open.

These houses are all big; most of them have swimming pools, and for legal reasons involving some kids maybe drowning in somebody else's pool, all the walls around people's property are of a certain height, and uniform. These walls are built of cinder blocks and capped with a red tile that makes them about six inches wide. They're so tall you can't see into your next-door neighbor's yard.

My cousins and I, as well as many of the neighborhood's our-age kids—of which there are literally dozens—have long used the tops of the concrete walls between houses as a kind of kid expressway that can take you into the backyard of any other house on our block. These huge yards, their bushes and trees and plantings, can feel teeming with kids, so it's never really surprising to look out a back window and see some friend's face motioning for you to open your window so they can tell you something that's happened that they think you need to urgently know.

We don't use the telephone, because every kid knows no parent will tolerate a phone call made after nine o'clock at night.

You get up on top of the wall from the roof of the bike shed. The wall's wide enough that, barefoot, you can practically run along the top of it like it's the balance beam in gym. You are also almost entirely hidden from the sightlines of the houses by the drape of what's left of the walnut grove, whose trees—at least through late summer or early fall—still have leaves on them.

I know Ted and Sylvia will be out, because they're always out, and so will Cheryl, who is just my age but already gorgeous in a grown-up way and so good at clothes and makeup that her mom's taking her over the hill to do modeling. Cheryl's popular with older guys who aren't even still in high school, so she is rarely home. Dougie, who's a year behind Jordy and socially retarded by his still being in junior high, will be there, as a kid his age has nowhere to go.

Dougie and his little buddies like to spy on us when Cheryl has friends for an overnight and we're getting out of our towel-wrapped bathing suits and into our pajamas after a night swim. We know they're watching, so we put on a show of pretending to strip to "Let Me Entertain You."

Ted's a tyrant but Dougie's so good-natured that he can be talked into anything, so I go directly to the DeCinceses' and climb down off the wall into the *V* of a certain fruit tree we use as our expressway's on- and off-ramp.

Dougie is friendly, interested, neutral. He doesn't even ask why I'm standing there; he just opens the door and lets me walk through to their all-white living room, where I sit on the white couch to put my shoes on before I go on out their front door.

John Philip Hudsmith has the kind of car certain boys always have— a '57 or some other similar year Chevy or Ford—and I can never pay attention long enough to cars to ever memorize the shapes and symbols and so must always read their names, spelling out *F-o-r-d* or *C-h-e-v-r-o-l-e-t*, to know for sure. His car has the usual new paint job and is buffed and waxed, the way this kind of boy's car always is.

He's been waiting under a streetlight on Oak Park with his lights turned off.

He flicks his lights at me.

Hey, I say, as I climb into the front seat.

Hey, he says back. No one else is in the car, which isn't the way we usually travel. It's about eleven thirty and mist is beginning to rise from the wide front lawns, a damp look that even smells of loneliness and always deeply spooks me.

Where to? I ask.

It's up in the hills, in Chatsworth. At that girl's house, the one who looks like you?

Oh, yeah, her, I say. At Brandy Cannon's?

I've been hearing about this girl ever since I was a freshman in high school. Her name is *Brandy Cannon*. A number of people—maybe eight or ten—have told me that she and I not only look alike, but we're both loud and funny and our laughs sound the same.

I've heard about her but have never been that interested in actually meeting *Brandy Cannon*, as this will show me what I remind people of when they look at me, something I don't necessarily want to know.

I also don't really get her name. I wonder why her parents named her Brandy, as no one is yet named this kind of really out-there thing. The name sounds lowlife to me, or like she comes, as I do, from a long line of alcoholics who think being drunk is *just hilarious!* as we do in my family, hence our million humorous words for *lushes, winos, boozehounds,* who've had *tee-minny-martoonies* or are *three sheets to the wind.*

It sounds like she doesn't really *go with* where she lives. In Chatsworth, kids are richer than we are. In Chatsworth, kids have horses.

John Philip Hudsmith, who actually goes by all three names, which is the kind of thing that makes me cringe, is driving west on Nordhoff, past the cornfields that will soon no longer be cornfields and the fruit stands that are now closed but have until recently been selling the last of the summer's fruits and vegetables. His name—or at least his going by it—clues me in to his being some kind of weirdo, as does the manner in which he's driving. He is extremely tense, though we're traveling down a wide avenue crossing largely empty streets and there's really nothing to be all that excited about. Still, I see his jaw clench and unclench; a little bulge first forms, then disappears as he releases.

He is also driving stiffly, with his elbow out the window, his arm resting on the door, so he looks as if he's completely relaxed, though he isn't relaxed at all.

Nice car, I say, as this is the thing you are supposed to say when you're a girl encountering some boy in a car like this, one with a manual transmission and tuck-n-roll interior that's still fragrant with the new-car smell. I say this though I don't actually give a shit about what kind of car a boy drives, and want only for it to get me where I'm going, which is, I always hope, far away from here.

John Philip Hudsmith anyway shrugs off the compliment.

Isn't mine, he says.

No? I ask.

My brother's, he says.

Nice brother, I say, to lend you a car as nice as this.

Not really, he says. He didn't really lend it to me. Then he turns to me and says, I actually more or less took it.

And this is when I smell his breath and realize that John Philip Hudsmith's been drinking and has also been chewing Juicy Fruit gum to try to cover it up. The smell of alcohol and Juicy Fruit or Wrigley's Spearmint is something I'm actually already acquainted with, though I don't yet drink and most of my friends don't yet drink, as we're still only in tenth grade but we all still somehow already know by teenager osmosis all the tricks of drinking: how you can raid your father's liquor cabinet and water the gin to fill it to the line he's marked on the bottle in grease pencil that's supposed to keep his kids from guzzling it.

And John Philip Hudsmith isn't one of the boys who's ever been to our house. Rather, I've seen him standing on the edge of things, listening, as I myself have often carefully listened while I was learning how to hide who I am in the disguise of a more regular girl.

Suddenly I know all about John Philip Hudsmith, who's a loser who's driving *shit-faced, polluted* in the car he's boosted from his brother, and that he likes me, it turns out, because long ago back in the Days of Yore before I became better at being a more normal teenager I was once nice to him.

This is so sad it makes me want to kill myself.

We're meanwhile cruising around in the foothills of Chatsworth driving up and down wide avenues of houses that are not yet built and he has the windows rolled down because he is supposedly listening for the sounds of the party, but there is no party up here because—as anyone can plainly see—these houses haven't yet been finished and are still only poured concrete foundations, with walls framed in, then stood up like the empty skeletons of lives that aren't yet ready to be lived and all this pretense is because John Philip Hudsmith is what in later years will come to be known as *really into me*.

Which I studiously ignore. I ignore him except to complain generally as if I were what I'm currently pretending to be, which is entitled. I tell him my stomach's upset, that I get carsick, that we're going to have to stop driving around in a minute and really find this party or I may be sick all over his brother's new tuck-n-roll.

John Philip Hudsmith is a great example of the type of boy—as I am only just now discovering—who will *always* fall in love with me, the Honors English–type boy who'll go on to college to major in literature and will want to write the Great American Novel without ever learning to write a single Good American Sentence. This boy will turn out to be gay and will want me or someone just like me—it will really make no difference—to save him from homosexuality. Or, if not gay, he'll almost invariably be Other, as my father was, which is to say he'll inevitably be in conflict about his identity.

Which is to say this boy will be sensitive, which I can't stand, since I'm already so sensitive I can't even stand myself, so sensitive that I can't bear to hear the sound of certain pretty common everyday words and phrases without feeling like I need to cover my ears and go *nah-nahhhhh-nahhhh* the whole while these words are being said to avoid the effect on my body of having heard these things said, which feels like a physical assault.

Which is to say John Philip Hudsmith will be nothing like Robert Burlingham, who's a clod but is at least *different* from me, which makes it interesting. Kissing a boy like John Philip Hudsmith, I already know completely, though I have no experience with this, won't be interesting, because people just like you are never interesting. It's too much like kissing Brandy Cannon or someone else who's somehow equally lifeless, being someone already too well known to your body.

I also know that John Philip Hudsmith, who probably will go on, because of his stupid name, to write really crappy plays that are just too honestly awful to even sit through, isn't really yet ballsy enough at fifteen-sixteen-whatever to pull the car over and park in some cul-de-sac of these still-half-built houses that overlook the dimmed-by-vapor lights of the cauldron of rising mist that is the San Fernando Valley in the 1960s. He can't put his arm around me and try to kiss me, which is—I know now—what this drive around town is about, so I keep chattering on about all our many mutual friends, who are actually *my* friends, not his, saying I really am not feeling well and if we can only get to this party, maybe I can get a ride home from Reggie and Steve. John Philip Hudsmith surely knows *Reggie and Steve!* because everybody knows *Reggie and Steve!* as they're football stars, and a football star is all a high school has in the way of famous.

Soon I'm telling John Philip Hudsmith he has to take me home, but he doesn't really want to take me home, though I am actually honestly beginning to feel sick, now that I've become honestly worried that I may end up raped or dead. At the very least my aunt is going to find out about this, in which case she'll kill me.

Up to my old tricks, and this one, I'm guessing, may actually do it. I've always managed to exist right on the margins of being just too *out there*, skirting along barefoot along the top of the wall along the borders of propriety always, right there teetering but managing not to fall off into the place Aunt Nan calls Beyond the Pale.

Boys in our family get shipped off to boarding school. I don't really know what they do with girls, but I am just about to find out.

000

I get John Philip Hudsmith to drive me to a gas station by telling him I need to use the bathroom or I will—*and I swear to God!*—throw up all over his brother's car, and he will—*I swear to God!*—end up having to take it to this specialty shop in Sepulveda where they get vomit out of the heating vents, and it's so expensive they have to take the whole console apart, which costs *the earth.*

So he drives down the hill and back along Nordhoff until we see a Texaco sitting in a wash of yellow light that looks as if it's been tinted by disease, and he pulls in and tells me that if I even speak to the gas station attendant he will drive away, leave me there, go directly to my house, and do a lawn job, which'll involve his driving his brother's '57-or-whatever backwards up onto the lawn, where he'll put the handbrake on and step on the accelerator to turn the wheels, which will then dig huge chunks of sod up out of the earth and pitch it back against the house.

Right, I say as I get out of the car and slam the door.

The attendant is wiping his hands on an oily rag as he walks from the office, coming toward the pump. The attendant is young and his teeth are bad, his face pimpled in the way of those who are new to California so their parents don't yet know how to plop them in the fresh air and sunshine and offer them fruits and vegetables.

Guy's bothering me, I tell the attendant. He's weird and he's been drinking and now he won't take me home. Can I use your phone to call my aunt?

Then we both turn as we hear the engine and the tires squeal; we turn to watch John Philip Hudsmith speed up and corner, skidding wildly away, driving as fast as he can but *with his lights off,* as if this is going to help him disappear.

I think about who I might call to take me driving around to try to find Reggie and Steve, but it's so late no parent will let me speak to their kid on the phone, and everyone will anyway still be out at parties or else over on Reseda Boulevard at Big Bob's, which is what we call that particular Bob's Big Boy—as opposed to Little Bob's, which is somewhere else.

But I actually already feel so tired and so completely caught, I call my aunt and tell her the short version of what has happened and where I can be found. Then I sit on top of the gas station guy's desk, drinking the soda he's gotten for me.

I think of what I will look like to her—some girl sitting on the desk in the Texaco that is lit up like a little frontier settlement on this foggy night in the middle of this place in the West, when we are still literally surrounded by cornfields and roads that go off into the night on the deepest blackest desert so you get the huge impending sense of what the pioneers encountered, those who walked two thousand miles only to arrive exactly *Nowhere*.

Though I cannot paint, I feel myself to be the inhabitant of some really lonely canvas. I'd have thought of a painting by Edward Hopper, had I ever seen one, but this is the American West, where we basically don't yet have books or paintings or many art museums, in that none of this is yet actually common, and what we have is the air and the sea and sky and everything that wasn't air or sea or sky was cast off and left in the muddy tracks of the wagon ruts.

Or I'd think of some other American painter—and it must be an American, since we're the best at this—who uses thick bands of raw pigment straight from the tube, so color's employed to make walls so high you can't see over them, and everyone's spaced just so along a certain grid, and light is actually then subtracted in order to describe what is, finally, a magnificent silence, which is what the universe actually thinks of us.

I see my aunt pull up in the station wagon that she prefers my cousins and I not drive, and I see the proud way she carries herself, the brittle set to her mouth, her handsome face. My aunt's cheekbones are elegant.

I go to the car and open the door, and she doesn't yell at me, and I sit down and she still says nothing. She has recently started wearing a huge clump of religious medals, one of which is the Virgin of Guadalupe that my father gave her one long-ago summer when he was sent to recuperate in Mexico at the home of the woman they call La Señora, one of the several times he cracked up.

My aunt brings her left hand to clutch her metals, which look like dog tags, then reaches over with her right hand. Her long fingers are tan, her fingertips are cold. Her hands are always fragrant from smoking cigarettes, a smell I happen to like.

She takes my hand in hers and closes her eyes in what might be a prayer of thankfulness, and when she opens her eyes I see that they're watering. This cannot possibly mean she's crying, since she and I are the same and we're stoic, as is my mother, also the other grandmother who's not a drunk. We're all Daughters of the Golden West and we all share these same tragedies, and these are griefs so huge they've long since served to dry our tears. I never cry and my aunt never cries, or if my aunt is crying, it'll take me years to find that out and years more to discover why.

7

Money Shot

WHAT IS BASICALLY most different about my generation is that we wear pantyhose. We're still required to wear dresses to school and cannot yet wear pants, but now—since pantyhose were invented—we can roll our skirts up at the waist so our knees show, roll them higher still so we expose whole areas of the flesh of our inner thigh, up into the shadows of what is hidden and what's never before been shown, and this has changed us not as a mere matter of style, but *fundamentally*.

What this means is, we are never going to have to turn out like *They* are, which shows not only in how we dress but in how we carry ourselves. By *They,* I mean our teachers, our mothers, our aunts, our grandmothers, who are repulsive, actually, if you stop to really think about it.

By *Them,* I mean *all* of them, *all grown-up women.*

When I am with my friends, I feel I've escaped into another country that in no way even pertains to *Them.* We feel we are inventing sex, as it has never occurred to *Them* and is a world that is ours alone.

I feel this powerfully: The rules of this country of ours, the one we will grow up to own, have changed, as has the language, and there are expanded boundaries for us that didn't apply to *Them,* and this shows most in how we talk, also in the striding way we walk. We no longer feel gagged and hampered, as if we can suddenly say the things that *They* would never even dream of thinking.

We may not yet have birth control, but we can feel it coming and it is coming right to us. We know these things without really knowing them, know them the way we suddenly know everything because we are the opposite of naïve, we are nothing if not *knowing.*

The news is electric. It's in the air; we pick it up by ant noise, and suddenly it all applies to us. The news says we're never going to be trapped as they've been in these little shitty lives of theirs that trip by petty pace from day to day so completely *pointlessly*: their driving the fucking tiresome carpool, their loading and unloading the fucking asshole dishwasher, their shopping at the stupid places where they buy their repulsive *ladylike* clothes.

We're never going to be stuck down into the Ozzie-and-Harriet, twin-bedded lives of American women in which they are told they both Do and Do Not like sex, equally and in the exact same measure, which is why they giggle at the word. Grown women who giggle make me so angry I want to stride over and slap their faces whenever they giggle behind their upraised hands, as if modestly. I *hate* giggling as much as I *hate* modesty.

This is what I imagine for myself: a world in which I can suddenly be able to *do* anything I want, which means my body will be able to follow my thoughts into far-flung places. I want to be able to go anywhere I can imagine going; to be able to follow my mind, which has already imagined itself out of here. I believe this means I will find my way to *freedom.*

My friends and I define ourselves in opposition to Them. My aunt tries to give me something someone, not my uncle, has given her—it's this filmy red thing to sleep in that simply perplexes my aunt, as well as making her slightly angry. Because it's insulting, I think it's probably one of my grandmother's twisted little gifts; its deep-down lesson is How to Keep Your Man, Though It's Probably Too Late Now. My aunt holds it out to me, as if to ask me what we should do with it.

I'm actually shocked. Even I know she would never wear anything that looks like this—it's *gross*, these see-through baby-doll pajamas that look like they're designed for a prostitute.

My aunt's too vexed and confused, so I'm the one to wad it up and walk it to the outside trash.

The giggling-behind-the-hand, baby-doll, half-virgin/half-prostitute cuteness thing is so *exactly* everything completely repellant.

They don't know what they're doing on this account because they're all twisted up in the Thou Shant's. My friends and I don't happen to care what God thinks, in that we don't believe in God, or if He does exist he should have known better than to come up with these *ridiculous* models, this *virgin* who has a baby (and my friends and I are like, We are *so totally* sure *that* did not actually happen) and her really faggoty-looking son. Their example is supposed to prove how spiritual we're supposed to be and that sex is bad for you.

My friends and I don't actually *think* so.

My friends and I are never going to be *repressed*. For one thing we're going to find things out, look stuff up for ourselves if *They* are too ashamed to tell us.

We poke around Cheryl's house and find the Kinsey Report hidden on the top shelf of Ted and Sylvia's closet, and we lie on their king-size bed to read it aloud back and forth, until this makes us think of Ted and

Sylvia doing it, which grosses us out, so we take the book out to the pool house, where Dougie and his little friends come to spy on us.

We intend to study up, become good at it. Jane Brown shows us what she practices with the younger boys she invites into her apartment after school, before her mother gets home from work. She demonstrates how younger boys can be controlled, how you have them lie atop you and you hook your legs behind their knees and spread their legs, which also opens you.

We practice this, also other positions. We read the words aloud, along with comic addenda and commentary, such as, Lick his asshole? And we say this *really loudly* so Dougie and his friends can hear.

That's so totally fucking *sick!* someone says, but we are able to say it, as *They* have never been able before to say these things without experiencing cosmic shame. Shame doesn't apply to us; shamelessness is part of the sheen in which we have wrapped ourselves.

We're going to actively allow sex into our lives, if only so we can shriek and laugh at what a fool having a human body tends to make of you. I look at the pictures in *Playboy* magazine with my cousin Jordy and his friend Paul—we've found it hidden in Dale Coffer's study while the grown-ups are outside by the pool, drinking their *cock*-tails, and why, I ask these boys, is it that drinks are named something like *cock*-tails, so they know I'm aware of their penises.

We three stare unabashedly at the huge jugs of the Playmate of the Month and her bright, invariably goldish hair, her dreamy eyes, her wet and slightly parted lips, while the three of us are lying on our stomachs right next to one another companionably. We're hiding behind the couch in the living room, then suddenly fighting and shoving—move *the fuck* over, you pervert, let me *the fuck* see—ready to shove the magazine under the couch if an adult comes into the room, which has grown dim in the twilight. I am older and I know more than they do already, and I take it away so I can read the letters to the editor aloud, especially the ones that say things like *oral sex* and *anal sex* and *climax* and *ejaculate*, saying this stuff aloud to gross them out, as they are—like Cheryl's brother—suddenly these *little* boys who have almost entirely been left behind by us.

Because my friends and I can say anything, we know we're *never* going to end up sitting at home, going nuts, smoking, drinking drinks during the Arsenic Hour, being counseled by the parish priest, who's in love with us but is too fucked up and repressed to swiftly step up to us and kiss us, as Father Bob should have done to my aunt, as she'd have made the best wife of an Episcopal priest the world has ever seen, which was probably even her destiny, which she refused—because of propriety—to step forth and meet, which is *a tragedy*, which is never going to happen to me.

We will never sit at home with our arms wrapped around ourselves as if to keep parts of ourselves from flying away into the universe, as my own mother did while becoming ever more isolated, more crazy, more lost from the Radiant Child she once was, the youngest-ever editor of *Pelican*, the humor magazine at Cal. My mom, who was once so obviously headed east, together with her best friends, Becky and Jo, to work at *The New Yorker* and conquer the Isle of Manhattan.

We will never be left home, locked in the house with umpteen kids, while The Men, who are firstborn and always six-foot-three and handsome and are therefore the most cherished creatures in our households, go out with whomsoever they want, driving off into the hot and glamorous night, whipping through the air in their new sports cars in badass colors.

This is our destiny: to not be withheld from our own destiny, and we will have birth control and we will own our *own* sports cars in badass colors, which we will drive with the top down and our *own* music blaring, and we will ourselves go out drinking with whomsoever we feel like and find *ourselves* in famous places, riding up and down in elevators with celebrities.

My friends and I will simply never turn out to be like the women in our neighborhood in the Valley, whose idea of being stylish strikes us as more and more grotesque, in that this includes wearing their hair in these ratted-up bouffant styles that are smoothed down, then pinned with infinite numbers of hairpins, then lacquered into place with hairspray. And they keep their eyebrows meticulously plucked—which is, like gardening, like washing up, yet another housekeeping chore—and their skin and nails are always perfect and their faces are held almost expressionless, as if they've been very expensively *burnished* of emotion, so you can't even come close to guessing what's on their minds.

Do the wives and mothers ever scream out during sex? I wonder as I lie outside in the darkest part of night, having climbed out my window to go stare at the stars from a chaise by the side of the steaming swimming pool, lights off, and I am thrilled to be by myself and in my wet underpants, thrilled—as I always am—to be where I am not allowed. I lie there listening to the night, but all I hear is cats making this ungodly noise, and it's because the males—or so it's rumored—have barbs on their cocks so the female can't slip off and get away.

My friends and I will simply never *become* these women whom we hate, who do not even resemble us, these women who have allowed themselves to be buckled into their cone-shaped bras so their breasts come to these weird, space age–seeming points, and whose butts are held taut and flat with girdles that have these strange, dangling-down clamps and devices that are supposed to clip together weirdly in order to keep your hose from sagging, so the whole underneath part of you is this bizarre feat of elaborate engineering that's obviously been designed to keep everyone's hands off you.

My friends and I are not like that—we feel ourselves and each other up.

Women's stuff is all weirdly menstrual and all about reproduction, and it's made of clamps and pads and rubber, and the bras and the underwear have this specific latexy, corsety smell that's like a scientific laboratory, or a hospital room, and so this is somehow the medicine we need to get *better*, and the Kotex we buy and then hide so the boys don't see them, girdles are the pink-plastic color of Band-Aids, which are supposed to look like skin but never had the slightest thing to do with the color of anyone's skin, as if the inventor of Band-Aids was too afraid to *look* at flesh without feeling that nakedness would make his eyes melt, and instead he went by the crayon in the box that was marked *Flesh*, another idea that has nothing to do with reality.

000

Our aim is always to wear as few clothes as possible, only two or three things. We need to be fast if we're going to get out of here. Everything about us is made for speed: Our short skirts are a direct challenge to the Powers That Be, so too our tight little sleeveless tops.

My friend Kat and I, who are on the girls' swim team, take long strides down the halls at school, brazenly lifting our eyes to those of the teachers who dare to stare at us. She's like I am, a half orphan, only it's her mom who's dead, so she's not well supervised. No one else has a name like hers, which is dangerous and therefore sexual because it's not traditional. Her name is actually Katherine, but she refuses to go by that, since this was her dead mother's middle name.

Kat and I have already been so deeply wounded, nothing else anyone does can touch us, which makes us almost impervious to harm. We encourage each other to act like this, becoming delirious with our own recklessness. She shows me how to shoplift. We go into a store, and while one of us—and we are monumentally self-possessed and exceedingly well spoken when we choose to be—engages the shoplady with this fake-adultish discourse, the other goes up and down the aisles, stuffing whatever she wants up the sleeves of the baggy hooded sweatshirts we wear after swim practice, or down the waistbands of our jeans.

We leave the store whooping, and the *lady*—and how I *hate* that word—knows she's just been so totally *had*. We whoop and scream as we run across the parking lot, as the shit we've stolen—which we don't even that much want—falls out of our clothes and we leave it there on the asphalt, which is even more *hilarious*.

People stare at us, we swear at them, we flip them off. We find ourselves on the highway, which is the abyss, as boys and men sense what we are, which is dangerous, and slow their cars to speak to us. We tell them to FUCK OFF and we walk out into traffic stopped at a light to walk along on the meridian divider, where we feel safe, going on down the middle of the highway like it's our tightrope out of here, and because we are propelled by tragedy—the early death of a parent—there is nothing to hold us here, so I feel that each of us may escape.

The world has never seen this thing before, though it has existed in the West—the American girl, the one who believes she can say or do anything and therefore feels untouchable.

We smoke cigarettes. Some of us can drive, and Kat and Jill and I all pile into Suzie's father's pink convertible Cadillac with its top down and drive to the beach with a paint-by-numbers canvas of Jesus' virtually life-size face riding along with us. We hold it in front of our own faces at a stoplight so that people glancing over will see that we've made a hole in the lips of Jesus with the point of a screwdriver just the size of a cigarette, so we can smoke through this hole in the life-size, paint-by-numbered face of Our Lord.

We end up in Malibu, where we pick up boys who are mildly shocked by us, which we find hilarious.

We are fevered, crazy, we feel like we're right on the verge of hysteria, and we've been good students in the past but now I am reprimanded in Honors English and am sent to the girls' vice principal for dress-code violations. I have to roll my skirt down from how I had it up at the waistband, and I get demerits for comportment; a couple more means a note home to my aunt, who will ground me. At lunch five or six or seven of us are made to kneel on a table to show that our skirts touch the tabletop; the teacher doing this hopes it will humiliate us, but we don't care and we comically contort ourselves to get our skirts to touch, and one of us, and this may be me, unzips her skirt to slide it down, and someone else leans way forward so her underpants show in back, and we are the opposite of humiliated because boys have begun crowding around to see, and now they look at us differently, and what *can* they do to us anyway—expel the whole tenth grade?

We feel hot to the touch, flushed with the day's excitement. The women at Sav-On stare at us as a group of us ding the bell to warn them that their store is being assaulted. There are now five of us, and while Kat and I, who are expert at sounding adult, talk to the ladies at the cash register, the others fan out in a way they cannot possibly keep track of. They aren't used to this kind of behavior from nice girls like we are, those who are white and who go to a good white school; we are these good white girls who are suddenly stuffing makeup and 45s down into our cutoffs.

It is *in defiance* of being good and because it makes these *ladie*s feel oddly powerless.

We enjoy traveling in a pack like this, the group in which our individual identities are submerged, and the women stare as we move down the street in close and laughing clusters that are tantalizing but also keep

us safe from men. The women stare as if we're very obviously conta-
gious, like it's smallpox we're carrying, as the Europeans brought this
kind of infectious disease to the New World with them and ruined innocence. These women know there is nothing they can do to protect those
precious to them, those who are not yet inoculated by experience and
who know no better than to be drawn to us, which would be their sons
and husbands, and we're told about being *prick teasers* and the dangers
to boys of *blue balls,* but we frankly don't give a shit.

We look like we're headed where some of us may be going, which
is the freeway exit in a certain town in the Valley that's called Reseda
but might as well be marked This May Well Be the Death of You, as
this is where the girls who've come to California on buses from other
places in the country end up when their other kind of movie dreams do
not work out.

My aunt *knows* all this but can't imagine what to do. She's never
had a teenage girl before, particularly one who likes the feeling of being
balanced there on the rim of the world, getting ready to tightrope-walk
off into complete nothingness because this girl has felt dead so long that
anything that makes her scared will also give her the thrill of being alive,
which is the opposite of the death-in-life she's used to.

As it happens, we live one town over from Reseda and we already
know all these men in LAPD Vice, and one is the brother of my friend
Mindy Dunnigan's father, Max, who works in The Industry but also
makes his money in other, more predictably profitable ways.

My aunt uncannily knows exactly which of my friends are being
well supervised. She believes Mindy Dunnigan's house to be what she
calls "an attractive nuisance," so I am barely allowed to go there. She
knows that on weekends, Max and Rusty Dunnigan take the smaller
kids on their cabin cruiser and go boating over to Catalina Island, leaving Mindy home alone.

I'm not allowed to spend the night at the Dunnigans', so I lie and say I'm staying at Suzie's or Jill's or Cheryl's. Kat's is off-limits because of her no-mom thing, as is Jane Brown's because her mom is divorced and works.

I'm sixteen and I know nothing about The Industry, aside from the fact that it doesn't seem very glamorous, that it's full of the kinds of people my mom calls Sad Little Men. Some of our neighbors, such as short, dumpy, bald Mr. Weymeyer, who is in no way attractive, are members of the Academy and so get to vote for the Oscars. I also babysit for Henry Mancini and his wife, who live around the corner from us and have twins, but The Industry doesn't impress me because nothing impresses me, in that I'm in a lulled and shut-down state that may have something to do with either shock or grief, though *grief* or even *sadness* is not a feeling I'd typically describe myself as having.

More than anything, either I feel the plain dumb thing that is being numb to all feeling or else I feel strangely tingly and anticipatory, which is something I don't actually feel in my mind, but rather in various parts of my body. It is slightly terrifying to feel sexual—a set of feelings that are in the body and that lie, I find, right next to physical hunger, as both sit in the heavier organs of the belly and well below the heart.

Something, I often think, is *just about to happen.*

I get to go on dates, as long as my aunt knows the boy. One boy takes me over the hill to see *Goldfinger* in Westwood, then parks on Mulholland so he can kiss me, but his mouth tastes off, some strange milkishness, so I make him take me home. Sexuality starts out okay but then veers off toward Band-Aids, turning so quickly from desire to queasiness.

And it's true that I almost never like the boys who like me, including the senior who asks me to his prom, but for some reason I'm pressured to go, though I don't know anybody in that grade and I'm horribly ashamed and embarrassed to do the prom-type shit I all of a sudden need to be doing: going to Bullock's Wilshire with my Grandmother Delia to buy a really humiliating dress, having to buy grown-up underclothes, going to a beauty parlor to get my hair *done* in the kind of bizarre updo thing that makes me want to pound the face I see looking back at me in the car visor's mirror.

So I go right home, take all the hairpins out, and immediately wash it and dry it and wear it my regular way, which is rolled on huge rollers so it curves a little under but mostly hangs down straight.

The whole prom experience is excruciating. I feel like I'm getting hives in my throat, feel like I'm being asked to act like something I have no hope of ever being—that is, this happy, pretty girl who'd feel honored to be asked to go to someone's prom with him. I know I am in no way ready for this mess that so reminds me that it's this bizarre, ritualistic prep for the satin-and-silk part of getting married and being A Bride, the whole idea of which makes me almost physically sick—how the white is supposed to reference how everyone's all *involved* in your virginity.

In fact, though I can say any manner of swear word, aside from certain derogatory words for *woman* (*cunt, bitch, twat*)—which are, for whatever reason, particularly sanctioned not only in my family but also in my own mind—I can't stand certain everyday terms that reference one's status as a person who is not yet sexually active, at least to That Unknowable Degree.

I suffer from Word Magic, which is what primitive peoples who cannot really tell the difference between the word and the act this word represents have.

I can actually barely stand the word *virgin*, for instance, which creeps me out, or the term *bridal suite*, or the verb *consummate*, or even the name of a drink my uncle sometimes has on Sunday mornings after we get home from church, which is called a *Bloody Mary*.

The sound of these words are abhorrent to me, in that hearing them uttered makes me almost literally ill.

I associate all this with *brides*, with what is obliquely related to everybody's cultural expectation of a girl like me: that I'm supposed to meet someone and withhold my body from him, and this is to trick him into marrying me so I can wear this stupid white dress (which looks exactly like what a baby is christened in) that is made of yards and yards of satin and lace, which strikes me as simply tacky.

This very profound aversion I have to the entire concept of getting married may go back to a basic misunderstanding I had when I was small and my mother explained what she called the Facts of Life to me, which I understood, she told me later, as everyone watching two people in church have sex in front of the rest of the congregation.

000

I'm sixteen. My friends and I know everything in our bodies and can say all words aside from the more normal ones having to do with matrimony, which sounds like a prison sentence, also other sickening terms, such as *mutual masturbation*, that we've read in Kinsey or in the sex manuals that turn up.

My friends and I at first know nothing about pornography, not even that it exists, though we live on the periphery of the vortex from which it swirls outward and is disseminated like sparks flying off a pinwheel.

Porn is being produced around us in warehouses and on soundstages all over the San Fernando Valley, and this is pre-video, so the porn part of The Industry still requires a motion-picture camera, film, and okay lighting, and film is really expensive and the whole thing costs *the earth*. Legitimate movie soundstages are used in the off-hours, so there's this other crew that comes around, and sometimes it's almost the same people who are moonlighting over here or sunlighting over there, working long hours and in grueling shifts. Sound, if it's used at all, is overdubbed, is only ever grunts and guttural moans, not plot lines, so porn can sell into any market, as these kinds of noisy cries never need translation.

And these actors and actresses are the same actors and actresses used in the real movies and commercials, those who came as if Los Angeles *beckoned*, since they were the best-looking girl or boy in their high school in Duluth, Minnesota, because California has *always* beckoned and drawn people forth to it, as the word itself has this magnetism and this promise that says you're just inches, really, from seeing your name six feet high and luminous.

As it was in my family in the Days of Yore, the word *California* will sound like destiny, but so far the doors of Twentieth Century Fox or Columbia or Paramount or Warner Brothers haven't opened up to you, and your agent has written this address on a little slip of paper and given it to you a little embarrassedly, and it's there off that certain exit in Reseda, a left turn and that quick right turn, and you find an unmarked back door to that certain warehouse because God knows you have to somehow pay the rent.

Besides, no one who knows you back in Duluth will probably ever watch these movies, which are still called *skin flicks,* as selling and buying them isn't part of a middle-class transaction and is still illegal, so even laying hands on a print of one of these requires knowing someone in Vice or someone else involved with the *underclass.*

I know about the underclass already because of my dad's run-ins with LAPD Vice. The word reminds me of the wild activity of sow bugs in the fragrant earth when you turn over a granite boulder.

Because these movies are really expensive, and your laying hands on one would depend upon your knowing someone who's well connected to this certain part of The Industry, someone like Max Dunnigan, who's a producer for commercials and has a brother named Frank who's a sergeant who works in Vice.

Even setting up one of these things to watch is really complicated in that you have to have an elaborate home-movie setup with a reel-to-reel projector and that kind of pearlized home-movie screen that flips over and pulls open from the top. Or you could tack a white sheet up on the wall of the den at the Dunnigans', which is an interior room that gets really dark.

Porn is still pure raunch, still plays to the most bestial of motives. There's nothing about it that says sex is a healthy part of the adult human experience.

This is pre–Mitchell Brothers of San Francisco, pre–*Behind the Green Door*, pre–*Deep Throat*, pre-Haight-Ashbury and our own hippie days, which will be this tiny window that lasts only a fraction of a second, and during which we will wear translucent dresses and tiny undies and no bras at all, and we'll be so totally stoned and dancing from shadow to shadow in the Panhandle, and convinced that no one would ever hurt us, that the day has dawned in which it's finally safe to be *a girl*.

So far, porn is almost entirely grim. Porn belongs to the underworld, and it speaks to the whore/pimp part of us, where everything is not as much about sex as you would think, and is actually more about money.

My aunt knows things aren't right at the Dunnigans', but she may not yet have a word for what's going on over there, except that her eyes flutter when we discuss it, which means her soul does not approve. She doesn't like or trust Mindy Dunnigan, who's been caught in the boys' wing of our house, making out with my cousin Graham, and my aunt's completely right when she thinks Mindy's probably one of those girls who's hell-bent on getting pregnant as a way out of her present circumstance.

Mindy is actually Max Dunnigan's stepdaughter, so she has a real father somewhere whom she's lost somehow, as I have lost my own. And my friends in high school have now, as a pattern, stopped conforming to the norm of the one mom and dad matched up and safely locked together in their chaste, twin-bedded Ozzie and Harriet lives.

I lie out in the backyard in the middle of the night and wonder whether women honestly do or do not like sex. I worry about what they think of it, that they can still—in the substance of their bodies—somehow remember how it was on the frontier that they were always, always pregnant, then often simply bled to death because of it.

Thinking about their grown-up physical bodies—the bodies of adult women (with all that secretly implied bloody stuff and the obvious risk of death implied in childbirth)—makes me queasy, in the same way as watery eggs.

The Ozzie-and-Harriet space-between-the-beds thing is simply confusing, in that it has resonance with my own experience, but I can't figure out if that resonance is even *real* or not. Do married people in other, more normal families *actually* sleep like this, and if so, what is *that* supposed to mean? The Ozzie-and-Harriet hiatus is also being laid down at the exact same moment in which the Kinsey Report is being read by my parents and my aunt and uncle and all their college-educated friends, who *act* like they're sophisticated, who are all trying to at least *act like* they are practicing heterosexuals, though they aren't—evidently—very good at it.

Because my friends' moms have started to be divorced, have started to work outside the house, as American women used to at least, before the 1950s got hold of them and told them to stay home with an apron tied around their waist and to live in the house with the White Picket Fence.

The Apron-Around-the-Waist trick is one sure way, as my mom has deduced from her superior vantage point of Ward G-1 in the State

Mental Hospital at Camarillo, to get whole hordes of women to completely lose their minds, which she tells me one of the times my grandfather drives Geo and me up to see her.

Beware, she tells me, The White Picket Fence.

Children are now growing up in what's called a "broken home,"
whose stigma, of course, also applies to me, though my own family situation at my aunt and uncle's is more complicated and hidden, in that the
household looks so All-American and stable.

My grandmother is clear that vice doesn't come from *her*, though
her blue-bloodedness has been polluted, of course, by her marrying my
grandfather, scion of an American Dutch family whose lineage goes
back to two drunken brothers so worthless that they were first thrown
out of an entire (and, by the way, exceedingly drunken) country, given
free passage from Holland to the New World, then tossed off a ship
slightly upriver from what is now Troy, New York, in 1644. The *burgh*,
or *hill*, in our august-sounding name comes from the slight rise in the
land where they lighted, which, my father always said, was in all likeli-
hood in fact *a midden.*

What we know about these brothers, Giesbert and Clyes, we de-
rived primarily from their arrest records, in which they were constantly
brought up on charges for public drunkenness or for fighting or for
stealing each other's pigs.

And my mom makes sure we know that almost all American
Vandenburghs are, in fact, descended from *both* of these two wast-
rel brothers, in that the same Henrys and Marys and Williams and
Margarets kept intermarrying their cousins all down through generations and centuries, which concentrated the affinity for *vice* that we all
seem to carry in our genes.

000

My friend Mindy's stepfather is either deaf or, as is said, hard of hearing, so he bellows at us, but then, he bellows at everyone. He has a huge head with a shock of sandy hair that he wears longer than most men wear it, which may be his way of trying to cover his hearing aids, which are big, flesh-colored, and conspicuous. His manner is one of manic, joyful yelling. He's playful, always hollering, braying, in that rounded-off way of those who can't quite hear the way the rest of us bite down hard on consonants.

His yelling is only another one of the ways this household is different from my own, which is very High Church, as my mother says, which means it's staid and quiet and so nonconfrontational that no one ever argues.

Max is all *involved* with Mindy and her friends. He gets into the pool and plays watermelon football with us, but we know we need to stay away from him.

The deafness has a congenital element, so a couple of Mindy's half brothers or sisters are deaf as well. There are a lot of kids in the Dunnigans' somehow patched-together household, the seams knit by Mindy and her younger brother's having taken their stepfather's last name.

Their house is only a few doors from our high school and is a natural hangout that Max Dunnigan has outfitted with whatever kids might want. The Dunnigans' swimming pool is deeper than anybody else's and has a slide and a springboard. The rec room has a pool table and a soda fountain that Max keeps stocked with huge commercial tubs of ice cream, as well as cherries and chocolate syrup.

We all *know* about Max without anyone's telling us. Mindy makes the "he's crazy" loop around her ear and says, Fuck you, Max, to him at full volume when he's not facing in her direction. We know what's wrong without anyone's telling us, because you can't ride in the front seat of the car without his putting his big paw of a hand on the skin of your leg that shows below your cutoffs, and his is a man's hard hand, strangely textured, as if the whorls of his fingerprints are somehow exaggerated.

But we think of a person like Max as generally harmless—as a Funny Uncle, though our own uncle isn't one of this variety—and it's our conceit that we can *handle* him.

We know about Max instinctively, know too that we're important to him, that he values us, that we can get him to do things for us and give us money and rides here and there. We're sixteen, we don't have boyfriends yet and we don't really date.

We are suddenly powerful. Max Dunnigan in some way fits in with this, in that we now have the power to attract a man like this and the power to repel most women, and this means that we'll never have to go live in the house that sits behind The White Picket Fence.

∞

I know all about all this stuff but still suffer from what feels like a very childish aversion, in that I honestly can't imagine really wanting anyone to fuck me.

I honestly mostly like kissing, but only the right boy. I like the power that being sexual gives me, his putting his hands on me in places that are not numb, but I don't want to be involved with this boy's dick, very frankly.

The times I do go ahead and feel his dick, I sense what he too feels: that his erection is bizarre, humiliating, that it *tells* on him, and what it says is that he's way more bestial than I am. A boy's erection is something that stands between the two of us and is in no way uniting.

But I do like kissing, as this is how I'm able to imagine which ones might turn out to be okay to go to bed with. *Going to bed with a boy* is the antique Ozzie-and-Harriet phrase that has replaced the one my mother uses, which is *sleeping with*. *Going to bed with* creeps me out slightly less than the other, more graphic terms do, which include *screwing, nailing, getting laid*. We don't yet call it *having sex* or *fucking*, and I haven't yet heard it called *getting busy, balling, jumping his or her bones*, or *doing the nasty*.

For me—with my gift of word magic and my very vivid imagination—kissing so totally *says it*. Kissing—as long as the boy smells good and tastes good—is like this little haiku of how the sex will be as soon as we get around to it, as kissing is like the sex *exactly*, how it will or will not be sloppy in the way of kissing a drunk boy, one who is inexact and noisy.

Kissing is the three-line note with all the pent-up nature of the real thing packed down into it. I'm really good at kissing, and if the boy smells good and tastes right and feels right, I withhold nothing. It has everything to do with smell and taste and fantasy, also with the really physical part that I more and more enjoy: all the softness, hardness, warmth, the texture of teeth and tongue, as if our souls are in our mouths and we can finally say the things that let us speak.

And kissing is, of course, what's missing completely from the movies Max Dunnigan sets up for us on the projector in the dark den at the very center of Mindy's house. I know about the economics because of Max and his brother, who works in Vice. We can easily overhear Max Dunnigan bellowing to his brother about this or that, and his brother shouting back to make sure Max can hear him, when they're getting drunk out by the pool, and why should they hide it, since no one's going to arrest them?

Because film and studio time are so expensive, there's this almost clipped, Charlie Chaplin-like, speeded-up rhythm to some of these movies, and the production values are all over the place because they've been made by all these different operations. Max's brother confiscates them in the LAPD Vice busts, then takes them to a warehouse that has an editing machine and a film printer, where they're copied before being turned in as evidence.

This is a giant joke between the two loud Dunnigan brothers out by the pool getting loaded—that Vice pervades everything at all levels of society, that it touches all of us.

It's Max who has set up the projector, as he has told us that we, being girls, are mechanically incompetent. When we come over to Mindy's to drink the Coke and Bubble Up that shoots from the armature of the soda fountain, he has it ready to go at the flick of a switch. I drink sodas at the Dunnigans' though my aunt doesn't allow us to ever drink what she calls soft drinks, in that they are, according to her, pure sugar, and we know she knows this kind of thing since she went to medical school.

Vice, I think, is what tells us about the activities that exist in the silence and hiatus defined by the space between the twin beds at Ozzie-and-Harriet's house. We don't want to know about Vice in our own lives because this embarrasses us. We so far have only the joking vocabulary with which to talk about sex. We think we are all virgins, in that none of us has had an actual boyfriend. We imagine we are virgins—though the word itself contains this very serious aspect of both tragedy and creepiness, in that it seems to say so much about our destiny.

The cock is so huge it tents the sheet and is found by the nurse who tiptoes in, as if not to wake him. This penis is strangely veined and old looking, unlike the boy penises of our brothers and cousins, which we've seen surreptitiously in getting in and out of swimsuits, and which are still what we think of as *clean*.

The lighting is terrible, so it's sometimes hard to decipher what you're seeing. The cock sticks out or it sticks up, and there is strange editing and confusion, and there'll be a couple of jittering cuts—with no narrative interlude or plausible explanation—and now the cock is being handled, now sucked. Now it is the mouth of the fully clothed nurse or waitress or secretary. The nurse or waitress or secretary sucks the penis for a while, then hikes up her skirt, climbs up on the man's body, and puts the penis inside of her, then rocks back and forth to ride it.

She rides it until she suddenly hops off. As the camera closes in on her face, she looks right at the camera and smiles. Then the penis starts to spurt come into her face through its little slit.

That's the Money Shot, Mindy says.

We all know she knows way too much about this, in that she's starting to earn money in The Industry. Last year she was working as a hand model, so her fingernails are always expensively manicured.

Wearing red fingernails, I somehow know, is a subtle sign of moral degradation.

Mindy earns money every time her hand is shown on TV reaching into the bowl to extract a potato chip. She mimes doing this. This money is called residuals.

We know nothing; we also know everything. We recognize this sex as gross, unattractive, and we say so to one another—that that guy's thing is just so fucking ugly—but we don't go home and we don't not come back the next week to watch the next one.

The movies, most of which are silent, show behavior that is aberrant, but we don't care. We are aberrant, if not in deed then at least in the wildness of our heated minds, which can think of all kinds of disgusting things that we might want to one day do or, better, watch as they happen to other people.

This is what the movies are trying to teach us: You let the cock come in your face. You smile like you're happy about it.

Or these movies may be about recruitment, I'm guessing, becoming initiated. The guy brings you to the warehouse where the film is made in order to pimp you out. This is The Boyfriend and he fucks you, but he wants you to fuck other people, too, while he is watching. He wants to see you do it. He wants you to do it with one, two, three other guys, all the guys in the warehouse.

Or a stable, a horse farm, may be involved. Can you do it with this many men for him? It's how he'll know you love him. Can you do it with the cowboy in chaps but no pants who beats you with a riding crop? Can The Boyfriend get you to let him do whatever he wants to you? Can he put you in the breeding crate while the little piglets, whose teeth are sharp, are suckling on your nipples?

The camera moves in on your face as the little animal teeth bite your nipples. Either The Boyfriend or the one he's pimped you to fucks you from behind. Your face, we notice, is deformed by what might be either pain or ecstasy.

That is so completely fucking gross, we say, but we do not not watch. We in fact watch movie after movie until we're strangely expert and can tell exactly when it's just about time for the Money Shot.

Will you do it with six convicts if The Boyfriend asks you to? Will you do with Mexicans? Will you do it with Negroes?

Are you willing to become his *thing*? these movies seem to ask, the one pure thing that no longer thinks or questions or needs to speak, that is only cunt to his cock, so he is cock completely and solely.

Would you whore for him? Would you stand on the street corner in a shitty part of Hollywood in the cold, wearing mascara that drips like you have been crying, and give him all the money you get for it? Is there no part of you he couldn't fuck or have some other man fuck if he asked you to?

The movies might be training, I'm guessing, on how to go out into the night and become one with Vice, to actually join up, as my mother says my father did, to stop thinking about these things and actually go and do them.

We might be being trained by Max, I guess, whom I now trust less and less, as there is something deeply wrong with a man who'd set these movies up for his teenaged daughter and her friends, and even though he's not there watching them with us, his presence is all around us.

Obedience is the moral lesson of these movies, which is strange because they appeal to the parts of us that are utterly unruly. We think we can handle boys, men, anything that comes to us. The movies say we need to learn a lesson.

◍

Boys never come to Mindy's house. We are girls only, are—I'm only guessing—virgins, and we kiss each other and suck one another's nipples but call it practicing and stay uninvolved.

There is something so odd and inconclusive about what passes for sex in these days in the San Fernando Valley, and I'm guessing that sleeping with one boy might not even do it when it becomes time for me to get rid of my virginity; I might have to fuck one boy, then fuck another—maybe a whole raft of them—in order to get rid of it, and I want it gone, its whole virgin, white-satin, bloodstained creepiness.

I don't know the boy who seems to be *up to this*.

◍

My aunt disapproves of Mindy's parents because they let us drink soft drinks and eat ice cream, and because they are not educated.

I always know who is and isn't educated based on my aunt's enthusiasm about my going over to whichever of my friends' households, as if a college education is the wall that needs to stand between our exalted selves and crass vulgarians like Mindy's parents, with their sweets and porno.

Rusty Dunnigan is a lunatic mom of a variety I've never before encountered. She's a disaster junkie who listens to police band radio provided by the Dunnigan in Vice. She regularly runs out to her station wagon without saying a word, leaving the little kids to us, and gets in to go drive to the scene of an accident. She collects pieces of the wreckage, taillight glass from a fatal car wreck, metal from an airplane crash. She keeps these in a special place in her closet, goes to get them if you act the slightest bit interested, and will tell you all about the scene as she came upon it.

She says it with a rapt, trancelike look on her face that tells you she's completely transported, her vision fixed on the cataclysmic moment, and I somehow know—though I'm actually too young to know this—that sex is somehow equal to disaster, equal to blood and death.

〰〰〰

The lesson of pornography, at least as I am taking it in, has to do with whether or not you prefer sex to be involving. You can stay out of it altogether, as if you were the woman being fucked, who looks at the camera and smiles as come splurts over her face in the Money Shot.

This is what I already know, though I have no way of knowing it: You can be a drug-addicted hooker and still be a virgin, in that it is possible to have sex *all the time*, while in your soul that resides in your mouth and comes alive only by Word Magic—in the saying of a beloved's name, for instance—who you really are doesn't necessarily participate.

The movies are brute in that they tell us what matters biologically: For the species to go on, you have to get the cock to come. The cock has to come. When the cock comes, the movie ends, as film and studio time are expensive. There is no plot to the stories except for that most ancient one—that it hardly matters whether or not the girl comes, whether she's enjoying it or is completely faking, so all that remains a mystery.

The cock comes, the action stops, and the film runs out, as there are no credits or trailers. The screen goes white. The projector makes the *clickety-clack* as the film comes off its sprockets.

ᗢ

The first time I ever have an orgasm, it's accidentally and completely noncontextual, while doing floor exercises in dance class for PE, a maneuver that asks us to straighten our legs, point our toes, then bounce our bodies forward toward our knees, and I totally know what this is because I am in no way mentally chaste. I'm not even interested in my own virginity and in no way value it, and if I could I'd just somehow skip over this piece of what has to happen or otherwise get around it, without having to go through *all that*, which is what my mother would no doubt call it.

My mother has somehow tutored me to be careful with boys, who aren't as tough as girls. This has to do with childbirth, and with the long road west, which makes Our People, by which she means girls and women, stronger, more solid at the core.

This is what I have, so far, to go on: Men and boys are a different kind of beast whose self-esteem is tied up in the size and shape of what I'll later think of as their Unit. White men and boys are particularly sensitive about this aspect of their anatomies, my mother either outright says or at least intimates, so we must never act to diminish them, as they've already been, she says, somehow diminished.

All the boys in my family have been circumcised. Boys are afraid, my mother says, because they've been circumcised, because they still hold in their infant memory the image of someone's coming at them with a pair of scissors or a bright and shining knife, which is why we are not to *criticize* men and boys, as—very honestly?—they're probably doing the best they can.

Boys, for instance, worry constantly that their penis and balls *can* fall off while they're sitting on the toilet seat, my mother says, a worry that—believe it or not—never entirely goes away.

These are the lessons I've learned about the Facts of Life. Men and boys are babies, my mother says, so we indulge them. You can fuck as many men as you can find, but this won't necessarily involve your psyche. Men and boys do much of their thinking with their cocks. Their cocks are what make men and boys *act up,* but it's the cocks that are doing this, so men basically cannot help it, which is what makes us fundamentally better than they are. Everyone actually wants the same thing, which is to get the cock to come, which is when everything settles down and becomes normal again.

Years later, a song I love captures the feeling exactly: We are fever, we are fever, we ain't born typical.

My mother's wisdom drifts back to me: You check the box marked *Other*.

8

A Continent of Grief

So now my Uncle Ned is anyway turning out to be a *cad* or *lout* or *bounder*. He's what my mom calls yet one more *Good Time Charlie*, and this is widely known in our family, though it is never spoken of.

My diagnosis? That he's as sick of grief as he is of the rest of us, so he's obviously voting in favor of his own happiness.

He's sick too of this big house with its wings that reach out and around, as if to snatch up all light and air. The house is being perpetually *added onto* yet remains too small and crowded with the unruly energies of all us kids, who are lately climbing out of windows into the hot dry night, fragrant with humus in the planting beds and the chlorine vapor rising off the swimming pool.

Which is to say, my uncle's jealous, knowing it is Graham and Jordy and I who'll escape from here most soon.

And it's anyway just one more summer's day in the baking heat of what he calls the Rat Race, and the air-conditioning's running continually, so he yells at us again and again, Slide that door closed behind you! Do you think I want to pay to cool the entire neighborhood?

Late afternoon fading into evening, the Arsenic Hour, in which they sit in the cool underwater light of my aunt's blue-and-green color scheme to have yet another polite but tense conversation, and all he's thinking of is how he's *got* to get out of there, drive away, go do something he really *wants* while there's still time.

And the thin marine light reminds him of church, of my aunt's good works, her piety, the seriousness of her purpose, all of which oppresses him. She's ten months older than he. He's begun to say aloud, It's what I get for falling for an older dame.

The suburbs. They're flat, monotonous . . . he hates it here, and I actually know this feeling, too, know how you might just have to strike out with your clenched fists and smack the front windshield of the VW that you're riding in as a passenger. My uncle's lately driving a VW Bug, so he sometimes gives me a ride to school when my schedule conflicts with Graham's. My uncle's driving this car because it makes him feel like less of what he calls an Old Goat. My uncle says *Old Goat*, then snorts.

Uncle Ned is in his late thirties. When my father died, he became the oldest adult male in our family, aside from one agéd grandfather on my mother's side, who—by Poor Mouthing, by invoking the Power of the Weak—has managed to contribute nothing to the upkeep of the three bedraggled, half-orphaned urchins.

My uncle, in inheriting my two brothers and me, is now financially responsible for a wife and seven children.

What does my uncle do? He goes to his investment club—they meet at lunch, so they call themselves the Brown Baggers. He becomes more and more successful at everything he touches.

He's more cheerful than he's ever been, something my aunt notices. He travels out of town more often and when he's in town drives his new car away from home as soon as he can and stays away as long as possible.

And his cheerfulness makes odd but entire sense to me when I come at it slantwise, not with my mind, but by thinking with my body. I understand his happiness in the deep way I now know certain other things: that you can, for instance, get the boy you're making out with to press on your belly right above the pubic bone when you need to pee, and the sensation is completely thrilling, in that you retain your power and your modesty, not letting him touch your breasts or skin, and that you can stop him, stop him just short of ecstasy, and the whole time he actually has no idea what he's doing.

This is what my aunt often says about a boy: *You poor dear dumb thing.*

My uncle wants to drive around in a new car with the windows down, zipping through the chunks of hot, sagey night that waft through the canyons on his way to Malibu, voices baffling wildly, then snatched away. There to sit with someone glamorous who *wants* him, who's paying attention just *to him,* who is enveloped with him in a dark cocoon of secrecy, eating with him in a booth in a seafood restaurant where he sits on the banquette and feels his heart expand, pounding to fill his chest, all the blood he owns crying, *Rise up! Arise and be free!* And she slips her shoe off and puts her stockinged foot in his lap, where he cradles the silk heel of it, and as they turn to watch the sun go down, he says simply, because he's a simple man, You make me very happy.

And as he drives away from the too-thick-with-grief air of the house that is crammed with just too many of us, he figures he *gets* to do this, as an American male of the Upper Middle Classes, because American males of his generation are taught to think they are entitled to such privileges, to an expectation of happiness. Happiness has begun to seem like a destination to him, a place that lies elsewhere. He needs to go there while he still can, he knows, to this place where he'll be able to somehow *enter.*

Because everyone who's been in the West for any time has his or her own sad story, and the tragedies—I can't help but notice—become hinges in the narrative, places where the story turns. This shift—once accomplished—sends the tale in a new direction. Tragedy, I notice, has a way of rhyming with itself or doubling, like my uncle's Republican investment club's principle of interest always being *compounded*.

Uncle Ned's grief is different from my own, only in that it's *his* story that this family is always trying hardest to keep from telling.

And his personal grief anyway so completely trumps anything any of the rest of us can come up with, that any of us have—as my uncle says—to *moan and groan about*. His story is so tragic, it lies like a great archaic continent that's been buried by Geologic Time, whose evidence is seen only in the jagged strata of the Overthrust Belt, rock slices shoved diagonally upward and that make no sense, and are therefore perfectly inexplicable to all but the most learned of scientific eyes.

The continent of grief underlies all of our lives, I'm finding, but it is studiously ignored in this part of the family, while my own mother—who, it's said, *indulged* her grief and was therefore *driven crazy* by it—will speak of nothing else.

My uncle's story is such ancient history, I have no memory of who it was who even told me about it, though it must have been my mother, since she's the one who will *not* not say whatever occurs to her to say, this being one of the main reasons she's been committed to a mental institution.

As her father says, Margaret, women do not talk like that.

To which she answers, Dad, honestly? Really? They *do too*.

The shape and nature of my uncle's grief is the story that's been buried since he was about the ages Graham and Jordy and I are now—fourteen, fifteen, sixteen—when he was away at boarding school. This is when he lost his mother, sister, and brother in a hotel fire. It was in his school's town. They'd come to visit him.

This grief, which I figure must inform everything my uncle does, is simply so huge that he can't bear to acknowledge it.

And my uncle, who is my aunt's husband and therefore not related to me by blood, is unlike the rest of us in this one very fundamental way. He's a Western *man*, so he somehow manages to keep the oxcart moving, to stand by his dad to bury the dead and *who knows where?* since this is the West, where we burn the markers as firewood.

Tall men. Each tall man turns, with his back straight and his upper lip stiff, and these two are Edward Snowden Junior and *the Third*. To do otherwise would be undignified.

My uncle makes a point of being optimistic, forward-thinking. This pays, he says, when you're a Republican and a businessman.

My uncle's smart but he isn't deep. He's also *proud* of not being deep. He'll tease me about it, saying it's possible in this life to be so deep that you completely lack a surface.

He says this to me as I'm reading Shakespeare aloud to myself, sitting in the kitchen alcove, waiting for the wall phone to ring, hoping it'll be some boy I like, and wanting to head off Geo or any of my boy cousins, who will, having nothing better to do, race to answer it.

Five fathoms deep my father lies, I read beneath my breath.

I never liked Shakespeare, my uncle says as he's digging through the refrigerator. He's hungry, he's looking for something, because he *wants!* he *wants!* he *wants!* He must scroll past old food, push beyond the half-eaten sandwiches my aunt makes Geo and Thomas save for later, for when they're hungry and are begging for a snack. He must get beyond the vet-pack part of the fridge, the special dalmatian medicine that's kept in there for Murphy's hot spots. The fridge is also the reptile and amphibian supply store, so he must sort through canisters of moths and mealyworms to try to find anything vaguely appealing to a human.

That's okay, Uncle Ned, I tell him kindly. Shakespeare doesn't like you either.

My uncle and I are fond of each other, though I have no idea why; we're as unalike as night and day. But we have the orphan thing in common, also that we're tough in some profound way, as each of us recognizes in the other. I admire his talent for happiness, while he likes what he calls my *joie de vivre*. But I'm almost painfully observant, while my uncle purposely will not notice things and so comes off as an anti-intellectual clod.

I have certain strengths, in that I'm not like Geo, whose plight now troubles everyone.

The truth about you, my uncle says, is that you're a strong swimmer. Not fast, but you continue to plod along—it's the steady pace that'll get you where you're going.

I'm a strong swimmer, but I am also like my parents. Being like my parents—this is wildly praised as *creative* or *brilliant* or *hilarious*, then right away derided as *alcoholic, outré, self-destructive, crazy*—is just flat-out exhausting. It makes me want to go to sleep and not wake up—not to die, just to get a rest from the constant yammering.

My being *artistic* makes me act in a manner my uncle thinks of as contralogical. He's a Republican, a guy, and the highest value for a man like this is a) to win or b) if you can't win, to at least save yourself from drowning.

When a riptide catches you, therefore, you need to know that you must swim patiently sideways, without panicking, swimming parallel to the shore until the current releases its grip on you. Even the strongest swimmer will be overwhelmed trying to swim back to shore against a rip as strong as the ones we know.

My father, who had his own sailboat from an early age, taught me another way. You may also save yourself, he said, if you relax entirely into the current and allow it to carry you out to sea. You float on your back, look up, admire clouds, become one with the cawing seabirds— you see them well and enjoy the ride and in this way come to completely know that life will finally prove to be much too much for each and every one of us.

I've let this happen, let myself be carried out to sea beyond the break line, knowing I am a strong enough swimmer that I can get myself back to shore. My uncle doesn't get why anyone would allow herself to go *backward*, and I can't explain this to him, the simple pleasure of sometimes allowing yourself to submit to the backward pull.

It's because he doesn't really get Shakespeare, how the witches warn Macbeth yet Macbeth still goes ahead and does the exact thing he's been warned against, because it's his fate to do that, so he's therefore drawn toward his own future. And he goes directly there because he really just can't *not*.

My uncle is Republican. It's Republican to think grim fate is what happens to the darker, angrier races.

I, who am contralogical, was born having to live my life in a manner that feels retrograde to Uncle Ned, as if, though I am still a child, I am somehow fundamentally older than he is. I understand the undertow, that he and I are passing each other on our separate ways out of here, I'm growing up even as he struggles to stay young.

I live in his house, eat his food, and am not a Snowden—not, therefore, his blood, which is somehow English. I'm a girl, a teenager, and sort of Dutch, and he's never had one of these before.

And I can't explain myself to him: that I was born in obverse, facing history by going in the wrong direction, and I look back into Deep Geologic Time because this *comforts* me.

My job is to memorize the lives of my dead and still-living relatives, and to keep them with me not only by bundling them up and dousing them with camphor, but also by remembering their lines so people will know which *roles* they played.

My mother talks a lot about *roles* these days, because this is how the people in her group therapy in the mental hospital have been taught to express themselves.

✹✹✹

It is 1963, and part of what my uncle does with grief has to do with Edward Snowden the First, his grandfather's being English. The English are, as my aunt and uncle's friends Michael and Sarah Burlingham say, a cold, stiff, and ultimately disappointed tribe— disappointed because they believed they were God, but it turns out they aren't—which the Burlinghams should know since they were born in London.

I'm always wondering what people like the slaveholders or the British, who went out to conquer the world, did with all their guilt, because I know guilt to be the cause of things. Guilt will cause the turn in the narrative, become the elbow in the story that says *this* happened, then *this* happened *because* of that first thing's happening, which is what we're shown in *Crime and Punishment*.

My uncle, who doesn't like Shakespeare, also doesn't *go by*—as my mother would say—Dostoevsky, in the way my own parents always have. Your father, my mother says, was pure Fyodor Mikhailovich, while my life is turning out to be much more Émile Zola.

But anyone who reads *Crime and Punishment* can feel how the two events—the crime of Raskolnikov and his being punished for it—are magnetized to each other across countless pages or invisible time or even a mass migration across an entire continent.

There is simply no chance that anyone's going to get away with it.

His mother, brother, and sister—which was *everyone*—dying in a hotel fire, and their only being in that hotel when it burned because they were visiting him? How can my uncle live with this?

My own father's crime was to have not been speaking to his parents when his dad—on a trip to Illinois to see certain cousins—died suddenly, of a cerebral hemorrhage.

Historians call sudden-death-from-a-cerebral-hemorrhage-while-off-in-Illinois-while-visiting-certain-cousins a *Contingent Event*. The California Gold Rush is cited as one of the Contingent Events of the Civil War, in that the financial institutions to which all that gold was shipped were in the North, so those billions of dollars of wealth went there to be used by the Northern bankers to invest in the factories that manufactured munitions for the Union Army.

And because I don't understand what people like my uncle do with their guilt—that his mother, brother, and sister died in the fire *while visiting him!*—I imagine he must be magnetized to its having happened, so I study him for signs of it.

It happened in a beach town somewhere south of us. The school sits—or so I'm forced to imagine, since he won't speak of it—on a hillside above the town. I imagine that the boys in their dorms, awakened by the sirens, would have gone to their windows in their nightclothes to see the embers being carried upward and back, past the tops of the eucalyptus trees planted around the grounds as windbreaks. They might have thought to worry about the trees, which carry such a huge fuel load that they sometimes burst into flame with a tremendous *whoosh* that sounds like a bomb going off.

But my uncle is a firstborn boy, his dad's heir, a charmed boy in a culture that worships boys. He's tall, good-looking, very confident. My family has long been adept at producing such men. Each woman is then raised to marry a man like this in order to have more sons like these.

So my uncle might have imagined himself to be lucky, even blessed. He was a man among men, and high up in what my mother calls the Mucky Muck, which is the Great Chain of Being, the English being anointed as maybe the luckiest race there'd ever been, until the Twentieth-Century White American Male was *finally* invented.

So my uncle, gazing out of the dorm window, would *never have imagined* that the bells of distress being rung in the mission of that seaside town were, that time, being rung for him.

∭

I'm reading, which is *allowed* on a Saturday morning, but my uncle comes in from their rooms in the adult wing of the house and makes a goofy face at me to mock my being studious. He thinks I'm studious but I'm not, as that would require being systematic and even organized in what I'm reading, and I am honestly neither. Instead, I read because a good story is the best way to escape from wherever it is I am.

Dontcha wanna go do something outside in the living daylight? my uncle asks.

Nope, I say. I talk through the mouth I can hardly open since my chin's resting on my hand.

Why not?

Can't, I say.

Can too.

Don't *want to*, then?

Why not?

Depressed, I say and glance up at him. I invoke the word though I'm in the wrong part of the family to say this, as this is the portion of the collateral descendents of the blah-blah-blah, Holland Society, 1644, so forth, that doesn't *go by* what my mother calls The Psychological.

All the more reason to get going, my uncle says. Get off your *bee-hind*! Go change your shirt. Isn't that the same shirt you were wearing last night?

No, I say.

Looks the same.

It isn't a *shirt*, Uncle Ned, I say. It's the top to my pajamas, I wear it *all the time*, and now I'm wondering how it can be that he's *only now* noticing.

Your pajamas? he asks. At eleven thirty in the morning? Where's your aunt?

Dunno. I say. Food shopping? Altar guild?

I mean it, he says. Go get dressed.

Noooooo . . .

Yesssss, he says, and while you're at it, brush your hair.

But I don't *want* to . . .

I don't *care* if you don't want to. My uncle says this through a blaze of straight white teeth, grinning as he speaks. Get going, he says. Go out and ride your bike. You and Jordy take the little guys. Ride to town, buy them all an ice cream.

Then my uncle takes out his wallet, from which he extracts a neat little fold of cash and begins peeling off bills. Money's new, bills feel sticky as he hands them to me, and the smell is loud with ink.

And since my uncle is as famously generous as my aunt is tight, he then remembers the others, who might want some of his money, and so heads in the direction of the boys' part of the house, calling, Did everyone get his allowance?

At the door to the kitchen he turns to grin at me, saying, I am a river to my people.

〇〇〇

I sulk and wear my pajamas around the house and won't wash my face or brush my hair, but only until something fun presents itself to do, in which case I can snap out of a pout in less than two seconds. My mother does not respect this quality of mine, that—depressed as I am and almost entirely defeated—I'm still eager to participate. I can even go somewhere sometimes and not completely hate it, go there and be almost entirely enthusiastic, which my mother really hates, since she and my father became almost curdled by their joint cynicism and she carries it on to this day, out of loyalty to him.

In my mother and father's lineage of our once august family—we're supposed to imagine given the grim state of the world—that committing suicide is a very rational thing to do, which I two- to three-fifths believe.

But now I live in a more or less normal house and have normal clothes and friends. I get dressed for school, then go out to the car and am carried along by the buoyant sense of my own weightlessness, having been released from the penitentiary.

Graham drives me and Jordy to school, and sometimes Cheryl DeCinces or Debbie Poor, everyone sitting on everybody else's laps. It's only cute girls, those Graham says are bitchen, who get to ride in our car.

We're teenagers. We're porous. We're like the chalk you dip into vials of stain in chemistry and allowing someone non-bitchen to ride in our car with us might taint us with their weirdo-ness. Our status as human beings is actually so frail even walking down the hall *next to* someone non-bitchen is enough to *implicate* you.

The car still smells vaguely of vodka barf from when Graham took it out and got *boozed up, creamed, schooled in the fine art of drunkification*, on the first weekend he was allowed to drive it, so the car now stinks mostly only when the heater's on.

So going to school is like being on parole and I'm good in school and it's fun for me and my classes are almost always interesting. My teachers encourage me, which may be only out of pity for all my assorted tragedies, as I'm so completely unlike my uncle that everyone almost immediately knows everything about me—I don't care, as saying this stuff is becoming more and more who I am intrinsically.

Every part of school is fun, even the complaining about the asshole teachers, even completely hating it. I'm really good at hating things. My parents were *anti* this and that. It's Lina who says this, pronouncing it *AN-tee*. Lina's my dusty grandmother, not Delia, but the one who grew up raising pigs and flyfishing on a ranch in Montana.

It's in Mr. Greenbaum's first-period Honors English that I am asked to go first one Friday in November when our oral reports are due.

I'm surprised but it's okay, because I'm prepared and I've worn something okay to school and my hair's all right, so there's nothing really that obvious that's wrong with me. I've always looked like such an essentially ordinary person that it's a shock to everyone—myself included—to have to witness the ways in which I'm not.

My major problem—the language of which I'll find out later, expensively—is that I am not *well integrated.*

So I go to the front of the class, confident enough of my bitchenness, with my skirt rolled up at my waist to show the right amount of thigh, which is not permitted but is allowed, and I smile as I stand at the podium and put my report there in front of me and look at Mr. Greenbaum, who's sitting in the back and reminds me of my father—but then, every man I'll ever meet who is in any way good or nice or smart or kind will remind me of my father. Then I begin to speak, when I notice that my upper lip feels strange, and I understand that this is because it has started twitching.

And because I am not *well integrated,* this happens without my experiencing any conscious sense of my own nervousness, and so this comes as a complete shock to me.

And this isn't some barely perceptible tic—rather, it's this huge, very visible twitch that I can both feel and see. I'm witnessing the horror of it on the faces of my friends, who drop their eyes, too embarrassed by my bizarre behavior to even look at me.

This twitch, which raises my upper lip in the way of a snarl, continues the whole time I'm giving the report. I stand there and I continue speaking, and because I'm already a good writer, it's probably eloquent. It's probably eloquent and is probably about Hell, because we're reading Dante's *Inferno*. I can write about Hell knowingly because I've lived through much worse things than this, but as I continue to give this report, I know this just may be the incident that defeats me.

After today, I already know, I'll be so un-bitchen that even *my own cousin* won't let me ride in the car with him.

I'm going to have to go home and beg my aunt to change schools, to transfer to Reseda or Chatsworth or enroll at Marlborough, the exclusive girls' school in L.A. where Grandmother Delia went, though then I'd have to wait for her to get drunk, then beg her to pay for it, get her to sign something, so she wouldn't take back having agreed to do it.

And Mr. Greenbaum, for reasons I don't get—since he's as kind as my father was, and I was my father's favorite child—allows me to stand there with my face twitching the whole time I'm presenting my six to eight minutes on Hell.

Hell, as my dusty grandmother says, is always *other people*.

I've studied the architecture of Hell, so I know that the seventh circle of the seventh level is where they put all the betrayers, Judas Iscariot, as well as all other suicides. And Mr. Greenbaum, whom I liked and who I thought liked me, has me continue to stand in front of the room while my performance is discussed.

What's the first thing we noticed? he asks.

That she was nervous? someone says.

Really?, I think.

And how could we tell she was nervous?

And now my face, which is no longer twitching, has become hot, wet and red, and it occurs to me that I may cry, though I haven't cried since I was nine years old and my father died, as your father killing himself is the sort of numbing event that will actually anesthetize you, so my teenagerhood is probably turning out to be way less worse than it might be for a more normal person.

My tongue feels really fat. I bite my lips, which are also swollen. My hands are blotchy, I see, and these are hives—I've never had hives before but will, from this moment on, be sporadically afflicted. I can't actually speak as the class continues its discussion of the anatomy of my embarrassment.

And I'm still speechless with humiliation at the end of the period so I take my time gathering my books after class and don't leave with my friends, who go on without me as I dawdle, maybe wanting to spare me the shame of talking about this incident or, more likely, not wanting my twitch-lip thing to spread to them.

The class is in a portable, with a door and stairs on either end. The main benefit of being in a portable, away from the main building of the high school, is that these rooms open to the outside and don't trap the goopy, boiled-cabbage-and-canned-spinach-trapped-underwater sea-grass smell of the cafeteria, which is so bad some days it's like we're being gassed.

Mr. Greenbaum is now thronged by over-anxious students who still give a shit about their grades, and who have gone up to him to get pointers on how to get a hundred—I so long ago stopped caring about *how to get a hundred*. I go down the back stairs. He comes to the porch of the trailer and calls to me, but I won't turn around. I'm too busy wondering if I can get transferred out of there and into Miss Lowenson's.

My next class is Mechanical Drawing, at which I'm excellent, maybe the best student in my section. I actually love the way this class requires us to draw some plain and uncomplicated thing, just this manmade object that is completely straightforward and in no way surprising. We must draw it from all angles and very precisely. I don't care that this isn't creative—I actually hate being creative, which only makes me more like my weirdo parents. All we must do in here is accurately render a metal plate or a four-inch bolt. Drawing like this is the most simple, meditative thing to do, and accomplishing it makes me feel profoundly peaceful.

I can go into this class and sit on my high stool at my tipped-up desktop and become entirely lost in the process of seeing this bolt, or whatever, really clearly and from every angle, and drawing it, then checking the measurements and proportions. I'm also working on my print handwriting, developing a technical hand that is blockish and neat and looks amazingly like that of my architect father.

I'd be entirely happy to stay in this class forever if it weren't for the boys.

Because of my brothers and my boy cousins, I am already completely used to boys, used to being treated, in fact, like a kind of honorary boy on the many occasions when I'm the only girl. This class, however, is made up of a different breed of boy: These either are stupid or have something else deeply wrong with them, in that they don't know how to be friends with girls.

What they do instead of taking on the assignment is waste their time trying to bother me, when this is the actual truth, which they're too fundamentally dense to realize: When your father kills himself and your mother gets sent to a mental institution, some jackass boys teasing you in Mechanical Drawing simply doesn't climb very high up the pain scale.

And their teasing isn't even clever; it's only *organized*, which means they're ganging up so that I can't glance past them toward the teacher without seeing all four of the boys in the row sitting opposite me, staring at my chest.

Boobs, one says.

Knockers, another whispers.

Jugs, one adds, and they're not talking to one another, which would make them turn their heads to the side, a movement the teacher might see. Instead, they're directing their comments at me.

Fucking assholes, I say, loudly enough that the teacher hears my voice, which is conspicuous because it's the only girl's voice, so it seems to float and carry. But the teacher has heard me, he more than likely can't believe it, so he asks me to tend to my work, which is consistently excellent, so he doesn't want to get mad at me. I'm still blotchy from the humiliation of Mr. Greenbaum's, and now I have to sit opposite these morons, who are basically too fucking stupid to live, and the one good thing about going to Marlborough would be that it's a girls' school.

I'm nauseated and I have hives in my throat, and I'm thinking I really do need to go to the nurse's office to get her to call my aunt to say I need to go home. Meanwhile, I use my fingers to comb my hair over my left hand and arm so it makes a curtain, I lean forward with my hand cupped like a visor to shield my eyes, and I look only at the sheet of paper that's masking-taped to my drawing board, and so make myself entirely calm as I enter my work.

Entering this work, or any work, is like becoming an atomic part of it, small to the point of being almost infinitesimal, so you are within the project and thus able to see the most itsy detail to the exclusion of all else around you.

I work, and all the while I keep my face down and my body hidden so they won't be able to catch sight of me.

〽

We're barely settled in third period—Señor Gallegos has taken roll and collected homework and is only beginning our lesson—when the principal comes on the PA to announce that President Kennedy, while riding in a motorcade, has been shot in Dallas, Texas.

Señor Gallegos is so stricken that he cannot speak to us. He simply sits down at the table in front of the class, holding his face in his hands, and we, who are embarrassed by this emotion, become completely quiet. Honestly, this room becomes quieter than any room I've ever known. It has something to do with the potential for all the noise that might come from thirty high school kids, and with our stifling any need to be loud or boisterous, we who are completely unaccustomed to being this quiet for long periods without direction, which only further emphasizes how quiet it is.

One person yells from outside in the hallway, but the whole school has been unnaturally muted, like a TV with the sound turned down.

This is the part of the sixties that is still almost exactly like the fifties, so children are still obedient, and though we're teenagers we still imagine we must obey our elders, so we are faced forward, hands clasped, silenced not by the enormity of what is happening to President Kennedy—or maybe to our whole country—but by the profundity of our own ignorance, because we *know* we have no clue, no inkling, no possible way of understanding any part of what's transpiring. We don't know *the first thing* about what's going on or what to think or how to act or feel.

The room is quieter than when we are taking an important test, as there isn't even the sound of a paper shifting or a pencil moving. This sense of the world on mute goes on and on, and the silence is compounding, and I'm not thinking about President Kennedy at all; instead, I'm trying to remember silences that might be analogous to this one.

The only other experience I have with a period of extended quiet is on Good Friday, when my aunt picks us up early from school and drives all six of us off to St. Nicholas Parish in Encino. We're supposed to have fasted by not eating lunch, which we may or may not have done. Once at St. Nicholas, we have to march in, hands clasped in front of us, to genuflect while crossing ourselves as we enter the pew, which is right in front since my aunt and grandmother tithe, something we're not supposed to know about but do.

Then we're supposed to kneel and remain kneeling for some interminable period of time, during which there isn't even a sermon to semi-listen to, to be quietly critical of, as we were when Father Church spoke of plugging in the Holy Ghost *like a vacuum cleaner!* or like any other *common everyday appliance!*

Father Church is who we got when Father Gerhardt left—Father Church is pretentious and speaks in what my mother calls the English Major accent, which means managing to sound round-voweled—she says it *vowel-ed* to rhyme with *hallowed*, as in these *hal-low-ed halls*. The English Major accent makes you sound like some poor kid from the wrong side of the tracks, she says, who's sent to Yale on the Poor Pitiful Me scholarship.

During Good Friday services there is no pomp, no music—all we do is kneel and kneel and supposedly pray, and this takes up some incalculable part of the four-hour service that's supposed to represent the Stations of the Cross.

And it being Good Friday and not Sunday, we are not dressed up, so the little boys—Geo and Thomas—have that playground smell that is dirt and sweat and their stinky Keds, and my aunt and my cousin Lizzie and I—like all the other women and girls in the Episcopal Church—must cover our heads. My aunt is an expert milliner—the hats she wears on Sundays are so stylish and amazing that even I am sometimes awed by them—but this isn't the day for fancy hats.

Today is all about only the darkness, which is the death of the Son of God, so Aunt Nan and I are in regular clothes and have lace mantillas on our heads. These are the black veils she and her mother buy on Olivera Street in Old Town L.A.—these drape over our heads and on either side of our faces, like auxiliary hair.

Lizzie's head is covered, too, but since she isn't yet confirmed, hers is this round lacy doily thing that's stuck to her hair with a bobby pin and looks like it came off the back of some old lady's overstuffed armchair.

The air in the church is thick with incense and the cross is covered with a black drape and some of us may have actually fasted, as we were supposed to, so our stomachs are growling audibly. We smirk when we hear them roil and grumble. Lizzie is sitting on the other side of my aunt at the end of the pew and is still a little girl and good, so she doesn't act up.

Though Lizzie doesn't yet misbehave, Graham, Jordy, Geo, Thomas, and I can all hardly contain ourselves once we begin to notice, while kneeling, how our bellies seem to almost be *speaking to one another!* One rumbles, another gurgles back an answer, and the next time someone's belly makes a noise, someone—and this is probably Thomas—starts trembling with laughter, and Jordy, who's sitting between my aunt and me, turns to me and announces in a church whisper, *Bowel sounds excellent,* which is the kind of pseudomedical phrase he's heard on some TV show like *Ben Casey* or *Dr. Kildare.*

And his saying anything about *bowel sounds* would have been bad enough, but he's pronounced it in Fred Harvey Army Bus, so it sounds like this: *Boooowel sooooooonds exsuuuulooont, Dooooktur Kooooolduuuuur.*

Froood Hoooovey Armooooy Booooos is a private language—I think Thomas may have been the one who actually invented it spontaneously on a car ride home from our grandmother's house at the beach. Jordy and Geo and Thomas were all lying in the way back of the station wagon like sunburned and sandy cordwood, pinching and shoving, as usual, when Thomas piped up to say, Loooooook, loooooook! It's a Frooooood Hooooovey Armoooooy Booooos. It sounds a little bit like Gaelic.

A Fred Harvey Army Bus, whatever that is. I've never been clear on this, except that it's something somehow old-fashioned, maybe something from Before.

Whatever it is, Thomas saw one on the freeway.

We speak like this mostly in the car, and mostly because my uncle really desperately hates it and will try to reach around to swat anyone who makes any kind of Froood Hooovey–ish sound like that. He also hates for boys to sing in falsetto—Oh, Denise, sooo-be-dooo-o, sooooo in love with yooooooou, Denise, blah-blee-bloooo.

But it's the thought of the term *bowel sounds* that has *completely* torn us down in church, and now we've all started laughing so hard we're completely gone, faces buried in our hands, our whole bodies shaking, side muscles cramping, hiding our wet faces, as the rest of the congregation, all seated behind us, must be wondering just what it is about the Death by Crucifixion of Our Lord Jesus Christ that makes Nan Snowden's little monsters, who occupy the most prominent pew, laugh themselves sick in church.

000

It's later in third period that the principal comes on the PA to tell us that the president has died at Parkland Hospital, and that we are now on an abbreviated schedule. The B-9s through B-12s are to go immediately to lunch, and the A-9s through A-12s will follow. After lunch, we're all to return to homeroom in order to be dismissed.

And I see that Señor Gallegos is doing what no one in my family ever does—aside from Grandmother Delia, who cries when she's drunk—which is weeping openly.

So we gather up our books and go to our lockers to get our lunches, to go to the cafeteria or back to homeroom, and there's this festive air of release and excitement. We're being *dismissed*, turned loose, which has never happened before. We're getting out of school and our parents don't know this, so there's a huge surge of energy that has nothing to do with what's going on in Dallas and everything to do with where it is in the San Fernando Valley we can go to get in some kind of trouble.

Drugs haven't happened yet, but you can feel them on the edge of things, waiting like the crisp paper wrapping on a noisy present.

And I'm heading across the quad to my locker when Greg Cox, who's a friend of my cousin Graham's, calls out to me: Hey, Cuz! We're all going to Big Bob's on Reseda. Need a lift?

Some of Graham's friends call me Cuz because he does, and this is when I realize that they're lofty juniors and a grade ahead of me, and because the lunch recesses haven't happened, the news of my spastic face hasn't traveled far enough up the beach to get to them, so I've been miraculously saved.

I'm still Cuz to them, still related to my Snowden cousins, and though word will eventually filter upward, the enormity of what's happened to our president has actually altered not only *now* and the future, but also the time that came before. My problem has been altered now, diminished by this event, which is *historic*, and it's just this pretty tiny thing that happened in the life of me and that time is already rendering insignificant.

ooo

The TV is suddenly on in every house I walk by, on in our house in the daytime, which has never happened before, and my aunt is almost entirely quiet, which is her no-nonsense way of dealing with uncertainty. People are saying maybe it's the commies who did it, since Lee Harvey Oswald is married to a Russian girl, though the Poors, who live directly behind us and are John Birchers, say this theory doesn't make sense, since JFK was himself a pinko.

President Kennedy was not a *pinko*, my aunt says. He was a liberal Democrat and Janet Poor is an idiot, and on that, she adds, *you may quote me*.

And strangely, we're allowed to hang out in the house, drinking lemonade, eating Fritos and stale Girl Scout cookies from a cupboard in the garage that my aunt keeps locked, and we're watching TV during the daytime because this keeps us home and out of the way of whatever might be going on out there, and Aunt Nan is watching TV herself, which she never does, and in any case we're not paying that much attention.

My aunt's distracted because my uncle's driven off to a Brown Bag lunch with his investment group, because they need to talk about what the death of the president is doing to the stock market. My aunt doesn't agree with his behaving like this.

And it's because she doesn't agree with his doing this, or maybe doesn't know for sure that he's coming home to eat with us, that she fixes a kid dinner that night, which is spaghetti and meatballs, the sauce made with an envelope of Lawry's, and a salad and french bread. All us kids love such a dinner, but my uncle can't really stand it, so we never eat this kind of thing unless he's traveling or out with Visiting Firemen.

My uncle doesn't like what will later come to be known as *pasta* but is then still known as *noodles* or *macaroni*. He doesn't like anything with all the basic food groups confused or mixed together, anything resembling a *casserole*, which is dreary, he says, and is what poor people bring to funerals.

It's Geo's turn to say grace. We say the same thing every night, which is Bless O Father These Gifts to Our Use and Us to Thy Service, For Christ's Sake, Amen, which for us is breathed in one or two exhalations: *Blessofatherthsgiftsouruse, usthyservisChristsakeamen.*

And dinner is tense because of the spaghetti and meatballs, which my uncle, who has come home to eat afer all, may believe is a form of vengeful cooking, so he's visibly miffed. Then he says he got a bunch of tickets to the Rams game this Sunday from someone in his Brown Bag group who's not using them, and he asks which of us are going.

Cuz? he asks, starting with me, as he's started down the right-handed side of the dining table, as the three right-handed ones lie to the right of him. I'm startled because he's never called me Cuz before.

Sure, I say, because it's my nature—if I'm not sulking—to want to go everywhere and do everything, and I've never been to a pro football game before and it'd probably be especially fun with my uncle, who's generous and lenient and might let us play KFWB really loudly in the car, and who can usually be counted on to buy us the exact kind of crap my aunt will not allow us to touch—for instance, Pepsi-Cola, which, very famously, is only sugar, which ruins your teeth.

Then I notice that no one else has chimed in, and I see my aunt glaring at him, her nostrils flaring. Edward, she asks, using his full name, which she never does, do you imagine a *Rams game* is actually *appropriate* under the circumstances?

He crosses his eyes, face gone slack and goofy, which is for the benefit of us kids. It's like he's been cartoon pole-axed and his head's about
to do a 360 on his neck, and he'll now lose consciousness like Elmer
Fudd when Bugs Bunny slams him on the head with some huge wooden
mallet, and the thought balloons will all be bubbling up like fireworks
full of the X's and exclamation marks of many blanked-out curse words,
and the soundtrack will be this lullaby played in twittering birdsong.

Then Uncle Ned immediately snaps out of it.

Oh, I never know any longer, he says—and his voice is thick with
sarcasm—what is and is not appropriate, Nan, so why don't I leave all
that *to you*? And he pats the meatball on his plate with the back of the
tines of his fork, and we notice that his food is entirely untouched.

And we're all just stricken, shocked, since the two of them never
fight and this sounds like a fight to us. The world's in chaos! My aunt
and uncle are fighting! The president has been shot!

Geo, he tells my brother, in order to change the subject, you don't
launch your whole piece of bread toward your mouth like it's a plane
coming in for a landing. You break it on your plate, like this, and your
plate is also where you butter it. My uncle demonstrates his classy
manners for Geo, as if to show my aunt he can use manners if he
decides to.

All right? my uncle goes back to asking, because Uncle Ned isn't a
person to be either sidetracked or dissuaded and isn't one to waste good
tickets to a Rams game when the seats are on the fifty-yard line.

Okay? he says. Who else is going?

But everyone is quiet, so he polls my brother and cousins one by
one—all the right-handed side of the table, then up the left-handed side—
and everyone, astonishingly, begs off, even Graham, who's a sports fan
and whom I'd completely counted on to go, even Jordy. I would never
have said I'd go if I hadn't assumed that at least my two older cousins

would be going, and now going with my uncle is like being in trouble *because* of him.

Even Geo and Thomas just hang their heads, though they'd ordinarily be the first to jump at any kind of fun, so in the end the tally says it's only me and my uncle, and I'm only now realizing the degree to which I've been so totally *had*.

Who is and isn't going to the Rams game the Sunday after the assassination of John Fitzgerald Kennedy becomes this hinge in the narrative, the contingent event, that place where the trail divides and some folks take the high road and others take the cutoff toward the Humboldt Sink on their way to Donner Pass.

It's like a referendum on their marriage, though this, technically and on paper, is still a strong and stable marriage that will endure, at least technically, until their last child—and this is Lizzie, who's now only eight or nine—leaves for college.

But it's as if we've discovered that this solid ground we're used to is a slip-strike fault, and right now something shifts and gives.

Which reminds me of the months that lay between the death of my grandfather and my own father's death, as it was during that period of time that I kept having the dream that gripped me with fear because it seemed to foretell the future.

I dreamed my parents were fighting, the road in front of our house was cracking open, and that my father was on the far side of the crack and our mother was on the same side as we were, with our house, and that as the crack widened, I had to choose whether to jump or not.

Because no one ever argued in our family. Because voices were not raised. This was not *done*.

My parents never fought, aside from the one time Welton Becket was trying to move my father to Dallas or Houston, Texas, to build these new cities, but these places were *nowhere*, as far as my mother was concerned. And Texas would have been a promotion for my father, in that he'd have been heading up a project group, but she wouldn't even entertain the thought or go on the weeklong trip Becket proposed to simply take a look it.

My mother had her principles and this was one of them: Texas was a shithole dump full of the most objectionable kinds of people.

He wanted her to at least go on this trip with him, but she said she'd never before set foot in Texas and wanted to keep this perfect record.

Our parents fought and their voices were raised, and this was such an unusual event that they didn't notice Geo and me sitting right there where we were hiding under the kitchen table.

They fought and he did not win and they stayed in California, where each together and separately came to grief and my father *cracked up*, and because he was not speaking to his father, it was Uncle Ned who had to fly to Illinois to bring my grandfather's body home on the train for burial, our grandfather having gone to Illinois to visit certain cousins.

And it was during this time—after my grandfather died but in advance of the day, which was the twenty-sixth of February, when my father took his life—that I kept having the earthquake dream in which the street split open and he'd be on the far side but reaching back to us, as if we could either save him or jump across and be with him. I loved my father, who, while sad, was also tall and witty and elegant, and was also a man, while my mother—and this was one of my family's deepest secrets—was already crazy before he died, so his death wasn't really what caused it, and I didn't want to be stuck with her, her insanity, so always, always, at the very last moment in the dream, I leapt.

〇〇〇

Not one of my cousins is going to the Rams game except me, as I've been totally tricked into this magnificent act of disloyalty to my aunt, who's miffed at me, but I can't do anything about it without being disloyal to my uncle, who's lately become one of my more ardent fans.

We have five more tickets to give away, but most kids' parents won't allow them to go, given that the country's in this terrible state and Monday's a national day of mourning, so we get it off from school.

When we get home from church that Sunday, my uncle has the TV on in the family room, and as we're setting the table for breakfast, we all see the telecast that shows that as they're moving Lee Harvey Oswald from one place in the jail to another, or maybe to the courthouse, this nightclub guy comes out of nowhere and shoots him in the stomach, and then Lee Harvey Oswald is also taken to Parkland Hospital, where he also dies, and this is when my aunt goes over and turns the TV off, saying, *That* will be enough of *that.*

So I spend a long time calling around to nearly everyone I know, and finally find that Reggie and Steve are allowed to go to the game, maybe because they're football players, or more likely because they've lied to get out of the house, and my friend Jane Brown can go, because her parents are divorced and her mother works all the time as an accountant at Kmart, so the rules of her house are written mainly by her two older brothers, who are twins and jocks. And my friend Suzie Witucki can go because her parents, who manage an apartment building, are alcoholics, so she gets to do whatever she wants.

My uncle likes Suzie and sings some college football fight song using what he pretends is her last name, but he says it as *Go, Windsock-i,* which may have something to do with the state of Wisconsin, or maybe not.

So there are the six of us at the Rams game being played in L.A. Memorial Coliseum, which holds a hundred thousand people. The day is beautiful, the sky cold and clear, and the stadium is pretty full, considering that the year before, the Rams had their worst season ever, as Steve and Reggie are pointing out; Jane Brown knows a lot about football, too, which she probably gets from her older brothers, both of whom once played football for our school.

My aunt was furious at breakfast at those who decided to go ahead and play this game even as our slain president was lying in state in the Capitol rotunda.

Too much at stake, my uncle said from behind his paper. He was eating toast and reading the inside of the newspaper, whose headlines were two inches tall and shockingly thick and black with ink. He was doing this though we're actually not allowed to read at the table.

You mean money? my aunt asked. My uncle shook the paper a little to straighten it and didn't answer her.

Before the kickoff, the announcer comes on the loudspeaker to ask us all to stand for "The Star-Spangled Banner" and to request that after it's sung, we all remain standing to observe a moment of silence in memory of our fallen president.

And we do, and it's the silence of so many that becomes profound, the communal hush of all of us being quiet together as the reality sinks in and what seems like the silence of the eons begins to envelop us, and it's into that silence that the Blue Angels fly.

The sound is deafening, like the sky is being torn open. There are five jets in the formation, and it's the Blue Angels' showing up that finally gets my uncle, who is a hard case and thinks he's been inoculated for all time against grief by what he went through in his youth.

But my uncle flew as a navigator in the Navy in the Second World War, and our president fought in the same war and in the same branch of service, so my uncle sees the loss of the president as his loss, too, and he puts his arm around my shoulder and we stand side by side, our faces tipped upward, as the jets—which are F-11s, as he'll tell us later, built not by his company, which is Lockheed, but by McDonnell Douglas—twist and rise as one thing into the perfect sky, a diamond that dips and tilts, and as it comes roaring back over us, a solitary jet veers off.

And in going way faster than the speed of sound, their wings are pushing the shock waves ahead of them, and as these waves build up, they'll actually fold sound back upon itself so the waves are physically compressed. What you hear in a sonic boom is the air breaking loose as all that that pent-up redoubled sound's released.

The air breaks and falls around us. Time breaks too, I've always felt, as the future comes spilling toward at certain times in wave upon bright wave. I understand that we are all subject to these currents and history as we never seemed to be before. Before, back when we thought the American story was the one about all the progress we were making toward our own perfectibility.

Instead, history is like gravity and it applies to us, and Time moves in one direction only, and this applies to us, and History is turning out to be the ghost that stands up like something out of Shakespeare and silently points the way we've come, saying this guilt too applies to us, we are not exempt from it.

The air breaks apart and the sound of that falls around us. Time is shown as a hinge that swings wide at a moment like this, when the door of the future suddenly gapes open, as if you've come to the edge of an ancient sea.

The death of the president is the same as the death of my father, I see, in that it is all one loss, as the Lost Flier shows, and I am different in that I became good at loss so early, which is what makes me like my uncle.

Time changes us. Before, as Americans, we'd thought we were oddly impervious to history and didn't really believe it even *applied* to us. Before, back when the story we thought we were writing had to do with how we were just like God.

2

A POCKET HISTORY OF SEX IN THE TWENTIETH CENTURY

9
Climbing Out a Window

SO IT'S ALL THESE years later and we're living in Berkeley and everything's the same, just as it is all also completely and utterly different. I am still the person I always was, which is the girl who'll be calmly going along, masquerading as responsible, then will simply find myself mildly watching as I begin to build the anatomically accurate body in my bed, then climb out my current window.

Building an anatomically accurate body in your bed, then climbing out a window, is, I've found, very much like what it is to be a novelist.

I am simply overcome, at times, by the need to escape my present circumstances, to strike out for The Territories, as my forebears did, which, if truth be told, might turn out to be even the most *unlikely* place, as long as it's somewhere else, *anywhere*, as long as it's just not *right here*. *California* seems lately like almost a state of mind as much as it does an honest-to-god *locale*, and if you're born here and raised here and you have virtually no relatives who were not born here and raised here, you don't even get to *go visit* people from other places, and so have no experience of Elsewhere. And California is such a long state from end to end and is so far west that you can drive for literally days without ever arriving anywhere that strikes you as a plausible destination.

So a place like Berkeley or L.A. will feel like it exerts an almost centripetal force on the soul of someone like me, a place where even the light can seem like something that etches the pavement with acid shadows, leaf-shaped, ghostly, tinting the lines and cracks in the concrete with the vegetable stain that speaks forever of brokenness.

And we're living in the big gray-shingled house Jack and I have bought on Virginia Street in the flats two blocks below Shattuck. This house has an old thick-trunked wisteria vine growing over an arbor that crosses the drive, and there's the falling-down building out back he's going to fix up for me as a writing studio. This shed was once used as a garage or carriage house, but it's much too small for my SUV, the seven-seat-belted mommy car I drive and drive and drive, making all these countless carpooling trips that involve hauling my two interesting kids and their interesting friends around to all these expensive, tightly booked, enriching activities.

Because I am perhaps predictably in disguise these days as one of those chardonnay-swilling, Volvo-driving, albeit left-leaning, very *bourgeoisified* Berkeley types—that everyone, including me, hates, though I break from type in that I'm much too much a student of Marx and Veblen and Flaubert to do anything so conspicuous consumption–ish as to actually *drive* a Volvo, and I cannot, of course, *drink*, given the sodden, oh-so-severely alcoholic matrix that's deeply embedded in my twisted helix wherein my genes are copied by the eerie legacy of the two so closely matched pairs of my very closely matching parents. And all this has been actually proven fairly recently in my going abjectly to hell over the recent dissolution of my marriage to the father of my kids, which—given *both* nature *and* nurture, given my shitty childhood, given what is clinically called *early death of a parent*, given all the other tragedies best enumerated as what my mom called all that blah, blah, blah—has very spectacularly failed.

When their dad and I split up, I sublet a house from a wine merchant who had an amazing cellar to which he graciously offered access, so while this man was off traveling in Italy and France, I became more and more deranged by my own grief and disappointment, and would dye my hair bright shades of mahogany or walnut—once, it was the deep purple of aubergine—and smoke cigarettes. And in trying not to weep until I dropped my kids off at Point A or Point B, I'd not particularly surreptitiously chew my way through the childproof caps of the bottles of Valium I kept in the pockets of my jackets. Only after I'd made it through the day and tucked my kids in at night did I get to *finally* sit down at the typewriter with a bottle of really fine pinot grigio. I'd be drinking as I was trying to write another novel, but what I wrote when I was drinking was—as has been said of the lesser work of Hunter Thompson—nothing but coo-coo spit.

∞

I was in graduate school when I met the man who would become my kids' dad. He was my professor, and he was *exactly* the age my father was when my father died. He was somewhat older than I was, of course, and gloomy and smart and strange, also cynical, also a little devious, which probably read to me as *mystery*, and all this figured so clearly in what was very obviously *in loco parentis*.

I had this conceit going from my childhood that I secretly *knew* what men needed, any man, one like my dad or even a more ordinary man, like my uncle. It was like whatever's the opposite of an Oedipal thing, but I do not mean Electra. It was this generalized contempt that I carried for the older version of what my mother called Our People, in that I knew that in being a girl I could so totally do such a better job of making any man happy than any actual *woman* could, so why didn't women not exactly die, but more just *move over* and get out of my way?

In that my professor in grad school's wife had just dumped him and he had these kids already, whose hems were falling down waifishly out of their homemade seventies-hippie-children skirts. But I knew how to sew, even hemstitch, and I knew how to make both chocolate éclairs and potstickers, so the professor's little family seemed to have such simple needs that I could so easily fill.

And Berkeley then may have been, and may still be, one of the best places in the world to go shopping for new wives and husbands, but it does often happen that it's the wife who dumps this kind of sad-sack guy and you see these men all the time in the produce aisles of Andronico's Park and Rob, with their little handbasket for one and their air of slightly unkempt, befuddled, hapless anxiety. Honestly, it takes about five seconds of shopping among the peaches and nectarines of the Park and Rob to find all kinds of prospects, and many of them have advanced degrees from really excellent universities.

My professor had these waifish daughters, one of whom was *exactly* my age when my own dad died, but it was at the very moment he confided that he was in psychoanalysis—then immediately clarified that this *wasn't* the New Agey kind of crap wherein you call your therapist by his first name and go out with him for coffee, but the old-world, Germanically accented, über-strict-ish variety that is actually the *Freudian analysis* that has you lying on the couch, reading squiggles on the ceiling, as my parents had, this being the therapeutic approach that was so entirely unhelpful, given the monumental troubles of the two of them—that I suddenly knew what my future held. It was when he pronounced the word *psychoanalysis* that I seemed to hear a heavenly choir singing, *Dun*-dah-dun-*dun*, in that *immediately*—and I mean *right that very second*—I was very deeply involved with him.

Within the fortress of this rule-bound and non-New Agey marriage, I bore my own two very interesting children and wrote a book I'm still proud of.

Jack published it. This is how I met him.

I'd written this book, which took a long time to do, and I was now completely torn down and really discouraged that I'd even live to see it published, as I'd become pretty sick with one of these stress-related illnesses that almost invariably afflict women of childbearing age, and mine was the one in which you suddenly become allergic to almost everything in your environment, including, and increasingly, the scent of your professorial husband's shaving cream.

So when Jack called, it happened that I'd been in bed in a darkened bedroom for more than a month with a raging headache, extreme light sensitivity, and a persistent low-grade fever. My husband was home to answer the phone. He told Jack I was sick, that I'd call back later.

They don't phone to reject your book, I said as I got up out of bed, phoned Jack, and began to feel much better almost instantly.

The rheumatologist I was seeing explained it this way: A wired-up lab rat in a closed box will, when repeatedly shocked, quickly die, but if you show this rat an open door or a little cracked-open window, *just the sight* of an exit will act to save its life and you can go ahead and zap it a hundred times.

It was during the editorial process that I started to get to know Jack, and so discovered that he, too, was going through a rough patch. It evolved naturally that I became one of his little cadre of sympathetic listeners, most of whom were women, all of whom were married or otherwise unavailable, so there was no blur in the distinctions. He'd call and ask one of us out to lunch, or maybe for a drink or dessert at Chez Panisse after his stop-smoking class.

That was when Jack was still sitting up in his beautiful house in the Berkeley Hills, huddled in a wooden folding chair in the kitchen by the koi tank, listening to the Giants' game on the radio and smoking cigarettes, while he waited for his wife to come home. Late spring through summer and fall, it was the Giants; then he changed and listened to Cal football. And if you talked to Jack on his home phone during that period—which I didn't, but so said Ross Feld, our mutual friend—you'd quickly realize Jack *really needed* to hang up, so worried was he that she'd phone that exact minute to say she'd decided to come home, but if she got a busy signal or the machine picked up, she'd probably change her mind.

Everyone who knew them knew she wasn't coming back, knew all Jack's endeavors were useless—his putting in a new and glamorous downstairs bathroom that opened onto a deck with a hot tub and a view through the treetops of the lights of San Francisco; his redoing the kitchen with the eight-foot koi tank, the Sub-Zero fridge, Wolf range, sinks, and cabinets all put together left-handedly in deference to this left-handed wife. No one said anything; everyone was being patiently mindful and respectful of his household activities, which had everything to do with the hopelessness of denial that rigs the mind with these strings of tiny icy lights like it's Christmas way off there in the coldest part of the darkest and most distant desert.

It already was the brand-new day, the bright harsh glare of the new reality, but Jack wasn't ready to go out into it.

So he and I'd have lunch and I could see his situation clearly, just as he could see what I couldn't see, which was the hopelessness of mine. I'd be bragging and lying, as usual, about my first having successfully raised myself, *despite all odds and with almost no assistance!* then having worked my way through college as an emancipated minor, since I'd been thrown out of my more extended family for the usual infractions, mostly having to do with my surliness and lack of gratitude.

And I'd be bragging and lying about how I'd made this fairly wonderful marriage to this really decent man with several advanced degrees from a truly prestigious university, when my physical person was actually increasingly allergic to him, which I made a point of never mentioning to anyone, including myself—this *good man* who was so good, in fact, he somewhat surprisingly imported his widowed mother from Queens to live with us, which was—*no! no! really, perfectly fine with me! No, really! I really liked* my mother-in-law, who was courteous and easy.

She actually was sweet natured and in her early seventies and in remarkably good health, discounting the fact that she was in the midstage of Alzheimer's disease. But I was becoming an expert on all the types and various forms of dementia, which are actually clinically interesting.

Exactly what the thinking was that had resulted in the importation of the Alzheimer's mother-in-law wasn't something I could recall, in that one aspect of my stress-related illness was this brain fog in which my own cognitive function was impaired and I had, by then, almost entirely lost all my problem-solving capabilities. No kidding, it manifested itself as an almost complete inability to properly sequence episodic time.

I'd need to drop one kid here, the other one way over there, while *concurrently* I'd need to be driving the Alzheimer's mother-in-law to her own daycare, which was in exactly the opposite direction. It was that these events were set up to take place *simultaneously* that always just vexed and stymied me.

I'd think about this for a moment and my brain would seize up, just as the hard drive on a computer freezes, and I'd stare mindlessly into the middle distance, thinking, *I'll think about this again in a little minute.*

I believe the decision making may have gone something like this: The Alzheimer's mother-in-law was living alone in her house, with nothing to eat but the ten-pound block of Poverty Program cheese in the fridge, which wasn't an object she or anyone else could decipher. Since she was increasingly childlike and I was already home with our two kids, who were also childlike since they were actually *children*, another kid-type person could be added to the mix, which I'd then handle with my usual jaunty calm.

Because I was actually unusually generous and good natured about everybody's frailties, as I was already completely used to fairly flawed, unusual, cracked, and spackled families. I was also good at finding the heartwarming story in any scene of domestic chaos, which was just such great material. And I could already riff hilariously on how my mother-in-law—who now lacked any kind of adequate ego—had taken to shadowing me around the house, humming mindlessly, or else it might have been little snatches of what can only be called *ditties*. She'd get one little ditty in her head—it might be the first couple of bars of *I'm a little teapot, short and stout*—where it simply stayed and stayed, playing on tape loop, and I'd be opening a couple of cans, doing two different tasks and trying to solve the puzzle of simultaneity, and she'd be humming and I'd be suddenly *overwhelmed* with the need to give our Cavalier King Charles spaniel the Progresso and feed my mother-in-law the dog food.

But no, really! she was only trying to be helpful! as she followed me from room to room, humming as I put a chicken into the oven, but when I would come back a while later to check on it, I would find that the little teapot had snuck in and turned the oven off because she still managed to think she needed to remember this adage, which was *Safety first!*

Safety first! she'd say, wagging a crooked finger at me as if I'd been trying to pull a fast one.

000

So Jack began taking me to lunch. Our lunches would be editorial in nature, and at one of these he told me I had handed in the *penultimate* draft of my manuscript, and I thought, *Great. Just my luck to have an* editor *who doesn't know what the word* penultimate *means.*

But I in fact was rewriting the book and did eventually rewrite it a time and a half, then another time after it was already in galleys, because the book in fact was all sprawling and stuttery and was always way too long and was never very good, but then it miraculously was and it was going off into the world, so we'd finished our editorial work but he and I'd still be strolling up Solano Avenue to this or that little restaurant as summer turned to fall turned to winter, and because I was still suffering from the lingering symptoms of the stress-related illness, including a sun allergy, I wore what can be described only as these fairly elaborate costumes whose style was somehow hip-hop crossed with Claude Monet.

I wore huge dark sunglasses and wide hats and long sleeves and full billowing dresses that fell to my ankles in black and gray. Because I was wearing zinc oxide on my face and arms in order to be able to swim, my professor husband had started to refer to me jocularly as Mrs. Vincent van Gogh, the joke being that my last name is Dutch, but also that I was (secretly) crazy. My being (secretly) crazy was one, in fact, of the rock-solid tenets of our marriage.

It went like this: I was crazy and artistic, so my judgment was skewed, just like some wacko Dutch painter who saw the world from this canted and weird perspective that had all the furniture pushed up into the corner of a yellow room. He was Theo to my Vincent and I'd be lost without him and I saw things wrong—my family was *crazy*, while my husband's was only *organically demented.*

And it was true that I also had recently developed an allergy to the thick look of the furniture in our house, which had been already completely furnished on the day the Mayflower truck arrived from Queens and unloaded all of my mother-in-law's furniture into the rooms of our house, so there were now rugs upon rugs upon rugs and tables shoved right up next to these other *really important tables*, if I cared about such things as *really important tables*, which I absolutely did not, and now every room was so clotted with furniture that the place looked like an antiques shop. And then there was also the mundane and everyday clutter of all the physical playthings children need, which were usually strewn in the first ten to fourteen inches of the understory of this forest for the trees, a mix of metaphors that was actually bewildering, since I have figure/ground problems on the best of days, and the kid stuff was often made of that bright plastic in clownlike primary colors, which gave the whole thing a really jumbled look that reminded me of my own mom's housekeeping, or complete lack thereof, and made me feel completely psychotic.

Because of my sun allergy, I'd been investing in actual hats, including one that had a name, which was Springtime, and was made by a genius milliner named Victoria di Nardo who had a shop in lower Manhattan. I bought this hat one day when I was actually dead drunk and it wasn't even noon by my body clock; I'd been out with the PR person for my book. She'd taken me to Victoria di Nardo's shop after we'd had lunch, at which we'd each had who knows how many glasses of champagne to celebrate my brilliant performance on a television show that had taped that morning at the crack of dawn. I'd flown in on the red-eye from Oakland the night before and they'd lost my luggage and there'd been no stores open that early in the morning and the show was scheduled to tape first thing, far off in this really desolate studio in Harlem, the same one they used to shoot Lucy and Desi. The PR woman had come to the hotel to get me dressed while the Lincoln Town Car the production people'd sent was already idling downstairs, and she'd had to knock on the doors of all of these neighbors of hers in her apartment building to borrow all kinds of different potential articles of wardrobe, since she and I had never before met and she had no idea what I might or might not want to wear, let alone what would even fit.

My book was a success, though I'd managed to give it the ballast it needed to make it mine, this being the way I needed to always fuck up in order to keep on being my own parents' child, so the first word of the first book I ever published had as the first word in its title the code word *Failure*. And in the world of publishing, they shorten titles to their first word or so, so while the whole title was *Failure to Zigzag*, I did hear people refer to my book as *Failure*, though I secretly called it *Zigzag*.

The success of *Failure* was an entire shock to my system, and I was okay to good on the TV show, and so went out with the PR person and got completely and utterly swacked and it wasn't even nine thirty in the morning Pacific Standard Time, which was where my body was. And it was only later, when I was completely drunk and shopping and was spending, oh, I don't know, *four hundred dollars* on this thing that wasn't so much a hat as it was Someone's Miraculous Creation Belonging in a Museum Somewhere, that I noticed—with horror—in the hat shop's mirror that not only was I wearing hand-me-downs from people I'd never met, but my face was still entirely made up in the exaggerated lips and eyes and cheeks that they put on you for TV, a look so awful I literally screamed.

〇〇〇

So back home, I'd still be going out to lunch with Jack though my book was launched, and I'd be hidden behind dark glasses and this $400 hat of mine, which had a wide brim and a fringe of raffia dreads that were almost exactly like a curtain, so while I could see him, he couldn't exactly see me. It was as if I were watching him from another room, as I heard him half rationalizing, patiently justifying, his wife's fairly wretched behavior, and he was so patiently *understanding* of her, which is—as I happen to know—how we all cloak ourselves from the terrible need to tower over our loved ones and rain obscenities down on them.

But Jack had been raised Baptist and was now a practicing Buddhist, so he didn't shout obscenities at women because he didn't shout obscenities at anyone. He really rarely used profanity, and I, too, was probably more carefully spoken than I really am, not saying, for instance, *Oh, for fuck's sake!* at the slightest provocation, because I'd fallen in love with him and wanted him to think I was a person of some kind of, you know, *quality*.

And my love for him was simply overwhelming. I'd never experienced anything like it—I was in love with the resonance of his voice and the beauty of his hands and the tawny color of his skin and the shape of his head and the almost Asian-looking slant of his eyes and the look of his muscular arms. His stories were always miraculously detailed, their endings always both deft and surprising. It was his shy and stately demeanor, and that he was an *enthusiast*. He was hopeful and enthusiastic about almost everything, yet managed to ardently despise his mother because this was realistic, in that she was basically a despicable person. This made no sense according to Sigmund H. Freud, but then, maybe Jack would be living proof of the entire disputation of Freud's lock-step, reductive, fatalistic theories, which had anyway never interested me enough to actually read them, and which I naturally resisted, in that these theories essentially doomed me.

Jack was courteous to his mom: he just didn't feel compelled to *like* her. She was manipulative, he said, and she was cruel. I take these two things as proof of evil in the world, he told me once: my mother and the Republican Party.

But he believed the best about almost everyone else and still thought the errant wife was probably, one day, coming back to him. He wasn't cynical. He had no idea at all of his effect on women. And despite his mother, or maybe even because of her, he actually *liked* women and had as many women friends as he did men. He seemed to listen to everyone with an air of respectful attentiveness, as if this person might have something interesting to say and he, Jack, was maybe going to learn something.

And there was no doubt that it was because I was already so sickeningly married and he was completely unattainable that made it easy for me to love him. It helped, too, that he did nothing to act seductive, in that acting seductive is so often fake.

In those days he'd walk me back to my SUV and open the door, and in his mannerly way that was in no way reserved for me, he'd close the door, then lean in through the open window to kiss me on the lips—but then, he kissed everyone on the lips, I'd noticed. I'd seen him kiss his own grown sons on the lips.

He'd kiss me, then say in parting, So, call me next week and we'll have lunch? and I'd say okay, but I'd be thinking, *But we just* had *lunch*. I didn't think this was *exactly* how the writer/editor relationship was supposed to go, but what did I know, since I'd never before been in one?

So we'd have lunch, then another lunch, and when I was back out on the road again a little while later, promoting my book—this may have been the paperback—it happened that, by sheer coincidence, Jack and I were going to be in New York over the same few days. It was purely lucky in that this happened through neither his guile nor mine.

Neither of us had any control over any of these events: that someone else had arranged that I'd be staying at the Westbury on the Upper

East Side, this being paid for by some media entity that can afford this sort of travel—and it was here, I'd discover, that a bowl of berries with cream and a pot of room-service coffee cost $28, *and this was in the 1990s!*—and Jack was going to be staying at the Algonquin, which was where he always stayed, where he had a sales conference.

As he walked me to the car, he asked me to call him when I got to New York, so that we could go out for coffee or maybe go to a museum together. Call me, he said, looking at me over the tops of his sunglasses, and maybe we can get into a little trouble.

10
The Least Little Push of Joy

IT IS MY PROFOUND belief that there is something wrong with me and that it's this wrongness that keeps me loyal to my parents.

I believe in failure. This means *failure* isn't anything I can really part with. My parents were just *so good* at being *such spectacular fuckups*— better than almost anyone. And I'm *proud* of this about them, in that these are *my people*, my own mother and my own father, those I was *born to*, and I have no real wish to ever let them go.

So *failure* profoundly appeals to me, as it feels both true and actual, and I believe in failure in the way I don't basically believe the Success Propaganda that people put out in their Christmas letters, which always seem to stink of the ink of faint Republicanism, and even if this stuff is verifiably, fact-checkably true, it still just doesn't much interest me.

Failure just seems like the more intimate and important news: that you're born, that then you die, and that life between usually stretches as one long grim trudge westward into the hinterlands, and that, sure, there are these bright moments of almost unaccountable joy, but mostly? mostly? it just is not that. Mostly, it's this story of restlessness and loss and dislocation, but it's also our very strangeness as a lost and dislocated species that accounts for our being funny, and being funny is what elevates us from the basic lies of the Success Propaganda, all that's humdrum and blah, blah, blah. It's being funny that's liberating, that actually saves us.

So it's that we are almost always just *so incredibly lost* that serves as my compass, my ballast, whatever dark, molecularly dense material that's placed in the hold of my soul that gives me stability in heavy seas, and this is why failure is so *valuable* to me and why I keep it stuffed in the most secret pocket of my jacket like a little thingy of Kryptonite.

This wrongness I come by genetically, in that it derives from why people like mine even ended up in the West, where the sun's blaze has suddenly turned against me and my skin has become bizarrely allergic.

The name of this condition is photosensitivity, which is a heightened response to ultraviolet radiation, but what I really think is that I've been oversaturated by the sunniness of the place and its relentless optimism, that my skin—and I have always somehow reasoned with either my belly or my skin—has now just basically *had it*.

I've always done an adequate job of masquerading as an ordinary person, having learned this by living with my aunt and uncle. I've learned to comport myself and think of this as *passing*. I have somehow even tricked this man I love into loving me, and this man isn't even someone flawed and broken and wrecked, like the usual guys who'd come around, all hangdog and slobbery, but someone I actually adore, about whom I was and am still ardent.

What's wrong with me is that I have so many conflicting things going on, and *all at once*, that I feel crowded, also lonely, also buffered and walled off and numb. This pertains to something I've read somewhere: that the dead surround the living, that our work in being alive is to serve as the beating heart of them, that the living and the dead are all *in this together*, that we form, in fact, one elaborated body, and for the moment we're the ones who are representative of what it is to *be alive*, which was once the job of our dead, and they are stationed only slightly off and out from us, but in close proximity, only occupying another intimate plane in time.

I feel them, the physical spirit of my parents, who are as fellow travelers on my journey, and I'm like Whitman, I believe, and self-contradictory—I contain *multitudes*. Though I often feel almost starving in my loneliness, I also am pressed by how everyone is always crowding me and how they're all loud, fractious, bossy, everyone pushing and jostling like we're all trying to simultaneously board this once-a-week train in some remote part of India. I am honestly *never* alone, and all I want—I believe—is to be left alone for one goddamn minute so I can maybe concentrate. I think if I'm alone for a moment, I can maybe hear the song someone might be out there trying to sing, and that this someone might be me.

The dead cluster around us, they depend upon us to keep them alive in our thoughts, and as we are the beating heart of them, they inform us of who we are. But we now have the human body upon which experience may still be written and that still may do useful work, and this is the holy function of our physicality.

We are the body and they depend upon our bodies to carry on enacting them, so it is with their will and urging that we go on into life to do these things we are destined for—they want us to because they know our bodies, too, will so soon be gone, and with them these physical pleasures. Then we go to join them, clustered as they are off in the vast forever, which is Timelessness.

So it could be that what's wrong with me is that my own family's time in the West is too brief, too thin, that our dead are so outnumbered by those who've walked here throughout millennia, and that people like my father and me—those of us who suffer from sensitivities, photo-istically or otherwise—cannot help but intuit this.

Our dead are simply outnumbered, which is why we're so lonely here. We stole this place from others, and others are better at witnessing the transparency of all existence. Ishi saw it. He was standing on a cliff overlooking bathers on the beach when he turned to Kroeber and gestured, saying wistfully, So many ghosts.

000

So I am living with Jack and my kids in this big gray house on Virginia Street in the flats of Berkeley, and everything ought to be perfect. We live only a couple of blocks from Chez Panisse and it's the boom in the middle of the '90s, tech driven, the Clinton years. With a Democrat in the White House, we can even *afford* to eat at Chez Panisse—if not downstairs, we can at least get a salad and a calzone in the upstairs café every once in a while.

Everything's fine, in theory—has never been more fine, in fact—in that I'm a novelist who's actually published a novel, a mother who has these two great kids, and never mind that the name of my book contains the word *Failure*. This is the kind of thing I keep magnetized next to the iron keel as a secret counterweight. I need weight and counterweight so I don't go get so ecstatic and joyous—and I have inherited from my parents a great talent for unadulterated joy—that I go flying off a roof somewhere.

I'm a *failure* because I am being *careful*.

And it ought to be easy to write another book, but it actually isn't. If anything, writing a second book is even harder than writing the first, in that I was supposed to have somehow learned how to write a novel through the act of doing it, but I obviously haven't. I'm shocked to find

I haven't learned the first thing about how to write a novel, nor am I a better writer.

I am not better—as a matter of fact, I am way, way worse.

What I'm trying to write about does happen to be something I actually know something about, which is having your entire life go stupendously to hell when you least suspect it, having shored your poor, frail, damaged, secretly waifish, really pretty adolescent self up in the fortress of a marriage to this really crabby old guy, who's like something out of a fairy tale and has this ogreish streak that you no doubt have actually exacerbated in him with your usual tricks and antics. And it was never really fair when all he really was was this rather old-fashioned person who wanted an old-fashioned marriage and who didn't go by the tricks of a person like you, with your newfangled sort of New Age-ish rules of being a Californian of your own specific generation—and it's true and you can't help it that you're one of the dread 77 Million Baby Boomers who are *always* changing the rules, and it isn't really because we've meant to, it's only actually that there are *so many of us* that when we decide something, more often than not, what we say goes.

This is the name of the rule we mainly go by: Majority Rules.

And the rules will be the same, the same, the same, then abruptly change, might remind you of is idling out beyond the breakline on the longboard you used to use, in that it was never exactly your own board, as it was junky and you had to sometimes share it with your cousin Jordy, but then at least you weren't always responsible for carrying it, as it was dinged and waterlogged. But you'd be out there face-first, belly down, just paddling around and basically waiting on the smooth, glassy, almost entirely placid sea, and everyone you'd be with, who were much better, more determined surfers, would be all pissed and impatient, but you weren't; you were happy enough to be doing nothing so much as *waiting*, as you had this great and confident talent for waiting, and what you were waiting for wasn't even the next big wave or the rogue one that would smash whatever's peaceful and Pacific, it was simply to be in this state of keen, buoyant, watchful, even extraordinarily alert *anticipation*.

And out of this watchfulness and sense of anticipation, you're writing about these two troubled Berkeley marriages, comedies of bad behavior among articulate, well-intentioned people, people who are smart, even basically kind, and who aren't exemplars of anything except folks who live in one or two very specific Zip Codes.

Which is basically just *so* not true. The book, very basically, is about sex, and you're writing it because it's occurred to you that most women don't write about sex at all, or if they do they don't do it very well, or they write from received notions that are basically lies, or from this uninvolved sort of philosophical Situation in the Sky, whose secret subtext is I'm Actually a Lofty Virgin Like Whoever the Greek Goddess Is Whose Name I'm Not Just Now Remembering, or they write from the *real down-low*, which is equally dishonest, as the secret subtext of this perspective is I'm Really a Whore, Which Should Make You Totally Want Me.

Or women write all purplish or silly and blushing or get gothic or medieval or do it with Space Aliens or become all mannered, elaborate, and Victorian, and all of this is just about equally irksome to me, and some of it makes me almost physically ill. Most writing about sex is so bad and soft core–ish and tame, which is to say conflicted, that I actually prefer the most hardcore of hardcore pornography because even if it is perverted in the eyes of some, what it *isn't* is dishonest; what it *isn't* is ulterior and creepy.

And you still suffer from the same old Word Magic, wherein Words and Deeds don't seem to have a really strong border that's particularly well maintained, so it seems like women who are writers and take all this seriously have some important work to do here, yet Your People, and by this you mean girls and women who are members of the 77 Million, are suddenly putting all these weird, really gacky words into their writing about sex, such as typing the letters that bump around, then clump together to form the clusters that spell out, really loudly, I HAVE MY PERIOD, when what you're wondering is, first, why is this something I really need to know? and second, why is this supposedly sexy?

And you suddenly realize that it isn't usually even *about sex* at all, that it's usually about shame, and that the creepy subtext almost always derives from shame, and that *everyone* is ashamed, and that we are all really so heartily sorry, and what we're sorry about is that we show up in these poor, flawed, sad, fundamentally mortal bodies, and this shame is actually something basic to us as Americans—that is, were we Pacific Islanders, we'd no doubt have our own special problems, but it wouldn't be this one.

And you realize you're ashamed as well, and that this shame is part of the secret thing that is bequeathed to you and you don't even know how you got it. Your own parents did do so many parenting things *wrong*, but teaching you to be ashamed of your human body wasn't one of them. And it occurs to you that it is because of their example that you've been able to fall in love, and that falling in love with a man who's in love with you and staying in love with this man are practically revolutionary acts, and that maybe you can write about sex from the delirious-falling-in-love-with-someone perspective, and that, having finally learned something about sex, you can maybe write something that helps to exorcise your own shame, as writing is the only thing that you've ever done that honestly feels completely helpful.

〇〇〇

This is during the Time Period, as my daughter says, and it is probably as a corollary to the economic boom, when every other marriage in Berkeley, or at least in these two or three little Zip Codes with which I have an acquaintance, has foundered or struggled and either does or doesn't come apart but rattles on down the road, and it is very often true that Somebody Else *is* involved, despite all these protestations to the contrary.

Somebody Else is usually involved. What people around here prefer to say is that it's a mutual parting of the ways, and My People, by which I mean the 77 Million—who honestly believed this kind of thing was basically beneath us—feel it's just so sickly retro, so sort of fifties, sixties, seventies, and clichéd to have Somebody Else Being Involved as a reason to wreck your marriage, which ruins not only your own life but also the lives of all your various loved ones.

It's almost *always* Someone Else, at least in my experience, and what this person's name is, frankly, honey? *Anyone* But You.

I believed it was beneath my basic dignity to have fallen in love with one man while I was married to my children's father, and I was so ashamed at the Glamour-Trashy nature of this not particularly original plotline, how it made me feel *exactly* like a friend of mine, a woman I really liked whose kids went to school with my kids. This woman who one week was laughing affectionately at how her truly diminutive husband, a man who in truth was as preternaturally small as he was almost astonishingly wealthy, needed to buy his suits in the boys' department, and wasn't that sweet?

That was one week. The next she was there in the carpool lane in her new sports car in a badass color, top down, and her car was being driven by her black, unbelievably beautiful, and almost embarrassingly studly personal trainer whose name is Marcus, and she was waving, waving, like she was on a float and was *ecstatic*, having just been crowned queen of the Rose Parade.

So I'm evolving this theory that this has something to do with the stats on my side of the 77 Million, all these women who have just turned forty or are turning forty in a little while, and how forty is the new thirty, or maybe it's more descriptively the new twenty-six, so we're all now acting *exactly* like we did when we were way, way younger, having basically missed this important step in growing up, and we're all back up to our same old tricks and acts of mischief.

So I've created these characters who enact these half-patched-together, semi-sociological theories of mine, my characters being composites or sometimes flat-out caricatures of the French I've met through my children's school, which is Ecole Bilingue, and the eventual publication of this book will result in some of these people's never again speaking to me.

I'm coming to realize that we are collectively—by which I mean both My People and the 77 Million—one of history's worst nightmares. We are *exactly* what everyone was afraid of. We are what happens when the woman side of the 77 Million takes control of Our Own Reproductive Destiny, then sets out to teach this simple truth not only to our daughters, but also to our sons.

The new rules are simple: Henceforth, we say, we refuse to bleed to death on the trail west, nor will we stay married to the man who walks into the house and automatically shouts at us, Hang up the goddamned phone.

So it's now actually the wives in almost every case I've personally encountered who have simply one day—and probably while shopping in the produce aisles of Andronico's—decided they've just *had it* with these poor, long-suffering, sad-sackish schlubs who walk around the streets of Berkeley with their advanced degrees from excellent universities, cringing, self-pityingly counting out their vitamins in their seven-day plastic compacts from the health-food store, as they daintily sip their decafs outside Café Romano on Shattuck, looking basically poleaxed or at least fundamentally and even existentially startled, as if they've been jolted with a psychic stun gun.

What My People, because of the rigors of biology, have caught sight of is something it was never possible to see before, and this is that the journey westward goes on and on, maybe infinitely, and there is amazing hope in this. We also know we basically don't need them, and they know we know that now, so what underlies the tattered souls of the solitary castoffs is this dark and growing desperation, as they measure out their herbal vitamins and count them one by one.

000

And it is the wives in each of the two marriages I'm writing about who one day, while gazing away into the middle distance, realize they must *get out!,* that they are at least profoundly and fundamentally bored, if not turned off, repulsed, and this is a deep secret in the straw poll of marriage in these, the last waning days of the twentieth century: Women who aren't happy in their marriages are no longer forced to stay!

But it's the husband in the one marriage who's fallen in love with the wife in the other one, though this husband is such a *man*, which is to say, dutiful and rule bound and Eastern, so blown down by the changes in the manners and mores of such an echt Californian place as Berkeley is turning out to be, which is kind of like it's California Squared or like California multiplied by California a hundred million times, all this California-ness pushed down into this one specific Zip Code made so tiny and dense, it'd fit into the size of the dot at the end of this sentence.

But I'm not getting anywhere with this book, in that my friend Ross Feld, who's a writer and an editor, reads a draft of what I've written and phones me to say, That, Jane, is perhaps the most angry book I have ever read, which somewhat mystifies me because—on account of childhood trauma, early loss of a parent, blah, blah, so forth—I lack what's clinically known as signal affect, in which a person may say and do these *really angry things*, such as indict one's former husband on the grounds that he's basically a total asshole, but the synapses or other neural connections are missing or at least blunted, so that while you *are* secretly really angry, you don't actually *experience* being angry, so you believe you are being fairly courteous.

And Time is ticking and we are riding this gigantic financial boom, the likes of which has never been seen, that becomes this huge rogue wave of economic prosperity, and the whole American century is winding down and everyone knows this century is the only one America will ever get and that basically we've probably blown it.

So I write and write and write and am still not getting anything done, so I regularly burn the whole fucking thing in the fireplace, which reminds me of my own parents and the nihilistic way they'd often almost *ritualistically* act.

And I'm always talking on the phone to my writer friends, as this is in advance of email and Facebook, and I'm being pointedly amusing to my own detriment as a writer and I'm driving to and from the French school where my kids are learning, as Jack says, to misspell in a couple of languages and I'm driving my daughter to soccer and my son to row crew, and there are days I drive so many miles that I get the mommy cramp in the calf of my right leg, from alternatingly braking and accelerating, and at times this is so painful and debilitating I have to get out of the car at a stoplight and hobble up and down on the asphalt to try to walk it off.

I'm trying to be a good mom and—in spite of leaving their father for another man—to not set a bad example, and I'm trying to not instill in my children shame in their human bodies and their humanly desires, so I will sometimes hear myself, at the crack of dawn, issuing these random, almost ad hoc instructions, as my own mother might have done, and I will say to the boys in the back of my SUV who are on their way to the Oakland Estuary to row crew, You guys all know about condoms, right? and they say nothing, so I say, And you do know what I mean when I say *safe sex*? and they say nothing, and so I go on, And you do know that when a girl says No, this actually does mean No? but there's no answer to even this, except the soft sound of their snoring, but I continue to tell them these things in those dark mornings as I drive, hoping that these things get through to them, as posthypnotic suggestions.

000

And it's right about here that Jack starts getting calls at home at night, proposing something that he might find interesting, but he says, Nope, he just does not find this interesting. He thinks, in fact, that it's a stockbroker making cold calls to try to drum up business, and Jack politely, because he's always polite, simply hangs up on him.

This isn't, in fact, a stockbroker and is, in fact, a headhunter from a really very famous executive placement firm that we've naturally never heard of, and Jack's hanging up on the headhunter only makes the rich man who has hired this firm want Jack all the more.

The headhunter finally has to call Jack at his office to have his assistant relay a message that *someone important* wants to speak to Jack about *something important*, but this is all so hush-hush and secret, he can give no other details. Jack is finally pestered into giving the important man two days in Washington, D.C., a single visit, for which Jack will be really very well compensated and that is actually only a consultation. So Jack agrees to be flown first-class across the country to stay at the

Hay-Adams, where you put your shoes outside your door at night and they reappear in the morning fairly *glinting*, they're so perfectly shined, and the shoe transaction happens by stealth and entirely wordlessly.

And so it evolves over one winter and spring that Jack is somehow inveigled into entering into negotiations with the important man, not a circumstance in which Jack ever wanted to find himself.

The man wants Jack to move east, but Jack doesn't want to go. This is because Jack—as he almost always is—is already in *exactly* the place he wants to be, which is living on Virginia Street in Berkeley, California, a couple of blocks below Shattuck, with me and my two kids, and his sons, who are now just about grown and are anyway out on their own, are right in our vicinity.

And we've just planted seven native species of grasses in the backyard of the house and he has plans for renovating the falling-down garage out back as my writing studio and he's trying to quit smoking with his friend Bob, so they go on yoga weekend retreats to places in Marin where they talk the whole time the yoga lady's trying to get them to practice mindfulness, and they talk but do not smoke all weekend, then get in the car to drive home, talking, and without even discussing it, one or the other gets the pack of Marlboros out of the glove compartment and they each automatically light up, and, still talking, they drive home.

Jack is different from me in that he never exhibits the rash need to sneak out a window and race off to another climate. In the rooms of Alcoholics Anonymous, the name given this urge is Pulling a Geographic, and you can trace it genetically all the way back on my father's side to the two drunken brothers who, in the 1640s, got thrown out of Holland.

The psychology goes like this: What's really wrong with you is all *external*—another way of saying it is, Everybody Else's Fault—so all you basically have to do is change your situation, then you can show up in this New World to discover what you've always secretly hoped: that deep down, you are basically fine, that you're even *more than fine*; in fact, there's nothing at all really wrong with you.

What's wrong with me, I think, is that I'm a *Californian* who lives in *California*.

◊◊◊

The *someone important* is the man who wants Jack to come to Washington, D.C., to start a publishing company, to which Jack says absolutely not. Jack's already fully and happily working as he has always worked, doing what he loves to do and at which he's actually good, which is publishing books that are actually worth publishing, in that you can actually read them and sometimes even learn something.

And Jack has recently hung new birdfeeders in the trees in our backyard—some of these feeders hold thistle, some suet, some a mix of seeds—and he now has a new little stack of bird books, so he can sit in the shade and smoke and drink his iced tea utterly peacefully while glancing at the illustrations, then read the descriptions, then stare through binoculars at birds who are only about six or eight feet away.

Look at him, Mom, my daughter Eva whispers as we watch him from an upstairs window. He says he's memorizing the differences in three different kinds of *finches*, and her tone carries equal parts awe and accusation.

And my son, Noah, and I have recently discovered that our hands already know masonry, in that we've learned without learning how to set bricks expertly by making a ballast of coarse gravel for drainage, then loosely mortaring it with layers of sand. We're laying a path in the backyard leading from the kitchen door out to where the birder sits with his iced tea and his *Sibley's Guide to Birds*, and there's a lemon tree in the backyard that blossoms year-round, so when you fling open the windows at the back of the house, the rooms explode with the scent of citrus.

But the important man has people, who keep calling. Because he's an important man, he isn't actually used to this kind of resistance. So we begin this sideways discussion of what moving there might mean, and we're trying to think of anyone we know in Washington, D.C., which is almost literally no one aside from Mark, who works on the Hill for Representative George Miller. Mark's from Jack's old softball team, whose name is The Minds. The name of the team is actually *I saw the best minds of my generation destroyed by madness, starving hysterical naked, dragging themselves through the negro streets at dawn looking for an angry fix . . .*

The name of their softball team is actually *the entire poem.*

But Jack doesn't want to go and neither does Eva, and Noah has started Berkeley High, where he is rowing crew and has his buddies, so he says, very definitively, that he actually *will not be going,* so it's basically me. I am, after all, the haunted one, the one who feels oppressed by my personal history, who can hardly even imagine a problem that might not be readily solved by building a body in my bed and going out to change husbands.

Because I just want, for once, to live somewhere that isn't *California,* all right? Because I'm like everyone else in my family, and all of us have something basically wrong with us, and whatever it is is the genetic glitch that says, *All right, let's pack up and GO.*

And the house on Virginia Street is located literally one and three-quarters blocks from the house on McGee Avenue to which my mother and father brought me from the hospital after I was born, and with the windows open and behind the rustles of trees and the rise and fall of birdsong—the flight call of the coastal finches is described as a soft and husky *jeeef, jeeef*—I can hear the Campanile on the campus at Cal toll-ing the hour, and the songs pealing from the bell tower, a carillon still being played by human hands. It feels like subtle harm is being done to me, as if I live in a room equipped with dozens of speakers but whose only soundtrack is the one that's called *My Loss*.

My mother has died and my parents, as ever, are crowding very close to me. And my older brother has moved east and my younger one has now vanished so successfully, it's as if he has been vaporized. Geo is now one of those individuals who no longer exist on paper in any kind of manner, and so is no longer counted in any census that isn't the head count of homeless on a night so cold that the bureaucrats debate whether or not to open the Armory. George Charles Vandenburgh, born August 28, 1952, is the last direct male descendent of the last direct male descendant, all down through the generations, and there-fore on the roster of the Holland Society, last of our tribe, and—like Ishi—gone.

And I have told myself that I will somehow be able to write of all this from Exile, because I can't shop in the produce aisles of the Park and Rob without being reminded that Berkeley, my Berkeley, the last place where my mother and father were truly happy, has begun to reek to me of generational doom.

∭

This person wooing Jack is wealthy in a way neither of us is used to—new wealth, but this in no way shows. That his taste is impeccable is illustrated in his single-minded pursuit of Jack, and he has Dürer's *Small Horse* sitting newly framed on the floor of his living room in town, sit-ting there even casually, as it's being placed here and there in anticipa-tion of being hung, and he has his better-than-the-Met's *St. Jerome* in the den, and the couches in the study are the exact shade of the silvery-gray coat of his twin Weimaraners so the dog hair doesn't show.

And when Jack asks him which book he'd most like to have published, this man says, *The Meditations of Marcus Aurelius*, and Jack thinks—or so he tells me—*This is surely the least frivolous person I have ever met.*

And the man has already searched out the world's most accomplished harpsichord builder and has had this man come to the United States to live for however long it takes to build his wife a harpsichord, and though the wife doesn't actually know how to play the harpsichord, the instrument is built and they both commence their lessons, but she once whispers to me when we're off in the ladies' room of a restaurant, But I have so little musical talent . . .

And theirs is their original marriage, which I think counts for something in this day and age. I find this out as I'm wanding them for what is secretly wrong with them, whatever it is that doesn't go in the Christmas letter and that they don't want anyone to know.

They aren't drunks, I can tell, since it takes one to know one, and they may actually be almost entirely viceless, which is its own kind of problem in that it makes you so basically unlikable. He once smoked cigarettes and now only occasionally, when tense, uses the most infinitesimal speck of Nicorette that he chews with the flat edges of his front teeth.

They are formal people but not pretentious. The wife, particularly, is gracious, which I attribute to her being a Westerner and coming from Oregon. She has the same things in her various houses—in the one in the District, and in the dressing room of the poolhouse at the farm in Rappahannock County, Virginia, where the hands, a married couple who have gone to college, raise organic fruits and vegetables for the rich man's various households.

The wife keeps this serviceable and modest clutch of really good makeup—one nice lipliner, a lipstick, moisturizer, and mascara, say— all neatly organized and on the same side of the sink so she'll know where to reach for it, and her robe is hung just so, and the people who work for them and travel back and forth from town to country, who are named, no kidding, Carlos and Maria, have worked for them for a long, long time, and it occurs to me that wealth of this kind enables these people to access what is honestly excellent, to lay hands on what they need, and to surround themselves with what's worthwhile, so they don't have to waste all the time the rest of us waste trying to find what we've just mislaid.

And there's no striving in the way these people are wealthy, I notice, and being really, really rich doesn't seem to make them nervous. Nor do they act belligerently cheap, as was the style in one kind of upper crust–ish part of my own family, who'd buy off-brand liquor to serve at a party and have it conspicuously poured from the cheap bottles, just to make sure the guests knew a conscious choice had been made to *in no way* seek to impress them.

We're at the farm in Virginia, having been swimming, and are sitting in the shade by the pool when the rich man asks me, Have you ever imagined living in Zürich? Then, without actually waiting for an answer, he turns to Eva to say, Would you like to own a horse?

11

My Intended

WASHINGTON, D.C., IS A Southern town, so Jack, whose dad was from North Carolina, immediately gets it in a way I simply don't. But then, he always feels comfortable no matter where he is, which I do, too, for maybe the better part of a longish weekend before the inevitable gut-wrench thing begins in me, the tiny thought balloon that rises and presses upward on the underside of my heart, insisting, *You are* nothing *like these people.*

He quickly establishes his habits, his routines and rituals, and does this bodily by putting his boots on the ground, finding a barber, walking to and from our apartment in Dupont Circle to his offices in the Army and Navy Club on Farragut Square, his going out to the gym with Mark and LeRue. This is the same one where George Stephanopoulos trains, and Mark and LeRue—who goes by Doc—go through the roster of all the sweatily famous, all huffing along on their treadmills, pointing out who among them either is or isn't gay, and who either is or isn't gay might actually surprise you.

But then, there are *many things* about this town that are truly startling, such as seeing someone working out at the gym while wearing an FBI T-shirt, and realizing that this person is *in no way kidding.*

It also startles me to understand that we've moved directly across the country to a place where The Young are so different from the way we were when we were that age, in that they're only twenty or thirty years old but already Mean Business. They're up really early in the morning, for one thing, and they're all very nattily turned out, as if out of Another Era.

It was back in the 1950s when kids were still expected to dress and act and think like they were nothing so much as miniature adults, and it was at this juncture that my own dear parents got off *that* merry-go-round and went to pursue their more personal preferences.

Now it's the '90s, but it's a little throwbackish. It's the Clinton White House and Brooks Brothers for all, the pantsuit thing, for instance? The girls getting those odd, stretchy, slackish trousers that are just like a guy's but tighter, and everyone's striding downtown with this great seriousness of purpose, briefcases swinging along in one hand, Starbucks in the other, and there is indeed this geographical slope to the city, so it is as I sit drinking my own coffee in my sloe-eyed writerly way that makes me look like a layabout who's floating facedown out beyond the breakline believing she has *all the time in the world.*

And they do seem to flow like water toward the mighty epicenters of power, being the White House, the World Bank, the Capitol, and the various August Institutions, such as Brookings, that—because I very early on identified power as one of the truly toxic elements—I know as one of those elements I've always needed to avoid.

And in Washington, it's also important to remember this isn't even *make-believe* power, like being the *maître d'* in some hard-to-get-into restaurant. This is real might, the kind that will unelect a lawful president and appoint a different one—a person who, in his emptiness, is *positive-ly dangerous*, who will go on to really fuck up the world by bombing countries, for instance, for transparently specious reasons, and, as we'll then live to see, by playing golf in his bland way as the money men ruin the world economy, remembering the man has ruined every institution he has ever touched, from the Texas Rangers to the Republican Party!

Which is why it's clear to me that we need to remember we really *do not* want another alcoholic in the White House, because, as the saying goes, you take the alcohol away from the alcoholic, but you still have the drunk, with his riddled alcoholic soul that he stuffs with any imaginable substance—all those pretzels and O'Doul's—trying to fill the nothingness, but there will never be *enough* of anything for a man like this, so he begins to abuse other substances, such as money or military might.

∭

So I sit on my perch, putting pen to paper, writing postcards home to California at a small table in the sunshine outside Kramer's Books and Records, a couple of blocks from where we live in the flat made from the first floor of William Jennings Bryan's mansion. Our living room is the ballroom in which he declared himself, in 1896, to be a candidate for president, running as a Democrat against the gold standard and what he called "the money men of the East."

And I am looking all larky and confident, which is one of my several disguises, and I am happy because I know almost exactly no one, and being in a foreign city knowing no one and barely speaking the language is one of my favorite states, as this is the way I *almost always* feel, and having it be externally true at least accounts for the strange-ness I feel in the produce aisles, where I don't actually recognize the fruits and vegetables. I shop at the one called the Soviet Safeway—long lines, no food—and am told I need to drive into Maryland to find a Whole Foods.

You cannot imagine the strangeness of this concept, that in order to buy good fruits and vegetables, you must *cross state lines*?

I watch all these young people being drawn forth toward Power, with their bright faces raised upward as the sun shines down on this very touching and beautiful city, which represents My America, which is actually a very moving idea, and I know that some very large percentage of these kids will be taken down by what they are moving toward, that they will simply be psychologically deformed by their proximity to it.

Nor should they even be *asking* themselves to handle that kind of intoxicant at such a young age—that's exactly the same as putting a weapon into the hand of a young man in the desert or a young man on the streets, then asking him not to fire it. So I'm always vibing them, going, *No! No! Slow Down! GO HOME! You're going the wrong way! This is your childhood! You don't need to act like this just yet. Go and despoil your youth.*

∞

I'm a little shocked to discover it's hard to make friends in Washington. It seems like folks don't really rush to make friends in Washington, as everyone's on his way from somewhere and in a hurry getting somewhere else, and this is because of the waves of changes in personnel brought about by two-year terms in the House and six in the Senate, and the various political administrations that come shuffling through, and the comings and goings of diplomatic postings—three years here, then four off in the United Arab Emirates—entire households of human beings who are right there before your eyes three-dimensionally one day, then magically teleported the next to the realm where they exist only on the front pages of the world's most important papers, or fourteen inches tall on the TV screen.

We live next door to Joseph Stiglitz, and I'm guessing I wouldn't *even mind* knowing him, as he's an economic genius and he'd maybe drop off a couple of helpful tips, but then these enormous moving vans pull up and overnight, this important person with his entire family of kids, cats, dogs, and canaries is simply—poof—gone, like Kevin Spacey playing Keyser Söze in *The Usual Suspects*.

And I'm often thinking about these things because I am often really unclear about what's even being discussed. For instance, what is an NGO, or what do they mean by an Inside the Beltway Mentality? I've only recently found out—and only accidentally—what a Beltway is.

And here Jack and I are, with our laid-back California openness that isn't fake, and we're suddenly trying to earnestly answer these really impossible, prey-driven Eastern questions, always asked so people can *place you*, get you, know where you *come from* and what you can do for them, and this tells them where to seat you—that is, Above or Below the Salt?

Because even the seating chart in a town like this is very deeply encoded, and this code is almost impossible to crack, since knowledge *is* power, and power in Washington honestly *is* the Drop the Bomb, I intend to totally *FUCK YOU UP*, Dick Cheney sort of *really scary* power that can tap your phone and kick your door in, like it's paying a whole country back for some imagined slight to some twit drunk's equally twittish father.

I once said to a woman I was only getting to know, Know what I really like about you, Jenny? You're one of the few people in Washington who'll actually say what's really on her mind, to which she said, Know what, Jane? This isn't what's *really* on my mind.

Washington is this class/caste–conscious kind of place that asks questions that are seemingly innocuous, but aren't. The first question asked is usually the hardest one, though it looks pretty easy on paper. It's this: *Where did you go to school?*

Jack, as usual, has an easier time of it, since he is way more left-brained and linear than I am. Jack's answer is Westmont College in Santa Barbara for two months, which is when he got thrown out for having a gallon of Dago Red in his room, left there by his roommate. Dago Red is what we then called Daddy Cribari. Jack got thrown out, though he did not yet drink alcohol of any kind, since he was a doper who looked down upon drinkers, who reminded him of his parents, just as I looked down upon drinkers, too, until I very seriously became one.

And Jack by rights *should* have been thrown out by those Christers, but for very different reasons—not for the wine that he didn't drink, but for the whole huge baggy of pot, which we then called dope, that was lying in plain view on top of his dresser, but Westmont didn't *know that* because the Baby Jesus Thought Police, or whoever was doing this dorm-room door-to-door patrolling, were *so out of it* they'd never *even heard* of marijuana, and this was this truly insidious place where they used Westmont kids to go up and down the aisles with flashlights at the movie houses in town to make sure other Westmont kids weren't in there kissing, which is just *so not* Jack, in that he is and was just *so too good* for that bunch of Baptist losers.

Jack's answer—his being at Westmont College for two months—is something he's been advised by his business partner in their prestigious literary publishing house to *never reveal to anyone*. You're to say nothing about your past because doing so is *self-revelatory*, which means people who know this would then have some kind of magical leveraged power over you, like they might then do what? *Tell . . . ?*

It's as if Washington has these fairy-tale aspects that have to do with belief, and this fairy tale's spell isn't easily broken, and this is why Jack is asked to sign a confidentiality agreement as part of his employment package, but it's *Jack* who is asked to sign the confidentiality clause, as I like to say—not me.

☉☉☉

In Washington you're never supposed to mention anything to anyone that is the least bit interesting or self-revelatory, those things that make you, well, unusual, such as the kinds of things I am always saying, which include: My father *committed suicide* and my mother was in a *mental institution*, one brother is *homeless*, the other one a PhD in Sociology whose specialty is *deviance*, and . . .

But you're not supposed to *say* these things, as they're embarrassing. You also don't, in this town, mention the entire realm of human behavior that has to do with secondary sex characteristics, which is why many people here seem to have slept through the pocket history of sex I used to pepper my son and his crew with as I drove them to predawn practice.

You wand folks for their sexuality in Washington and get this odd, bland no-reading-whatsoever; it'd be like *nnnnnnnnnnnnnn* on the Interesting Meter—no spike, no blip, no nothing.

There are whole huge realms of material, I guess, to which I am not supposed to allude, so allude I inevitably do, in that I start chirping this random stuff and sound to myself like birdsong, like a whole chorus of coastal finches, *jeef, jeef, jeeeefff.*

What are you working on, Jane? I'll be asked, and I'll say, Well, *awwwwctuallly*, I'm working on a book called *The Etiquette of Suicide*, and it's about how this subject is still so taboo that it's rude to even *mention* it, yet suicide is so pervasive in our society that almost everyone knows someone whose life has been irrevocably altered by the act of suicide, in that the violent and unexpected death of a person—particularly one who's young—changes, it's estimated, the lives of at least thirty people forever, and *my father* killed himself, and . . . .

And I'm not supposed to mention that my husband spent a year or so supporting his bride (first wife, not me) and infant son by traveling in central California as a professional bowler, though this seems *vastly* more interesting to me than does the neutered-seeming guy, the satellite male (who gives off an Interesting reading of *nnnnnnnnnnnnn*) whom I am invariably seated next to at some Table for Twelve, which is the way Washington does these things, and a Table for Twelve in a room full of Tables for Twelve is a really terrible idea, since its physics preclude your talking to anyone aside from the two other Below-the-Salt types you've been seated next to, and everyone will have impeccable credentials, and that always makes me feel the intense need to excuse myself, saying, Pardon me, I'm have to go find the *ladies'* room so I can . . . (smile at them, they smile back at you) . . . *go kill myself.* Then I wander off to look in closets, pat walls and curtains, looking for the Secret Exit, and do eventually find a bathroom, where I dig through the lint at the bottom of my bag looking for *anything*—the merest crumb of Xanax? a Benadryl?—with which to somehow alter my consciousness.

Which is one of the more terrible things about being a not-drinking drunk: how you're still so *hypervigilant* about everything in your immediate surroundings.

〇〇〇

I came to Washington as a TS, a Trailing Spouse, as I am laughingly informed by one of the VBs—or Valium Blondes—I meet. These women are always gorgeously preserved, if somewhat later-in-life divorcees, who've been summarily replaced. They might be anywhere from forty to seventy or even eighty or ninety—you can't ever really tell. What I can tell is they are *bitter! bitter!* about what I cannot imagine, since if they wanted a new guy they could just so easily go find one in the produce aisle.

This VB is a realtor who's trying to sell us a row house in Georgetown that's three stories tall but is only twelve feet wide, and is—sure, sure, I'll admit—completely tricked out and luxe (she calls this *aaaawwwllllll the bells and whistles*), but it's on the market for three-quarters of a million dollars, and I mean it is literally *twelve feet wide* and this is the reason: It was built to accommodate human beings, long ago, who were *being kept as slaves*, and when I say something about this to the VB, she looks at me as if to ask, *What's the* matter *with you?*

Washington is just plain nuts about the TLAs, or Two- or Three-Letter Acronyms, because they're confusing and often actually inscrutable. An expression like *trailing spouse* is always said in this droll, Sally Quinn–ish, insiderlike accent that shows it's intended to be funny. It's like saying the Clintons have spent *their entire lives*, my dear, in government housing, or that so-and-so-forth—Adrian Fenty—lives on the *other side of the Moat.*

The Moat is Rock Creek Park. It's generally true that the more Sally Quinn–type people—by which I mean the white, affluent, connected—live on the left of the park as you study it on the map, while on the right side you will find *your teeming masses*, oh ah ha ha, hee hee hee . . .

Because I'm a TS, I basically do not count, which is basically okay with me because I have always enjoyed this Flaubert-type remove and invisibility whereby I can observe the bourgeoisie and make my caustic comments. As a Trailing Spouse you're supposed to be like a dark shape at the bottom of the important person you're lucky enough to be married to, in that your job is essentially *grounding*. You're like the shadow that Peter Pan lost and had to get Wendy to reattach to him.

There are many other world-weary and droll sayings regarding spouseness here, such as this one: *Washington is full of powerful men and the women they married when they were young.*

My being a TS means that Jack and I aren't necessarily even seated at the same table at a dinner party, where he is off there, Far Above the Salt, with the other interesting and important types. Because my husband actually *is* interesting to talk to, I always longingly track where he's seated at any banquet or social gathering by watching the butler carrying a silver tray on which is perched a single glass of shimmering iced tea.

Jack doesn't drink alcohol for reasons different from my own. He was maybe nineteen years old and bowling professionally—this was after the getting-thrown-out-of-Westmont incident—when he suffered the crisis of faith that resulted in his becoming a practicing Buddhist. Now, by my lights, there are *plenty of people* out there who are married to people with PhDs from really distinguished schools—I, in fact, used to be one of these—but *how many people* can go to an important cocktail party of really influential people in Washington, D.C., and brag about being married to someone—and a Buddhist yet!—who, while bowling for money, once scored a 297, which is just three points shy of a perfect game?

So, this being Washington and I being nothing if not adaptive, I've begun to develop my own verbal defenses, one of the best being to bury whatever small truth I might be willing to reveal in *reams and reams* of distracting paper.

So the answer to the question And where did *you* go to school, dear? has begun to provoke in me this long Faulknerian disquisition on any number of ranging topics, starting off very naturally with suicide,

suicide, suicide; then, normally enough, veering off to include how Ronald Reagan closed the mental hospitals in the state of California as a cost-cutting measure, sending the mentally ill back to their *quote* communities *unquote*, meaning the mentally ill now get to sleep under freeway underpasses and eat out of Dumpsters and panhandle; then moving without pause to the state of public schooling in California versus that of the District of Columbia, where our daughter is in middle school; then ranging outward to include the education of our various sons—my one, Jack's two—and where they went or are currently going to school, as Where Your Kids Go to School is just another way the Anonymous They of the District of Columbia have of Placing You. And I eventually get to the part about my own kids' French/English bilingualism and why we couldn't use public elementary schools and how this had to do with Gann-Rudman of 1977 and the ruination of one of the best systems of public education ever devised in the history of man, ruined—as everything else has been ruined—by the crazed, bloodsucking, starfucking right wing of the Republican Party, which is evil incarnate. And I sometimes even go off on how my great-uncle, who was in the State Department in oil-producing countries and *very obviously* CIA, came to rescue me from one of the more unlikely situations in which I found myself, as a young person living alone in an incense-scented beachside cottage, writing pretty excruciatingly bad poetry, going barefoot, usually wearing only a silken sarong over my bathing suit, and being constantly stoned, and how this CIA great-uncle, who found me with his spy connections, hauled me back to college, where I was enrolled over one weekend because he was, as my mother liked to say, Rather High Up in Administration, and this was somewhat like what would these days be called An Intervention.

So I was sometimes more or less enrolled *almost against my will* and attended first one state college and then another and then yet another one, and by now even I myself have *no idea* how I came to be speaking of these things, since I too have completely lost my place.

Point being, I have *no idea* why I picked *any* school I have ever gone to, aside from when I was a little kid and it was the one I walked to with my brothers because it was right down the street from our house. I once very literally went to a certain college and got an advanced degree because—as I was in the basement of the library, researching law schools—this catalog fell off the shelf and sprang open to the pages that read: Creative Writing, San Francisco State University.

My college education was complicated by the fact that I'd been kicked out of my family—the legal term is *emancipated*—for one or another infraction and, let's face it, I was like most seventeen- and eighteen-year-olds in that I had *no idea* what I was doing and had no long-term goals and was completely incompetent at making any kind of Life Choice and had absolutely no guidance, so I chose what was actually a very terrible school for me. And though I had that Inevitable English Major thing written all over me, as if in Sanskrit in amber Indian henna, I'd still impulsively Change Majors in trying to escape what was so very obviously my destiny, and I'd change to Pre-Med or Pre-Law or American Studies or Pre- or Post-anything that wasn't Art or English so I wouldn't turn out *exactly* like my parents.

The first school I went to turned out to be only good at things that started with the letter *A*, such as Animal Husbandry, Aeronautical Engineering, Agra Business, Architecture . . .

HA! I think, as I'm thinking about it. *Maybe* that's *it*. Maybe I was thinking, *If I go to a school that is mostly guys*—and the ratio at this school was about nine boys to every girl—*and some of these guys are architects, maybe I'll meet someone who is exactly like my father, and I can marry him and we can have three beautiful children, as he and my mother did, but this time, we won't fuck it up . . .*

But instead of meeting anyone attractive in architecture at Cal Poly, San Luis Obispo, I seem to have zoomed outside the ART, ARCHITECTURE, ENGLISH lines—which were probably all way too long for me to have the patience to stand in—and I seem to have gone on down and gotten in a much shorter one at the other end of the alphabet that enrolled me in ZOOLOGY, which was lucky for me, because this school was good at zoology because it had *actual animals.*

Which is maybe where I met the animal husbandry guy with whom I was suddenly raising nineteen pigs and two steer, this being another of these boyfriends who had something tragically wrong with him; in this case, it was that he didn't read, and while he was smart enough, his intellect was not *elastic,* so he'd go on stolidly to become a Large-Animal Vet, just not with me.

And I'd invariably get thrown out of my dorm if not school or this or that portion of my family for some minor infraction—if not for the jug of Daddy Cribari or the building the body in the bed, then for some analogous and equally stupid thing, for Hours or Demerits or other sexist crap that was just then finally being extinguished.

I'd get tossed out of wherever for me being me and for doing the kinds of things I *always* do, which is whatever impulsively occurs to me.

◌

So in Washington, when asked the where-did-you-go-to-school question, I just meander along anecdotally in this almost impossible-to-follow manner, trying in my open, honest California way to point out some of the interesting detours here and there, with side trips and excursions.

And how about when I went to school for one small piece of one semester in San Diego County while living on an avocado ranch? This was during the era of the two Simultaneous Davids, these being boyfriends I had who were named the same, so when I got a dozen roses with a card at Christmas I didn't know which to thank?

And how the time I quit college *entirely* for a whole summer and my school—this was Long Beach, where my CIA great-uncle was dean of international studies—didn't even realize I wasn't coming back, because I'd gotten this great job at the phone company at Ninth and Hope in downtown Los Angeles? This was no mere *summer* job, this was a *real* one that might lead to a really promising career, the kind of thing some women simply did. If you were one of My People and wanted a good job, it was just widely accepted that you could go work for the phone company.

It was even a traditional thing to do if you were trying to start behaving like a grown-up. You got a job at the phone company, which was considered a *women's company* because there were about seven women for every man, and you'd live modestly and buy dresses and shoes that went together at the May Company, and carry a neat little virginal handbag to hold your lipstick and your compact, and there you'd stay for the rest of your life.

The phone company—since Jack and I are roughly the same age—is what I was doing just as Jack was getting thrown out of Westmont College, getting his girlfriend pregnant, getting married, then going out to bowl for money.

And it's true that my path and Jack's often did seem—in retrospect—to have crossed and recrossed, then run parallel for a time, as if we were on the same trek. It's as if we were California Indians of roughly the same language grouping who might have glimpsed each other far off there, in our mutual future, and—while never actually speaking—would have known, if our eyes met across a room, to give each other that little chin lift of recognition.

The phone company—and there was only one then, remember? as this was before the Great Age of Deregulation—was the way some people, you know? *lived* in those days, which really interested me, if only in a touristy, shallow sort of way, like you could time-travel to the 1950s.

It must be the way gay people feel when they try to act straight: If they just *practice* hard enough, it'll begin to one day get a little easier, except that something invariably comes along to completely fuck you up by revealing the More Real You.

Because certain parts of what we might call My Surroundings would always then begin to intensely bother me, like that the elevator in the phone company building was, to my mind, unsafe in that it had no interior doors. It was an old-fashioned apparatus in which the doors slid closed on each floor, but inside the cage of the elevator itself there was just this folding grate at the front controlled by a Colored Gentleman, which is exactly how this man would have thought of himself, as he was elderly and though this was a good long while after Civil Rights had supposedly extinguished Jim Crow in the workplace, this hadn't actually even begun to happen. Also, it's true that people can't just readily completely *change* the things they call themselves in certain circumstances, and the phone company, when I was working there, was one of those circumstances.

For instance, no *Negro* or *colored* women worked there, I'd noticed, except at night on the cleaning crew or maybe doing data entry, and there were no Hispanics, who would have been called Mexicans, because they, of course, could not be expected to speak English, and all the regular or *white* women I worked with got off by the seventh floor, while the men went on up in the elevator and worked on the higher and more important floors.

So this elevator grate was supposed to keep you from sticking your fingers or hand through and potentially doing grievous harm to yourself or others, so I decided—as the daughter of a suicide and of a woman locked up in a mental institution for almost a decade for what was probably no more than the kind of grief you encounter in Greek tragedies, which is *epic*, also universal and therefore, like it or not, almost perfectly understandable—I didn't want to ride on said elevator, and began walking up and down the seven flights of stairs to and from my desk, minding my own damned business, which was doing a job at which I truly excelled.

This was manually alphabetizing some or another item; it may have been data entry cards done by the women who came in invisibly in the night and who probably thought of themselves as *gals*. My job was something completely rote and normal, which I really enjoyed, as it was the exact opposite of being creative, which had always seemed like a pernicious illness or malady that might eventually get to me.

I did this job and had a really wonderful boyfriend who was perfect in all ways, smart and funny and well read and good looking and tall and curly haired, and he looked to me like Paul Newman, aside from the fact that Paul Newman was actually short, which didn't read because he had such presence.[+]

[+]Paul Leonard Newman, born on January 26, 1925, in Shaker Heights, Ohio, and who died in his home in Westport, Connecticut, on September 27, 2008, was, in fact, rather short, a fact I have firsthand from the time Jack and I met him and Joanne Woodward in a receiving line at the Hollywood premiere of *Mr. and Mrs. Bridge*, the movie made from the Evan S. Connell novels Jack published. Jack wore a tux to this premiere, and I had on a black dress spangled with about a million tiny rhinestones that might have *cost the earth*, as my fancy grandmother would have said, had I not got it cheap at Loehmann's, but the panty hose I bought that day on Rodeo Drive cost, no shit, *fifty dollars!* and this was all the way back in oh, say, 1990? Joanne Woodward was wearing a plaid pantsuit, and Paul Newman had on blue jeans and a soft, washed-many-times light blue work shirt open at the collar to show his white T-shirt underneath, so Jack, in black tie, leaned over and whispered to Paul Newman, *I feel like I should be parking cars*, and Paul Newman put his arm on Jack's shoulder, man to man, and whispered back, *I never know what to wear to these things, either . . .*

So I had this perfectly ordinary life constructed, wherein I was working at the phone company—and no one, including my CIA great-uncle, could *make me* go back to school and be an English major—and living simply in a nice normal working girl's apartment, with a normal workaday job alphabetizing shit, the kind of job other people would actively *not* want to have because it wasn't *creative*, when I had no wish to be creative, seeing what being creative did to my parents, who were honest to God killed by it, which is why Allen Ginsberg spelt this place Amerika, and my parents were too *creative* to live somewhere spelt Amerika . . .

So I'd be trudging up and down seven flights of stairs to the lunch-room, bringing my lunch in a paper bag, its top neatly sealed over with a folded paper napkin tucked inside, the kind of well balanced and healthy Californian lunch I'd have made for my own three children had I married one of the regular, nonsuicidal, and less sexually conflicted architects I might have met at Cal Poly but didn't.

000

So Long Beach came *after* Cal Poly and *before* San Francisco State, okay? as I'd be trying to explain to whoever'd been stupid enough to ask me this question at a cocktail party in Washington, D.C., and by this time this person's eyes would be glazing over and they'd be scanning the room for someone else who could in some way *help them* with their Career Advancement, which I very obviously cannot, because the real question or subtext almost always being asked by people who want to get to know me might be more succinctly put as: Who Do I Have to Fuck to Get Your Husband to Publish Me?

And I'm using the term *fuck* here nonliterally, that is, not to connote actually having sex, as my daughter might say, or actual physical

contact of any kind, since Washington is one of the least libidinous places I've ever been—reference the *nnnnnnnnnnn* thing that goes on all the
time. And this is *not just me*, as I came here as an okay-looking woman
and the getting of boyfriends, some of whom overlapped and even had
duplicate names, has never been my particular problem.

And I am also from *California*, where we have, as cultural inheritance, a certain *je ne sais quoi*, yet in Washington, D.C., I'll go for days!
weeks! months! and have no one, absolutely no one at all, emit any kind
of buzz on any sort of frequency that isn't *nnnnnnnnnnnnnn*, and believe me, I am really adept at scanning all these really odd and particular
interpersonal frequencies, even those that have nothing to do with me,
which is one of the few things you get from being *literally* psychoana-
lyzed by a *literal* psychoanalyst, *analysis* meaning spending six and one-
half years lying on a couch four times a week, listening to oneself really
expensively saying all this ridiculous crap.

The sexlessness of Washington, D.C., feels positively eerie, as if it
thinks in its own mind it's the 1950s, as if anybody cares whom you go
to bed with! No one cares! No one cares whom you do or do not sleep
with unless *it's children* or maybe *chimps in the National Zoo*!

And one thing I really do think my generation can take credit for
is really successfully driving our tractor trailers over the CDs that contain all the random encoded data referencing the manners and mores
and popular culture that might grow back by sci-fi increments from the
1950s! which is why the right wing of the Republican Party, which worships the *1950s* as the Last Normal Time (for White People) and completely lacks a certain *je ne sais quoi*, really hates our collective guts.

∞

So I am trudging up and down seven flights of stairs at the phone company, having the perfect boyfriend with whom I am actually in love, and this is a huge relief since you really never know—when your father kills himself and your mother is sent away to a mental institution for almost a decade—whether you're going to turn out to be so ruined that you're incapable of loving anything more complicated than a goldfish.

And I have shoes that go with the dresses I wear to work and I am driving my very own brand-new VW Bug that my maternal grandfather, a banker and staunch contributor to the Republican Party named Virgil Elmo White, has helped me buy by paying the some-amount down payment, after which I pay my own monthly car payment of $54.93. And I am really well on my way to this certain secure middle-classness, and have even semi-convinced myself I resemble a girl some guy who resembles my boyfriend might want to marry, and when he goes away to Mexico City to study Spanish over my phone company summer and writes me, he calls himself *tu novio*.

According to my smattering of Spanish, this translates as *your intended*, though I may never bother to actually look it up.

There are a couple of tiny little glitches in the perfectness of my paper doll–like life, such as his being, well, gay (though this is *pre* or in advance of our actually calling it that), or his having at least this sort of twilit sexuality, as the only lover he's had—and I actually did and do deeply despise the word *lov-ur* and wish no one would ever use it for any kind of reason, but what other word do we really have in American English?—is a man.

Because he and I also aren't actually *sleeping together*, as is said back then, as this is way back in the Twentieth Century, which is a more modest and decorous time.

000

So if Time is a river into which you cannot step twice, I've arrived at a bend in the river where there's a jam-up because the river has frozen and the ice floes have simply backed up upon themselves and glacial formations are being thrust skyward, in that the Time that exists at the phone company is still pre–Civil Rights.

It is the Civil Rights movement that has begun to move us all toward the future. This is happening everywhere, not only in the South, and it has begun to liberate not just blacks, but all of us, to go and do all kinds of things that will be completely disapproved of by Virgil Elmo White and my CIA great-uncle, because they are the kind of tall white men who are *used* to being in power, and no one gives that up willingly.

So the Colored Gentleman who mans the elevator and wears the white gloves to open and close the grille and mind everyone's comings and goings does so with a little subservient, hunched maneuver of his head and shoulders that I know stands for his deep and abiding hatred of All Y'all White Folk, also the Very Horse We Rode In On, which was actually a railroad train that was called the Industrial Revolution.

This man's despising me is another reason I don't want to ride in his fucking elevator.

Point being, *my intended* is conflicted, but so what? *Everyone* in my family has *always* been conflicted—we are all these twilit, questing souls, which makes us interesting and seems natural to me, and I, unlike my father, may actually get to live long enough to discover who I am and what my true nature is made of.

Point being, being conflicted is *our tradition*; my own father's being conflicted was why he *kept* getting arrested, in that some of us are simply constitutionally incapable of *not* doing the thing we're not supposed to do, which is—when the spirit seizes us—climbing out a window.

∞

So *mi novio* is conflicted—so what? I'm totally down with this. He and I don't even have to discuss it, and have evidently formed this wordless agreement that we will conduct this mutual fakeish-romantic, completely sexy but sexless–type 1950s thing that looks good on paper.

And it is not that we are not mutually and even ardently attracted to each other, which we are, but this exists in the complicated part of Twilight, in that there are all these shades and gradations that no one wants to hear about, so we name ourselves into these boxes that say Gay or Straight, in order to gain control of what—in the Twentieth Century—used to be thought of as this *great big deal.*

Which isn't actually even true to human development, which I know from having simply flipped through the pages of my Zoology textbook, which is only to say, the tadpole you start out as isn't necessarily the frog you become, given shades and gradations.

But *Other*, of course, is not what anyone high up is actually going by in those old-fashioned days when I am working at the phone company while *mi novio* is off learning Spanish in Mexico City, only to come home in late August to say he has fallen in love with his Spanish teacher, and I have no real way of asking if this is a man or a woman or to really know which would be the more devastating answer, and my heart is legitimately broken.

But he wonders if he and I can stay *tangential friends* because he really likes my mother and my brothers, with whom I am now suddenly living in this kind of hippie-ish house a few blocks from the beach, decorated with furniture from all our rich and well-traveled relatives' basements and garages, so we have really beautiful if dilapidated old things: careworn old Persian carpets and a coffee table made from a teak door shipped home from Indonesia after a diplomatic posting.

My brothers and I all sleep on mattresses on the floor in our own rooms, and we've hung the windows with Indian-print bedspreads we get at Cost Plus Imports and that emit this certain dusty and exotic reek of Elsewhere, which shows us to be well raised and to have turned out to be what our parents intended, which is Bohemian.

And because we are now Bohemian, I learn to make ragout and Quiche Lorraine.

We're Bohemian except for our mom, who—and we must struggle to remember this—was raised as a somewhat spoiled only child and now requires her privacy and so is off in the back of the house, which is her own private quarters, where she has her own bedroom with a private bathroom, and a screened porch that is like her sitting room, and this area is sacrosanct. Our mother, who is the lady of the house, presents only when she cares to present and comes forth from her realm almost regally, like the Empress Dowager.

She has regular, honest-to-Jesus furniture that actually matches, including a bureau, a proper bed, a chest of drawers, and even a decorative runner made from the mud cloth of a certain tribe in Africa to cover the top of the bureau and disguise its nicks and scratches.

She is extraordinarily modest in terms of her person in a way I have never before noticed, and she never emerges from her rooms unless she is completely and neatly dressed in hose and heels, a skirt and a sweater, like she might have worn in college. She also carries her purse around with her, in which she keeps her cigarettes, and this may be one of the few vestiges or signs of her having been a mental patient for such a long time, and the times, they are a-changin' and the ice floes have given way and our mother has been delivered back to us intact. She is just very astonishingly *here*, completely lucid, and startlingly together.

And in this house, whose common rooms are really crazy and chaotic, an enormous amount of alcohol is being consumed by everyone but me, and drugs are being taken by my brothers, but privately, because my mother does not approve of drugs, and the only drug I use is this truly unbelievable amount of caffeine—I drink dozens of cups of black coffee every day—and the truly astonishing number of cigarettes I smoke, because I can see no daylight between myself and cigarettes, cannot imagine that I ever didn't smoke or that I might ever not smoke again.

I also take the diet pills they give you at the health center if you go there saying you're feeling, you know, low—saying the regular shit, like how your father killed himself and now your *novio* has run off with his Spanish teacher, so you're feeling a little . . . ?

And I am not kidding that they give you amphetamines, saying, *Of course* they're a crutch, but if your leg were broken you'd use a crutch, wouldn't you? and I think, *Well, that makes entire sense*, and I go home and pour the entire bottle of pills into a pile onto the teak coffee table that was once an Indonesian door, and my brothers and I pop them like Pez and we talk and talk and talk. We talk all night and all day until the drugs run out, and then we crash and sleep for days in a row, and it is in this circumstance alone that the three of us together can actually out-talk our mother, who suspects substances and stays largely off in her rooms, listening distantly, disapproving mildly.

She tells us later it's the most astonishing babbling sound, not unbeautiful but indecipherable as human language, that it's as if her three children have somehow been transmogrified into two dozen chanting Gregorian monks.

000

The night *mi novio* breaks up with me, we drive around while I am supposedly deciding whether he can still hang out at my house with my amazingly cool mom and my totally bitchen brothers, who are both so interesting and hip that all these fantastic people want to just drop by and sit on pillows on the floor of our living room at any time of the night or day.

And this is in fact a magical time, and Will has only just come home from Europe, via Greenwich Village, and is now enrolled in college. He was in Germany in the Army and has an amazing gift for languages and has read Marx in German and has been totally radicalized according to the Frankfurt School and has been given back to us as this preternaturally worldly and really attractive person. He is so well read and he sets about educating the rest of us in what is actually important and so gives me and Geo a reading list and conducts study sessions, and I read these books, or mostly do, and Geo doesn't because he probably can't, as he's already off picking up sailors on the pier and is sort of a rent boy doing who knows what with them in the $1.50 triple features.

And because Will's a few years older and seems to know what he's doing, he becomes this charismatic leader of student protests who is part of the governing body deciding whether we will occupy the college president's offices, and Geo tags along, just like in the Olden Days, and he is like a brilliant innocent who has this mysterious aura of humor and knowingness, which makes him impossibly cool. And Geo has also already been Inside, as my big brother and my mother and I have had to spring him from what is an Actual Institution, and this, in these days, is a badge of honor.

It's like an open house all the time. You stop by. You stay. You crash on the floor of the living room on laid-out pillows and no one ever wants to leave. Our house is just four blocks from the ocean, and with the windows open, you can hear the wave action on the shore, and all these friends of ours begin to arrive from all these different places in the country and widespread parts of our lives and everyone is intermingled and everyone gets along and there is no class or caste or snobbery and no one is ranking on anyone; no one is asking, *But did you graduate?* Everyone is just together for once and listening to music. Everyone drinks coffee and wine and beer and smokes cigarettes and goes into another room to smoke pot or hash, in deference to our mom, who prefers that both drugs and sex be performed discreetly and—*if you don't mind*—out of her earshot.

When Will and I are both enrolled in college, classes hardly matter, as we are closing the schools as soon as the government tries to open them and opening the schools when the government tries to shut them down. They are *our schools*, we deeply feel, so we believe we get to use them to launch ourselves as this massive assault on the Establishment. The kinds of political actions my older brother leads involve the United Farm Workers, and he's in organizations that are marginally communistic, and we put our bodies on the line for all kinds of actions and go to a peace march with the name of a sympathetic lawyer inked in ballpoint on our arm, then raise our hand if we're willing to be arrested.

Because it's always been important, in fact, to be willing to be arrested if it's for the right reasons, which is something my parents taught me and something I, in turn, have taught my son and daughter. It's important to remember that it was the children who were arrested during the Civil Rights movement, because if their parents had been arrested, they would have lost their jobs, and we need to be arrested because it wears The Powers That Be down and uses their manpower and their resources, because this is the way we break them. We are willing to be arrested over and over again, and when you are arrested, you call the ones who love you, who then drop everything and rush to the station house to bail you out.

So when my mother and brother are arrested together at one action or another, they call me and their voices are entwined and they are singing "La Marseillaise."

※

What has happened to Time over this single summer is that it seems to have suddenly cracked open, and from this place where the frozenness has broken, a whole bright and beautiful future has spilled, everything surging, roiling, alive with possibility.

The Powers That Be are tacitly finished. We have identified them as being positively evil, in that all they can ever think to do is cause another ceaseless war in which they always manage to economically benefit, and theirs is the terrible reality that we refuse to honor. This is something we are now collectively deciding and we are the 77 Million, so what we say goes.

We are interested not in power, but in the realm of skin on skin, the realm of the intimate, the place where one actually living human opens his or her mouth and says one true thing to another living person and even saying the word *fuck* feels defiant of the Old Ways, which are destructive and calcified and Republican and oh-so-bank-president and oh-so-CIA.

And we are simply such a huge demographic group that we know we now get to change a couple of important things.

By now I've had the antiwar argument with my Grandfather Virgil, the banker and staunch Nixon-ite and contributor to his political campaign, and another similar one with my Great-uncle Bobby, and I've begun to notice that I am now not being invited to family functions that traditionally have excluded my mother. It was when my father died that my mother began to be excluded; then she went to the mental hospital and—according to many in my family—was never seen or heard from again.

What that Time Period is suddenly producing is what you come to in art: People seem even more real than real, in that everything is suddenly heightened and alive and every moment matters and everyone begins to suddenly understand that it's allowed and even required that you write what you really believe and not what is merely expected of you and draw what you believe and say it and show it and *behave* vividly, as if you imagine yourself alive. And it's now that you suddenly understand that it all actually really *applies to you*, that you really will get to one day ride in a taxi down a snowy street on your way to the Met in New York City, having accidentally ended up on the other coast in the same patch of time as Your Intended (even if this is somewhere off in the brackets of your mutual future). This is when your own life suddenly snaps to and can be seen as containing the great themes that literature contains and you suddenly understand that history *pertains* to you, that history is what is happening every single day and that what is written in books is put there only to point this out to you.

People are suddenly brave enough to be saying or at least trying to say *true things* and do *true things*, and to get arrested for the right and not specious reasons, and this feels like you can suddenly breathe, which feels almost dangerous because it means you have to actually trust yourself, and suddenly in America we are no longer these fakeish, shallow, paper doll–like people, but have become the brave ones who will risk something, and it is exactly then that I begin to love my country.

⚈

I make my former *novio* take me to the liquor store to buy me a bottle of wine, since I'm not yet old enough and in my house they drink mostly beer, and I'm figuring it's right about now that I'm going to start to behave alcoholically, which is, after all, my destiny, but me being me, and basically a fuckup even in *fucking up*, I forget the bottle on the floor of his car.

I have a couple of things on my mind, the first of which I tell him before I get out and slam the door.

No, I say.

The answer is actually that no, my family and I have come through all this hardship as this one tight little unit, and *some guy* isn't going to stop by every now and again in order to enjoy how unusual we are just because I now live in a house full of these cool-to-the-point-of-bitchen characters who are as entertaining as anyone in someone's stupid play.

And he likes my family because we are, you know, so twilit and original. Because he's been raised in the upper-middle-class humdrum stupid repressed conventionality we exist in defiance of, and because he particularly likes my effortlessly hip mom, as *she's exactly* who this kind of guy will always go for, in that she's so vivid and extreme.

No, I say, he cannot continue to hang out with my family after disdaining me.

Because I can suddenly see him for exactly what he is and what it is he has meant to me, and I suddenly hear in him *the condescension* in his deciding he has found it in himself to admire my family for their, what? Unusualness?

Nope, I say, he has to go on now and figure out on his own what he's about and what he is and isn't actually into, and about this I actually have no idea.

And anyway while he was away in Mexico I have undergone a transformation, and under Will's spell and guidance I am now this hippie child whose hair is impossibly long and almost infinitely curly, and I am going around barefoot, dreamy, and often stoned. And I am wearing my high school prom dress that was, no shit, sewn at home by hand instead of being bought at Macy's or Bullock's. My dress is this long flowy thing made from dark-green-with-pink-flowers-all-over-it *hopsacking*, a fabric that got me talked about and that I chose in ironic protest against, you know, all that is Prom Night and all that boysie-girlsie conformist crap that killed my father.

And I have anyway also been fired from the phone company after being brought before the Safety Committee for my practice of climbing up and down seven flights of stairs.

This being the safety committee's reasoning: *No One Else, Jane, is doing this, and what if you trip and fall down and we never find you?*

I am fired not for climbing up and down seven flights of stairs, per se, but for sitting in that meeting frozen with rage, knowing these are exactly the kinds of *bitches*—the committee is all women, and I know that the word is like a physical slap to the face of My People, which is why I use it rarely and only advisedly—who would have actively scorned my mother, so I refuse to sign the thing they've drawn up, which is A Written Safety Committee Conclusion, together with its Order to Comply.

So when I slam *mi novio*'s car door on that chapter of my life, forgetting the bottle of wine, what I actually think—because my heart is legitimately broken—is that I don't hate him, in that this isn't really *his fault* any more than it was my father's fault to have been born in a society that wasn't mature enough to accept a person like him. But because I have been such a complete and dismal failure in my last really ardent attempt at what is called in my family *conventionality*, as I step into the street, what I think is: What now, for fuck's sake? I have to go be a *writer*?

12
Research Methods

IT'S JUST THAT I AM intrinsically so *like* my mother, in that we are just so *bad* at being feminine, so I come of age imagining that I am not a real girl at all, but am rather a transvestite version of a girl, more of a Holly Woodlawn or Myra Breckinridge, this beautiful (to me) creature who is only a semiworking replica of what a girl would approximate, like I am this girl disguised deep within the soul of a man who is somehow only *in costume* as an adequate girl.

Given my okay, even All-American good looks and my somewhat upbeat and well-adjusted demeanor, it is even *more* confusing that I harbor the secret that I am a cross-dressing man or—even more im-probably—a heroin-addicted lesbian hooker who stands in the smear of neon-wet street corners in Hollywood with mascara weeping down her face. You just wouldn't *get this* from looking at me, in that I am what is called *high achieving* despite all my various, *you know* . . . ? my *blah blah blahs* . . . ? as my mother would say, then draw in the air with her cigarette. In my mother's somewhat musical-comedic take on things, we might refer to these as the Tra-la-la-ge-dies.

I am simply so *An-tee* Girl, Lina would say. Lina is my dusty, Daughter of the Golden West great-granddaughter of the Prairie Schooner pioneers grandmother, as opposed to Delia, who's more proper, one, who was more Daughters of the American Revolution. But from both sides everything is saturated with this sense of dripping oppressive history and altar guild and Girls' Friendly Society and the Heroic Nature of Suffering, and it just makes me sick, in that it has all these expectations about Our People packed down into the subclauses of the membership requirements, and I do not want to have to even *know about* these clauses and subclauses, let alone try to qualify, so I immediately bring up the Tra-la-la-ge-dies, the Suicide for a Dad and the Mental Patient for a Mom and so forth, almost immediately on any interview or college application.

I am very closely identified with all kinds of transgressive behaviors, and I never have much of a damper on my mind and barely have one on my mouth, so I tend to say things as they come to me. This shows me to be my mother's daughter, though my respect for her defiance of conventional society is offset by an equal and opposite force that works in the reverse direction, which is that I honestly often cannot stand her. And one of the reasons I can't stand her is that she's so terrible at doing feminine things, which must be the way boys feel when they notice their fathers have no guy skills, like they've been essentially robbed.

And it's not that my mom isn't maternal—oddly, she is. For instance, she worked in the first integrated cooperative nursery school in the country and was, as she always claimed, very good at it. This was in Berkeley, when Will was in preschool and I was a toddler. People were being told, she said, by the medical establishment that the educated woman, the modern woman, wouldn't want to be *bothered* to breast-feed her baby, as bottle feeding was so much more scientific. My mom didn't *go by that*, as she liked to say, so she nursed all of us defiantly, saying all that was part of the Larger Plot intent upon intruding into all aspects of our private life.

And, of course, telling American women not to nurse *did* turn out to be a marketing scheme designed to sell infant formula to middle-class women, by promulgating the notion that only *the lower classes* fed their babies in that primitive way, as if they were animals on the feedlot.

But it is clear to me that I, like my mother, am coming of age conflicted over what I think of regular, missionary-position, Ozzie-and-Harriet sex—that is, nice-polite-little-white-girl sex, boring sex, which is the only kind of sex that a nice little white girl (which I am currently disguised as) is supposed to be interested in having.

I have boyfriends because—like my mother before me—the having of boyfriends doesn't turn out to be my own special problem, but I've been raised so counter to having respect for Ordinary Sex that while my body participates, my mind seems to dwell in the hiatus in between the twin beds. I'll be doing one thing, which is having okay sex with some okay-at-least-on-paper boy, but I'll be thinking about, for instance, having sex with an entire cadre of Indians as some kind of ritual sacrifice, or having sex with cowboys in the hay barn, and I know this isn't the kind of sex Real Girls are supposed to be having over there in the sector of what I tend to think of as Conventional Society.

Instead of Being Here Now, as the Buddhists say, I'll be the skinny, drugged-up blonde the LAPD will pick up and require to suck one of them off as the other one fucks her in the ass. I'll also be oddly aloof from *all that*, thinking of it as Screenplay or Poem, on which I'll be essentially—even as I am having good-little-white-girl sex—mentally doing an *explication de texte*.

I'll be this girl within a man dressed as a girl, imagining being the woman who's been stopped by the cops in a routine traffic thing and fucked two or three ways from Sunday in a city park in the evening, and these cops would be being really elaborately courteous to me, calling me Mrs. Van de Veer or whatever, and this story, a version of which I read in *Playboy* magazine, is *supposed* to be condemning police brutality—I noticed—but it so very obviously has a completely different intent, which is as pornographic as the movies Mindy's stepfather showed us.

Will says *Playboy* is designed to be read by Episcopal priests so they can get off and still feel good about themselves. This is how this works: You read a story about what assholes the cops secretly are, but what the story is *really* about is the same old thing, which is how to get the guy to come. It is also telling us that the woman, who is helpless because she is handcuffed, is secretly excited, too, so the story that is *supposedly* about being against rape is actually saying something also in favor of it, though anyone who's ever been raped knows that this isn't what rape really is.

I am just starting to suspect, but don't fully know, that this is a plain fact regarding our *imagined* pornographic experience: Most of us do not want the actual *visceral* experience of the things our minds can dream, in that it serves us well enough to allow our minds to make the imaginative leap, which allows our bodies to follow, as if we were, instead of listening to music, in fact singing along.

But I *feel* like my father, feel that this is my own more true experience, that that is *me* getting arrested in the bathroom of the Lighthouse, that I *am* the heroin-addicted lesbian hooker standing on the rainy street corner in Hollywood, that it's *as if* it really happened.

As if? There's nothing about that life that is the slightest bit *as if*.

But I've come of age just being so closely *identified* with sexual misfits, with homos and hookers and fags and mental patients and drug addicts and drunks and poets, of course, and painters, if they are the real things, and just any kind of social misfit, anyone with a sense of Otherness that will keep them out of the D.A.R. or the Holland Society that when I read the words of Allen Ginsberg's *Howl* aloud and he says, I am *with you* in Rockland, I am so totally *identified* with my mother, who is—even as I read those words—very literally locked away on Ward G-1 in Camarillo. Except that I have this essentially middle-class piece of me that worries about essentially middle-class things: that I don't really *want* to have to fuck a bunch of guys who smell bad and don't actually appeal to me, that I don't *want* to go to Ward G-1, where you actually don't get to sit in your private room that's painted in soft pastels and crack up in this genteel manner and sip tea with milk in it and compose broken lines of poetry, and I can't actually paint—as I happen to notice—and my poetry, when I deign to write it, is just so frankly bad.

000

I have no tolerance for alcohol, and there should be no surprise in this, since my family is so completely and diligently alcoholic that we're like certain tribes of American Indians, in that we probably have a genetic pedigree. I get drunk at a carnival and am so instantly messed up and disinhibited that I almost let some boy I've just met fuck me, and from that safe, drunk, porn-star place I often inhabit when it comes to sex, I'm thinking, *Good, at least this'll get rid of my by-now-bothersome virginity*, and the only reason he doesn't fuck me in some bushes is that my body—at fifteen, sixteen—*itself* rejects him; it begins vomiting convulsively, proving that it takes a certain strong constitution to stand on a street corner in Hollywood and get in the car with whomever it is who stops, who is not, as a class of person, going to be Richard Gere and you aren't going to turn out to be Julia Roberts and the entire experience is, very honestly? really brutal and unattractive. It's brutal and I'm a person who is simply too sensitive, many days, to be able to leave the house even to go shopping for fruits and vegetables.

One day a girl I know from my part-time job asks me if I want to double-date with her and go out with these two guys who're a little bit older, who want to take us to this fancy restaurant. I say okay, though I immediately begin mentally equivocating: What does it mean if they take us to this fancy restaurant? That there's a Monetary Transaction involved reminds me of pornography and Reseda, and how we're all in one way or another always going to Reseda to fuck someone whose real name we do not know, and how Mindy continued to get *residuals,* and exactly how messed up *all that* turns out to almost always be.

But I go out with these guys, who're excited because I'm young, and this woman, who's a little bit older and who's named Teri and who comes to work, I've noticed, smelling of sex, doesn't like the way I look when I meet her at the restaurant. I'm in one of my Persons in Black Period, one of those times when I shop only at thrift stores and I buy couture—but from the Olden Days: Chanel, Valentino—and I wear little rosy-tinted sunglasses everywhere I go, inside and out, and strange quasireligious symbols that are charms, in actuality, from a very personal religion. I think I look bitchen, but Teri gives me the once-over, as if to say, *Is* that *the best you could do?*

And these guys, too, who *are* honestly older and who travel for business and are in town as Visiting Firemen, look at me and then at Teri and raise their eyebrows, as if to say, *Where the hell did you get this one, Central Casting?*

And we're drinking our drinks at this Fancy Place, to which I'm supposed to be excited about having been brought *on a date,* but which impresses me about as much as the floor. A date means these guys are paying. It's also what you call your trick when you're a drugged-up lesbian hooker, which—in this particular moment—I feel it'd be way more honest to go and be.

And I'm thinking, *Yeah, they're paying, but* for what, *exactly?* And I happen to know, because I am not stupid, that this fancy meal at this fancy Italian restaurant is going on their expense account, when it suddenly hits me: *Oh, I get it! These guys are married!* Teri goes out with these *married guys* when they come to town, and that's what they are paying for, and it's exactly like my uncle and exactly like whoring, except it goes on their expense account so it costs them personally nothing and so, as women, we are spared the standing-on-the-street-corner-in-the-neon-rain part of this transaction, which is—in fact—the part that appeals to me most, even as their wives, glancing at the credit card bill, are spared the outrage.

We're drinking our drinks and eating the appetizer, which is calamari, when I say, So, you guys are married, huh?

And the three of them look at me like I've issued the kind of string of profanities that used to get my mother slapped back onto Ward G-1 in the state mental hospital: shitfuckfuckingcocksuckingmotherfuckingmotherfucker. And Teri coolly asks, Now, Jane, why would you want to bring that up? And I suddenly remember, too late, that she's technically my boss.

Why? she's wondering. And I honestly would have launched into the whole long story of how my aunt, after all these years of what actually constitutes abuse, has recently told my uncle she wants a divorce, and he doesn't want to divorce her because he wants the Both/And part of being an upper-middle-class White Male—*both* the wife and family and the gag-reflex White Picket Fence, *and* the glamorous mistress on the side. My uncle's is one he's promoted from Las Vegas showgirl, who is what the women in my family disdainfully call "the little blonde cute one," and I'd say all this at this dinner, except I've noticed that my throat has begun to close.

Because I've started being allergic, not just to the more exotic things, like calamari, but, as my allergist has recently told me, to almost everything.

So I say, Sorry, throat's closing, gotta go, and I get up from the table, taking my little jet-beaded bag, which is like something my mother would have carried when she was still going out with my dad to fancy Beverly Hills parties in the 1950s, and I go outside and hail a cab.

Which shows that if I ever do have to start earning my living as a prostitute, I'll starve.

◯◯◯

From the boy at the carnival, I learned that I should never get drunk with anyone unless I'm completely willing to let him fuck me, and eventually I do let boys fuck me. I have lots of friends from school who are guys, and I'm good at being friends with guys—it's from growing up with brothers and boy cousins—but these boys just don't particularly interest me.

So I go to Ozzie-and-Harriet bed with them and they fuck me and I think of other things, which isn't exactly their fault, in that they seem to lose a piece of their bestial edge by being friends of mine.

I only like boys who are kind and intelligent and sensitive, because I myself am kind and intelligent and sensitive, but I meet a boy like this, and he just isn't *interesting* to me in *that way*.

It's that he isn't enough like an animal, I'm guessing, or enough like some porno guy who is cock only, or enough like a faceless-seeming brute of an LAPD Vice–type person who'd brutalize a girl in a breeding crate. I have this memory that may not even be a memory, but it's something I believe I've seen, of going to a party where there were all these hay barns and pig barns, and being at this thing called a kegger, where beer is served in big cups and someone's car radio is playing Jim Morrison's "Light My Fire" and the guys have rigged this barrel on four ropes thrown over the rafters that's got a saddle on it and is positioned in the center of the barn so a girl can ride it. I guess guys are riding it, too, but this doesn't seem to be its point.

The point is that a girl's encouraged to get on this saddle in the center of the room, and to try to hold on while the guys at the corners pull it so the barrel tips and bucks as if it's a horse, and it's to get these girls, who are wearing tight T-shirts, to become more and more helpless and to eventually scream, while there are all these guys in the room who more and more want to fuck them.

The guys I know are nice and would never do this. The boy I'm with in my memory or dream or whatever it is is nice and is uncomfortable with the way the cruelty in the barn is becoming tightened down and concentrated as everyone gets drunker, and he says, Let's get out of here, so we do, but that porn-star, whorish part of me that's completely impervious to risk stays back at the barn and watches as ten or twenty guys fuck the girl they've locked in the breeding crate.

◍

So, noting that I am having this usually-not-hot sex with guys, and missing the piece of childhood that says you aren't supposed to *do* certain things, I guess what my problem is is that I am Other, in that I'm not cut out to be a Practicing Heterosexual.

I have gone to bed with all kinds of boys, but not yet one I'm in love with. I'll traditionally fuck my boyfriend, then his best friend, which often seems the friendly thing to do. I usually do this in a serial fashion; the one time I do it concurrently, I find out the true secret of the threesome, which is that someone is eventually going to feel left out. And these are two young men who aren't yet particularly experienced, so they don't at first get that they're using my body to get at what they're really all about, which is fucking each other, which is what does finally occur to them, which is such a jolt to my vanity that I stay in bed for three days, watching the Miss America pageant and having a nervous breakdown.

So I decide I'm probably gay, which makes sense since I've always had lots of friends who are gay, though this is the 1970s and being out, though not unheard of, isn't altogether common. My mother's theory these days is that everyone's simply acting out what she's always already known: that we're all Other, which she's lately calling Bi-Homo-Momo to let everyone know she has no intention of taking all this seriously at this late date.

I figure being Bi-Homo-Momo probably runs in families at least as much as being a drunk and sort of in-and-out-of-crazy seems to in our family. My mother almost famously says that it's fairly easy to *go* crazy but it's actually difficult to stay that way, and in the twelve years since my father's death, she more or less has cycled through the worst of her craziness and now goes around sounding more sane than *sane*.

Not that she actually approves of much of my behavior, which strikes her—I'm guessing—as not really settled down. She doesn't like me, for instance, going to bed for three days and watching the Miss America pageant after having suffered some boy-related heartbreak, and she doesn't approve of my not washing my hair and my habit of not getting dressed all weekend, lying around reading and writing poetry, which she says is, frankly, not particularly good. She doesn't approve of my taking whites with my brothers and staying up all night talking, or reading *all of* Walt Whitman's *Leaves of Grass* or *all of* Emily Dickinson aloud, or anything I'm doing that has started to seem extreme and probably makes her worry about my turning out to be both creative and chemically sensitive, which my mother, quite frankly, just really wishes

I would not be. My father was like this, suffering as he did from what they call Pathological Enthusiasms.

It's as if she and my father have already suffered enough for those sins, and can't one of the three of us just go to *law school* and earn an honest living? And she'll whip around and stare at me, as if I'm the most likely candidate.

The house my mother and brothers and I are living in is starting to crowd me anyway. We have a dog named Angus, a wire-haired retriever that my mother says reminds her of something covered with pubic hair. And when the guy I'm sort of dating comes to pick me up, Will asks, Hey, Richard! Whatcha got in the bag there, Richard? Will and my mother have a way of making people feel all overawed, usually by the spectacular nature of their verbal pyrotechnics, so Richard stumbles and stutters and says, I went to the fish market and got some prawns so I can make Jane a risotto (and we do have this plan to go to his perfectly respectable apartment, where he's hung Renoir prints, to eat dinner and listen to classical music), and Will says, Well, sheeeee-it, Richard, I was hoping you'd brought us drugs or that that is—at least— a bag full of condoms.

But I don't actually like Richard in that way, nor does he like me, and he basically just wants to talk about his girlfriend, who's gone away to school in Moscow, Idaho, but my brothers and mother have begun to seem like this huge weight around my neck in my process of trying to be the person I'm in the process of becoming, whoever that is, in that I have absolutely no privacy.

So I move out and get this perfect hippie girl's apartment, and I start grad school in literature and continue to have these unsatisfactory relationships with boys and am thinking I'm probably Bi-Homo-Momo, in that I have all these English major–type friends who are gay, in that being gay seems to come so naturally, and all I have to do is tell the story of LAPD Vice and what they did to my dad to have the whole gay world, such as it is, open to me.

And this is a better, happier world in oh so many ways, so alive with humor and solidarity, and people on the outside of the gag-reflex White Picket Fence are simply so much funnier than the normal ones, who view things from that dead center where they try to get in order to be safe, only to then find out they're dying anyway.

I've just started grad school, and of course it isn't in law or medicine or anything useful where I might pay a mortgage or earn a decent living or even meet someone who'd marry me who'd be in law or medicine and earn a decent living. I've turned into the consummate English major, of course, even though this is already an almost perfectly useless degree and I hate poetry that rhymes and the kind of poets—I think of them as *faggoty*—named Byron and Keats and Shelley. I like almost *nothing* English, in fact, past the age of Shakespeare, except Dickens, whom I'm a little ashamed of liking since I can't remember ever reading him and only know the stories from my grandfather's practice of reading Dickens aloud. I like one poet, Gerard Manley Hopkins; four writers who are British, W. Somerset Maugham and Evelyn Waugh (Waugh because he's both witty and nasty); George Orwell, because he's such a good writer; and E. M. Forster, because he's nice.

But I'm enrolled in a preliminary class called Research Methods, which will test us to see if we have what it takes to get a PhD in English, and I'm already deciding I will not ever be able to do this. Research Methods necessitates your learning how to look up shit in the library and take notes on three-by-five-inch cards, which seems to me to have nothing to do with literature. You also have to do this almost impossible research project that has this Catch-22 element, in that you first have to find someone who has enough citations pertaining to him to do a hundred-citation bibliography, but this also has to be someone simultaneously so obscure that no one has yet published this bibliography, which seems to me to have nothing to do with reading.

I hate this class and am about to drop it, but then I find the mad poet John Clare, who teaches me all about what the Enclosure of Public Lands did to ordinary people of Great Britain and confirms what I've always known about the English lords and ladies: that they're a bunch of snobbish shitheels, like my Grandmother Delia, to whom I'm currently not talking for political reasons. I've stopped talking to everyone in my family who's Republican and who supports the Vietnam War, which is trying to take my poor, psychologically maimed brother Geo and make him go fight in it. At first, Geo was addicted only to the small bottles of Coca-Cola, but in no time it became all manner of drugs, also alcohol, also picking up sailors at the pier who paid him money for unspeakable random things.

When they institute the lottery, Geo draws the number three, so my mother, Will, and I hire a lawyer and go to testify before the draft board and file appeal after appeal, saying our dad's dead and our mother's been in a mental institution and he's our little brother and can't they tell just by looking at him that The Military isn't the place this particular boy *really needs to be*?

Meanwhile, I am needing to find all these citations and then write a hundred-page paper not *about* John Clare, exactly, but more about what it's like to *research* John Clare, which is—I'm deciding—exactly what's wrong with sex, in that it's never sex, exactly, that I'm experiencing; it's something that exists more in the vicinity of sex, that somehow *has to do* with intimate relations, but that is weirdly drained of all but the Ozzie-and-Harriet aspects.

And this is in the summer in the evening in an un-air-conditioned classroom at Cal State Long Beach, which I deeply feel is a mediocre public institution that is somehow quite beneath my exalted, though shaky, sense of self-importance, and I'm taking this class only because this boy has fallen in love with me—and *why*, you might ask, since this very obviously is not going to turn out very well, as he is working nights, and part of the reason that he loves me is because he loves my mother and my brothers and is brotherly to me, which I so totally get. So I'm in this class but am not good at it—I've already worked at the phone company in Downtown Los Angeles, which is where I *so got over* being good at alphabetical order—because I see one letter and almost immediately begin to fixate on how to move the *h* so it comes *before* the *g*.

This place is mediocre and our professor sucks so much that his seminar on writing this scholarly bibliography has only seven people in it. The class is so small that I can't even hide in the back and write my wretched poems about being a miserable person who wants, three-fifths of the time, to kill herself.

A friend of mine is also in the class—Roseanne Larissa is someone I know from undergraduate creative-writing classes. She's Italian and is from North Carolina, where I never realized smart and sophisticated people live, as that is not what the Anonymous They would have us believe about the South. Roseanne is very pretty and has long, thick, beautiful brown hair that is naturally straight and big blue eyes and a smile that crooks off to one side. And her parents are both educated, as is said in my oh-so-snobbish family, so she speaks not Oakie or Arkie but in a soft Southern drawl that comes and goes as she wants and that you can sometimes hear only imperceptibly, which makes it all the funnier when she says things that are so right on, which is when you start to get how really, really smart she is.

She said things in the poetry-writing class we took together, in which, almost every day, we had to discuss whether or not Bob Dylan and John Lennon are as great as Shakespeare.

Nah, she said, but Bob Dylan's probably as great as John Lennon, who's probably as great as Dylan, but we are just gonna have to wait and see.

The way Al Jolson didn't turn out to be *actually* as great as Jesus, I said, and Roseanne turned to look at me, and she and I knew *exactly* what the other one was talking about.

She once said, Trying to make a poem with abstract words like *Love* or *Truth* or *Beauty* is like trying to build a sand castle using only water, which *exactly* pointed out what I could never stand about the Romantics.

I dislike these poets so much, I don't even like the term *romantic*, which reminds me of Ozzie-and-Harriet sex and the gag-reflex White Picket Fence aspect of living in what I've lately begun to think of as Amerika.

Roseanne is really, really pretty and she's as loud as I am and her language is as profane, and she confides easily and naturally and talks about exactly the things white girls usually will not speak of, saying, for instance, that honestly, the reason she's just not into having sex with a man isn't that she doesn't like men, but that she doesn't really want to have anything stuck into her vagina, which seems to me to be a pretty good reason to be a lesbian.

Her girlfriend is a type I've heard about but never knew before. Josey's dad was in the Army, and Josey herself stands as straight as if she's always at attention. Josey's obviously like the guy in this relationship and Roseanne's like the girl and, very naturally, Roseanne gets to have nongay girlfriends.

And I am technically so nongay right then that the boy I'm living with is thinking we should get married. I don't want to but don't want to tell him this, as I'm afraid it will hurt his feelings.

But Josey doesn't like me as much as Roseanne does, no doubt, because she's a really serious person and is in graduate school herself, at UCLA, which is no doubt more rigorous than what Roseanne and I are up to, which seems stupid, as if we could do it with our eyes closed if we decided it was worth doing, which it so clearly isn't.

We're always being hilarious and loud, much of which comes from the pressure of trying to behave in Dr. Crawford's seminar, to listen to his completely idiotic droning about what you write on the three-by-five-inch cards. I've already had him for Shakespeare, and he's such a terrible teacher that he almost ruined Shakespeare for me, except I realized I could go sit in a study carrel in the library and play the Nonesuch recordings done by Laurence Olivier and the Redfords, listening on headphones as I read the words on the page, and I could suddenly *hear* the language, as it began to make sense to me.

Speaking of who should and shouldn't be brought up on charges for obscenity: a person like *Dr. Crawford* being allowed to teach *Shakespeare?*

The class is so terrible, it makes me think I will die from it. It is simultaneously hard and boring, which is what I've heard about law school, to which I've actually applied and been accepted, though I don't really want to go.

Because the class is so hard and boring, people drop it continually, so now it's down to only the four of us.

But Roseanne and I still show up. We're both good students, even if people don't instantly recognize this, since we're usually having too much fun. Josey doesn't really approve of fun, in the way certain men don't, the way they'll come along and ask girls to settle down and grow up and get a sour look on our face and unpack the groceries and put them neatly away and have another baby and, by the way, bleed to death—if not literally, then at least psychologically.

Roseanne and I just really like each other. The only things wrong with this are that I'm not gay, and that she and I are both involved with other people.

We like each other so much, which is—I realize—not what I often feel about my girlfriends; honestly, you can't often even get to know someone, so hampered are we by what we are and are not actually allowed to say.

The boy I'm not in love with who works nights is really kind to my mother and brothers, so he seems like the person I probably ought to marry. But I'm smarter than he is, for one thing, or at least I have this protective thing going on with him whereby I don't want to get out and really gallop around in my intellect while I'm with him, so that I don't, as my mother says, make him feel diminished. This is one of the reasons I probably won't go to law school, another being that I don't want to, so here I am, concentrating on Dr. Crawford's Research Methods, but this is also something I have no real interest in doing.

This boy has recently intimated to several friends of ours that he and I are engaged, but I am so uninterested in the relationship that I'm not sure I've heard him correctly.

I'm hanging out with Roseanne so much both before and after class, including when I'm stopping off at my mom's to see Will or her or Geo, because theirs is a really fun place to be as long as you don't have to live there, that my mother distinctly does not approve of Roseanne, or more precisely, of the me-and-Roseanne part of my relationship with Roseanne.

My mom and I have always had these struggles over what I think of as the soul of me: She both does and doesn't want me to live the entirely conventional, settled-down, middle-class life that has always eluded her; she believes that the middle class, being married to what's called a *professional* in my family, is a safe place to stuff your daughter.

But she and I now have enough of a normal mother-daughter relationship that when she wants me to do something (like go to law school), I'm unlikely to do it, and if she doesn't want me to do something (like hang out with Roseanne constantly), I'm likely to do it more.

And I don't actually get it, since Roseanne is like one of the friends I know my mom had in college when she was at Cal and was the editor of *Pelican*, and she went around like she was part of the three musketeers, Becky and Jo and Maggie. Becky and Jo were—in everybody's estimation—Top Girls, so why wouldn't she want the same for me?

But then, I've started to notice my mom being jealous of any woman or girl who's ever shown any interest in me—my aunt, certain teachers, various faculty members—as if my loving another woman can in some way come between the two of us, which strikes me as ridiculous, since I all but channel my mom, since the good and bad of her are all but woven into the warp and woof of me. This channeling is my strength. It is also the reason I cannot stand myself.

It happens because no girls in my family ever have any sisters, so we never learn how to be friends with other girls, or to talk to them or share or be honest, and having no sisters is the reason I'm actually afraid of women and not afraid of men.

Men, as my mom has pointed out, are pretty simple. Usually they just basically want to fuck you, or they both do and don't if they're conflicted, or they totally don't, which is why it's such a relief to be with a guy who's gay.

000

One night in Dr. Crawford's class, Roseanne and I are trying so hard not to laugh at a fly that's droning above his head, a fly that every once in a while lights on the brown saran doll hair of his toupee, that we have to avert our eyes. We start to write notes.

BORED! NEED A DRINK!

NEED TO DRINK HEAVILY RIGHT NOW! MUST BE DRUNK RIGHT NOW OR I WILL KILL MYSELF! WILL KILL SELF IF I DON'T LEAVE AT BREAK AND GO SCORE DRUGS!

ME TOO! I NEED DRUGS TOO!

YOU HOLDING?

NO, YOU?

NO, BUT AM GOING HOME TO GET *IMMEDIATELY* DRUNK. WANNA COME?

And this is a night with a fat full moon that hangs out heavily over the water of the interior channel where I often swim the half mile or so across and back in the moonlight, methodical strokes that are not fast but get me where I'm going, so I swim across in my not-fast-but-serviceable backstroke, then home swimming freestyle, and while I'm in the water I am so completely calm and at peace that I feel I could swim forever because these sturdy, patient strokes of mine are taking me away from here via the river that is never the same river twice.

Roseanne and I come home to where my boyfriend, who wants to marry me and has recently moved in, isn't home and change into our suits—she borrows one from me—and we're shy as we take our jeans off and take our shirts off over our heads. She has a tiny waist and slim, boyish hips, which are a turn-on, but her breasts are large, even pendulous, which isn't actually my thing. She's athletic and I'd expected that she'd not be so big on top, which is stupid—I realize—because I'm comparing her to a boy, which is actually what she is not.

We open a bottle of wine and take it and our wineglasses and our towels down the street to the beach, where we don't actually get in the water, but instead sit on the end of the pier.

I haven't kissed a girl since back in the days of the Dunnigans', when Max was showing us movies and the four or five or us would sit there, owl-eyed and suspended in that twilight before we were what is called at the Health Center *sexually active,* and we were simultaneously turned on, overwhelmed, and disgusted, our bellies roiling with the edge of nausea that feels like desire. It confused us that we'd seen these scenes, acts we did not necessarily approve of—like getting semen shot in your face and pretending to lap it up like you like nothing better than that—but we hadn't looked away. We reacted, but only by making out with one another in the most mild way, unwilling to let the other see any true emotion, as what we were feeling then, and for whom, was just entirely too confusing. Our pants were wet, but we called our kissing and feeling each other up only *practicing.*

And now Roseanne and I are kissing, but she—I realize almost immediately—is much more animatedly into this than I am, which is, frankly, very often my problem. So we kiss, and she and I take the tops of our bathing suits off and sit on the pier in the moonlight, and I feel the weight of her breast but it doesn't excite me, which I'm afraid she's going to be able to tell, but she is talking, saying things I'm worried about her saying, since I am—as Josey imagines—frivolous. She's saying she's thought about the two of us and how we can maybe end up together, and she's saying these words in hot breaths as she's kissing my face and neck and breasts, which I'm thinking about and much too carefully noticing, which is what's always wrong with me: I'm like this observer of my own life, not a legitimate participant.

And now she's telling me heated and confessional stuff about Josey's being jealous of me, and how we can work around that because they aren't necessarily all that exclusive, or maybe I can get to know Josey, too, which I don't actually want to do, in that as much as I admire Josey—who's a little older than we are, also fluent in both French and Spanish—she's too much like all the other scary women I've ever known who'll let you babble on and on but be secretly judging you without their ever telling you what they themselves are thinking, except you do know this: This is one of Our People who is not actually On Our *Side*.

And Josey and Roseanne have these terrible fights over, for instance, who used whose hairbrush, which simply confuses me, because wouldn't one of the reasons you'd want to be with a girl be that you'd share your stuff back and forth? This is exactly the kind of thing I get in trouble for doing in my own relationships, in that I'm always making this kind of mistake, like borrowing something I'm not supposed it, because I can never tell which of the old-fashioned rules to follow and which we're not expected to go by anymore—for instance, fidelity, which I basically don't go by—and with a person like Josey, who is really sort of a bitch, I'd already be in deep, deep trouble.

What I want in a relationship is to not be afraid of this person, which is what Roseanne and I have, but also what I have with the guys I go to bed with. I want to not be afraid, but I also want the thrill of transportation, to be taken somewhere new by a person who feels and thinks and is at least as wild in his or her mind as I am.

And so it's revealed to me that I'm not going to turn out to be a lesbian, at least not right this very instant, and after a while Roseanne knows it too and knows she has to go home to bossy old Josey, who's no fun and who fights with her over who used whose hairbrush and the mundane Ozzy-and-Harriet part of life invades everybody's life, as I'm only now beginning to realize. All of us, no matter how out-there our lives might seem on the outside, have to get up in the morning and make our beds and go about living our day, which was always my aunt's basic point, that sex is just this part of things, not the entirety.

And Roseanne gets it, and it's sad that my being a lesbian or not has so little to do with the love I feel for this girl, my admiration for her beauty and the lilt of her accent and her astonishing intelligence.

As my aunt would say, Life isn't fair.

And Roseanne and I agree we'd have made an amazing couple, better than I do with this boy, whom I do not want to offend, and we're walking home from the beach, still in our suits with our arms wrapped around each other, imagining how great it might have been, when she asks, Am I not worried? And I say, Huh? And she says, About what people will think?

This is still the 1970s—as I seem to have forgotten—so there's still this societal overlay that hasn't been removed, and gay men and lesbians do not yet kiss or hold hands in public, as Vice is still around and Long Beach is a really conservative place, so you're taking certain risks.

That this is your neighborhood, Roseanne says. That they might see us?

I am startled to have been asked the question. This is the deep-down secret of my life: that I don't *live* here any more than I've lived anywhere since the day my father flew off the back of a building and I then, almost immediately, went to live in Other People's houses. Four people—my mother and father, my big brother, my little brother—are the only place I have ever come from and the only real home I have so far known, so caring about what people think in Long Beach, California, in some year in the mid-1970s in the middle of the Vietnam War wouldn't actually *occur* to me.

No, I say, I don't care. I look at the blank rows of houses in which blinds are drawn and the bluish light of TVs enunciates the body count, as the war goes on and on and on. I *can't* care, I tell her.

You know what my father always said? I ask her. The public is an ass.

In truth, he once told me, no one usually even notices what you're doing. And I feel myself, right then, to be almost entirely his daughter, in that I feel impervious to what my mother calls Public Opinion, and if it happens that people fall in love with me, this is their fault and not actually my own special problem.

13

A Pocket History of Sex in the 20th Century

A CHILDHOOD GRIM as Dickens—odd to have lived it in such a naturally beautiful place, those few blocks from the ocean. Years of strife, one tragedy, then another one, then a grief that just settled in, becoming so profound and sedimentary it'd put you in mind of Geologic Time and the epic way in which everyone will ultimately lose everything.

Which reminds me of history, of the boyhood story of a friend of mine, a chieftain's son, and his having to walk out of Namibia as a fifteen-year-old because he had worn either the red tail or the white. And these designations—I could never recall which was which—were no more meaningful than the colors of football teams and were a difference without distinction invented wholesale by the European colonists, all these boys being Bantu and all members of one nation. Yet *the color of his loincloth* was used to determine whether this boy would stay home with his baby brother's beautiful mother—also married to his father— or be force-marched into exile.

Another story of tribalism: how those who own everything encourage us to fight amongst ourselves so we won't notice them perpetually robbing us.

My friend, Bahimwa Kapute, ended up in a Quaker boarding school in Philadelphia, where he learned to dress in a suit and tie and have the most impeccable manners. Thence to San Francisco, where he went to college and lived in a rooming house on Divisadero Street. And he was almost exactly my own age, each of us born at midpoint in the American twentieth century, and I liked him in the way I would always actually prefer the boys I'd never go to bed with.

Nor would Bahimwa have wanted to sleep with me, since he was a shy and stately African and I basically did not attract him. I was just this poor kid with a rich girl's name, living in a cold city yet unable to afford a coat, so I went about buried under layers of boys' cast-off sweaters, a look someone later called "drodgy." I was in grad school, working as a ticket taker, popcorn maker, one-sheet hanger in an art-movie house a couple of blocks off Polk Street where Bahimwa was projectionist.

And I was typically in a relationship with one man yet having an affair with another, going upstairs as the last reel ran to fuck this other projectionist on the stereotypically dirty couch in the owner's office, hurrying to get this pathetic, sordid lovelessness over by the time the dinger began to ding—we'd then dress and lock up, and he'd drive home to his wife and nine-year-old daughter.

The nine-year-old daughter seemed an important detail, since I was beginning to watch the way history did not so much *repeat itself* as *rhyme*, and nine was the exact age I was when my father killed himself: *Ding!*

And Bahimwa—who was an honest innocent—would have been shocked by this behavior. Because he liked me and thought I was a really sweet, smart girl, which I actually deep down was, and a *good person*, as he liked to say. Bahimwa still believed in decorum, in verbal modesty, as did I.

And do.

And anyway, he was much in love with Aretha Franklin, also still very ardently involved in his imagination with the very young mother of one of his littlest brothers back home. He would always become somewhat stiff and formal at this point in the telling of his story, saying, But all this transpires in a very orderly way, as is accustomed by our kinship system.

Unlike the mess you all have here being what Bahimwa was no doubt thinking.

This woman was beautiful and not much older than he. She'd picked Bahimwa as her favorite and cuddled him and once removed a cinder from his stinging eye by opening the lids with her fingertips and swiping his entire eyeball with the softest motion of her tongue.

My God, he said, eyes closed now against the thrill of that particular ecstasy.

There were also two Pakistani men who rotated through as projectionist, and neither of them was interested in me, either, though the younger, smaller one was a flirt and tease who believed I harbored all kinds of wild imaginings about what and who Muslims were and what they would and wouldn't eat—when I actually had never thought much about Muslims one way or another, except to misguidedly imagine it might be Muslims who thought having your picture taken with a camera could steal your soul (or did that actually have more to do with depicting a deity?). The short one told me that both men had written on their resumes (which were virtually identical; honestly, their names may both have been Muhammad, if I'm not merely elaborating) that it was possible for a Pakistani man to work for up to a twenty-eight-hour period without sleep. Though I now wonder if this was yet another of his jokes at my expense, since I did still believe just about anything that was told to me. He may have been saying that the idea of *Muslims* to a person like me was analogous to what Flannery O'Connor in *Wise Blood* called *a trick on niggers*. She actually had one of her characters say this, of course, a character who was describing the historical personage we know as Jesus Christ.

That this devout Roman Catholic would have a redneck, white, protestant lowlife proclaim the Historic Jesus as something invented as *a trick on niggers* was about the most shocking thing I'd ever seen a woman—or anyone—write. But it also seemed so poetically *true* as to sound like something my mother would say, something that would make people snap their heads around to stare at her, wondering if she was going *in* or coming *out* of the door marked PSYCHOSIS, and I've always wanted to have an occasion to quote it without the travail of having to write an entire doctorial dissertation in which to plunk it down, as the phrase does encompass so many intricate levels of blasphemy.

Which is the kind of thing I was always wondering while lying upstairs with the formerly fat, white, married, Midwestern projectionist, whom I never particularly liked. I would wonder how the Pakistanis came up with that particular number, would be guessing that it was never scientifically measured, that it was meant metaphorically to state that a Muslim wasn't a total loser fuckup, like the now only-pudgy white guy. I knew his wife. She and I were both just so much *better* than this man, so much smarter and more attractive.

She had a good job at Blue Cross and was supporting him while he imagined himself a novelist, which wouldn't have been that bad had he been any good. But he read books by Henry James and wrote these labored stories whose one main point was to make nuanced, nasty observations about how acute and far-seeing this narrator, who read Henry James, was—at least in contrast with everyone else who hadn't read Henry James. That this work did manage to sound like some strangled version of Henry James only made it worse.

This ass thinks you need to write like Henry James from way out here? I thought. From the wrong side of the country and the *wrong end* of the twentieth century? It was such honestly awful writing that, after reading only the first few pages, I knew I needed to break up with him. I'd anyway only fucked him because he imagined himself a writer and held himself in high esteem.

But he was a pig, I saw, a commoner, while I felt myself to be more the princess of a displaced people, like Bahimwa's. My childhood felt analogous to Bahimwa's, huge in dislocation and events. In these cinematic tales of tragedy and heroism, it's always up to the children to go forth, to somehow walk out through the scorched earth that is a childhood without a childhood.

∞

Because I was a girl, I knew I needed to carry my body carefully. I felt precariously balanced, walking lightly across a strange landscape that might be like *a minefield*, but I don't much like putting it that way, since I am not Princess Di and have no actually living experience of *a minefield*, so I call Will. He was a soldier in South Korea, where the whores of Seoul would abuse him by spitting on him if he passed them by, not persuaded enough by their allure. He'd walk by, not interested, so they'd call him Number Ten G.I., a Ten being the worst thing a person could possibly be.

I'm wondering if my brother might have walked point in the U.S. Army.

Was our childhood, I ask him, pocked with misery as a minefield, or more dark and cartoonish? More the graphic novel with that wide-eyed wop, remember him? That little Italian orphan kid they called Dondi?

Nah, my brother says. Maybe it's just my mania, but I remember large parts being delightful.

That's because you're more like Mom and the two of you were delightful, I say. For one thing, you could talk. For another, you weren't suicidal.

Right, Will says, if that works for you. This is what Will always says when he's on the phone with me while simultaneously IMing or participating in some online chat-room situation.

So I back up, restate, because I'm honestly interested.

Were you suicidal? I ask.

I was suicidal once, my brother says, popping back into focus. It was the second or third time I'd started my PhD, he says, and I was still married to Michelle. Lilah had just been born when I started sleeping with always just *the least likely* person in my program. Once, it was this hundred-pound former gymnast named Bonnie, who was really chalk to my cheese, and she dumped me. And I immediately started drinking again, as I always would when I was washing out of this or that PhD program by sleeping with another of these really unlikely women. This was at Irvine. I figured I'd show her by going to the bell tower and throwing myself off. I was drunk, of course, but not so drunk that it didn't occur to me that killing myself over some hundred-pound former gymnast, who was, by the way, inane, was a really stupid thing to do.

I, too, have almost never been suicidal; it feels like an indulgence. I believe myself instead to be this precariously balanced mobile, a gizmo of Alexander Calder–like self-invention. Bright metal, wires, and springs that don't really go together, and huge pieces, of course, that are very literally missing, but I have walked out carefully, as Bahimwa walked out of Namibia, because walking out is the only thing—aside from lying on the trail to die—you are allowed to do.

Wherever I go, I still feel hounded and pestered by the clattering footsteps of all the sundry members of my dead and still living family, this entire *population* that is always popping up inappropriately out of a Stephen King–esque graveyard of creepy, cartoonish ghoulishness. They are *loud* and extreme, and seem to exist in caricature, being expelled from an overstuffed VW or crawling out of a Sgt. Pepper–like hole in the floor or dropping from the attic, like Gregor Samsa cockroaches in clown shoes.

And they are often brilliant mimics, these Westerners, these round-the-campfire storytellers, so I feel taunted and mocked if I ever think I *might* get away from them—also for my slight belief in my own small sad joy, a tiny faith in my own delightedness, about the notion that even one of us could imagine one day getting on a plane and flying off to land someplace that isn't just still more and more *California*. I keep it hidden in one hand that I shove deep into a pocket, a hope as bright as the light of Tinkerbell.

Because we've been here so long, our family has become ingrained and turned into really bizarre creatures of this place, wizened by the bright aridity that doesn't go with our skin tone. Our skin is quite wrong for this place of light and space, and hope is no longer the doctrine to which our family subscribes. And we are so totally representative of the dominant ethnic grouping, so typical, too, of our kinship system, these tall, fair-skinned northern European types, deeply depressive, defeated, all completely alcoholic.

So I don't drink and I do not take drugs, though everyone I know is suddenly washing down handfuls of all manner of substances and shooting shit into their arms and sticking it up their noses with what seems like reckless abandon.

Hey, I think, *you behave like that, and something really bad might happen to you . . .*

Anyway, I am already completely addicted to heroin and cocaine without ever having to try them. I've been emancipated from all family support and own only a single pair of shoes that are shaped like hamburgers, shoes that the man who called me *drodgy* refers to as my Little Man Shoes, and am anyway already so addicted particularly to cocaine that I feel entirely *at one* with it, as if there is no difference at all between my own substance and my abuse of this substance.

I am nothing aside from my addiction, except that I can't afford it.

And while I've slept with plenty of boys, a few men, and a couple of girls—but never a grown-up woman—and am actually not all that prudish, I don't want my addiction to some drug to be the sole determinant of whom I let fuck me.

Alcohol is at least legal, but I just can't drink. One of my more recent doctors, who's actually the nephew of John O'Hara (yet another hopelessly alcoholic American novelist) and is named for him, calls this condition being *clinically sensitive.*

I just can't do what these other people are all doing—if I did, I would lose my mind.

If I drink, I lose all sense of the world's verticality, my brain goes reptilian, and I am instantly lost from linear time. I once drank wine while trying to follow a recipe on the lasagna box. I was having an English professor over, a woman my mother jealously called Mrs. Poetry. Her name was actually Professor Dora Polk, PhD, and she was from England and was a Fabian socialist—she gave me Waterford crystal one of the several times I was either briefly married or engaged, or on some analogous occasion. Dr. Polk, oddly, believed in me—I had some kind of hokey-though-paid TA-ship under her, whereby I had no responsibilities aside from my own writing, then going by one department of Our Institution of Higher Learning every month to pick up a check from a certain window.

I'd invited Dr. Polk to dinner at my neat hippie girl's apartment as a thank-you, and it is completely typical of the abject nature of my really quite riddled self-esteem—I think of it as the part of the Calder that is the formerly beautiful copperish sheath that's now shaggy with bullet holes—that it truly astonishes me that I can still reach back through the dark halls of time and hear this woman, whom I admired, whispering her few curt British words of encouragement.

I saw how drinking immediately ripped through the metal of the Calder I'd been balancing so carefully, how it sapped me of strength and even the most basic kind of reason, made me now *completely nihilistic*, and how this happened *absolutely instantly*, so one moment I'd be this sweet, smart, well-compensated girl cooking in her neat hippie-ish kitchen, and the next I'd be noticing how little the order in which adding the fucking ingredients actually mattered to the Act of Committing Lasagna, lasagna being another of the huge raft of items that simply do not in any way existentially matter, as my mother would say, not even the *tiniest fucking bit*.

So I am both from here and from elsewhere, both the red tail and the white, and always oddly new to my most recent place of exile. My brothers and I arrived on a refugee ship filled with such real and cartoon orphans as Bahimwa and Dondi, which is strange because this is actually the same place we've always been, except that now the rules are changing. This is California, where the rules are always changing, the manners and mores morphing, so you never know what is right or wrong—just that it's different from what it was just yesterday. It is *crazy!* which might be bad or good. Someone is hung up, uptight, straight; one day that's a compliment, the next it's an accusation.

For a while it is all New Games, in which aggressive energy is pushed down and subverted, when someone will put a huge, heavy rock in front of the bathroom door, holding this door open. The bathroom is right off the main room where the party is going on, so the New Gamers can watch you run the humiliating video behind your eyes as you're trying to figure out how much you really need to pee, and whether moving the rock is even possible, or if maybe it isn't time to leave this party, to go home and find some new friends, some friends you actually like?

And the words for things are changing, so you never know what the more accurate thing to say is. What something is called is always different from what it formerly was. Sex isn't *making love*, but is it really *fucking*? Isn't it more *having intimate relations*? Were these relations even *intimate*? Here, as in other important arenas, I always feel like someone struggling to learn the language.

And we are suddenly nonviolent and we are vegetarian and we are reading Gandhi and thinking hard about not wearing leather shoes, though we go ahead and do it, and our not being meat eaters has to do with the bloodlessness of sex, which, while friendly enough, is also actually passionless and perfunctory.

So I am trying to learn to live by the laws and rules of the new Western world, and these have everything to do with Time Consciousness and successfully completed goals and monetary success and high status and achievement.

I know only that it is important to try to follow instructions, and that two of our most basic instructions are You Share Rides and You Do Not Take Intoxicants, though sex is one intoxicant still being pretty freely shared. It simply seems to suit me to work in close tutorial in the new guidelines, so I seek out tutors and often sleep with them, and I fall in love easily and well with all of my friends, and these friends are often boys, even as I am also sleeping with a man like the projectionist, whom I do not much like, though sleeping is, of course, not what is ever going on.

I once notice a body like his in the San Francisco MOMA, when the museum is still on the second floor of the Herbst Theatre, down the street from city hall. It is a small bronze, a squat, thick-thighed sculpture Matisse did in 1900, called *Le Serf*. The figure is armless and seems almost animal—penis and ball sack full, belly sticking out, bottom lip drooping. The man seems as elemental as one of the hundred Russian words for dirt, a heavy-bodied thing that looks like it was dug from and is returning to the earth.

I am young, so I tell myself, *This is what a man must be.*

And I understand our *kinship*: that he is alcoholic, *of course*, and therefore afflicted by gravity, as is everyone in my family. And since he's read books I haven't read, I believe he has something to teach me.

It's so easy to notice, in the Inevitability of Retrospect, how like the casino girl Susan Sarandon played in *Atlantic City* I am, the one who washes her hands and arms with lemons to take away the smell of the oysters she's shucked, how yearningly she asks the elegant old man she's just about to go to bed with if he will teach her things.

And I am someone so completely and even naturally alcoholic that a single beer or a glass of wine lights me up internally like a jar of shook moonshine, a substance I tasted once in the moonlit night of a Tennessee parking lot out behind a printing plant. *This is the Deep South*, I was busy telling myself, *and this is the wine of their communion.* The pure grain alcohol shimmers in that eerie light—hence its name—and drips viscously from within the lid as something so colorless and lethal, it might remind you of gasoline.

I ended up making out with some other traveler in the backseat of someone's car, no doubt utterly humiliating myself. But I didn't go to bed with this person that time, didn't get pregnant, didn't get venereal disease, as I was being careful with this vessel that was my girl's physical body, knowing it had a particular destiny. And we, the Big City guests, were such completely foolish assholes as to be in Tennessee touring this printing plant with locals who were *so clearly entertaining themselves* by winding each of us up and turning us loose upon ourselves. They knew we thought they were hicks, so they were acting exactly like the stage rednecks we needed to speak slowly and carefully to.

Tribalism. And just one more case of Us Versus Them, and of the Dominant Culture's (of which I was still obliquely representative) hanging onto the belief that it was *winning*, that it would *always win* when up against Our Inferiors, which meant anyone marginalized, anyone poor or dispossessed or rural, Bantu or Pakistani.

Or female.

෨෨෨

I'll make out with some publishing boy but am meanwhile honestly only into Mrs. Poetry and her ilk, my wont being to fall almost instantly in love with any of the better-looking senior faculty, any man or woman who might be able to teach me even a single thing: that, for instance, the comma goes inside the quotation marks. And this person, who might or might not be married, is always completely inappropriate, given the terrible discrepancies in power and proximity-to-power between the two of us and the very obvious vibe of my status as a waif, my Little Man Shoes, my no coat, my no parents.

I love the kind of English professor who is, of course, married, but this is the part of the seventies in which the sixties are still alive and we aren't yet all hung back up and we still share rides, still occasionally hitchhike or live communally, as these activities make us feel young, free, and European. So we might still fraternize across the class/caste discrepancies, and some great-looking professor will come sit on the grass of the quad with what Will always refers to as A Group of Us.

And it is always A Group of Us, as these are deeply communal times, which are actually wrong for me, since I hate being in any group for longer than a minute or two, as I have the most intense need to pay way too much attention to every detail of every single individual.

So I'm able to fake Group Think for only a little while, whispering to ask which page we are on in the Big Book, only to have some tiny sparkling prism thing in my Calder start communicating with me by wireless from high in the armature, issuing an SOS of warning.

Fuck the lasagna, it says. We need to get out of here and go drink Antisocially.

I am porous, clinically sensitive, and the stress of anyone's special needs makes me marginally psychotic. I am balanced pieces that move in the wind and have no proper spatial boundaries. I am a chameleon and the elements are reflective; they mirror the surroundings, enabling me to disappear so completely that *any* group becomes yet another place where I can lose my mind.

And what other people are doing during This Time Period is being really sure of themselves. They admire psychosis, which does seem a fairly rational reaction to the United States of America's current government, which seems to have traduced us into an endless war and are yet again unwilling to enforce anyone's civil rights, aside from the tall white men of northern European extraction that my own family is so good at producing.

The Dutch are some of the tallest people on the earth, on average, reasons for this being usually ascribed to a combination of national wealth, nutritional habits, quality of healthcare, and genetics. The Dutch are admirable in all ways. The Dutch can also, as was always said in my family, drink *like fishes*.

I could never fall in as one of these fellow travelers of psychosis, as there is almost nothing about actual insanity—with which I have more than a slight familial acquaintance—that I find in any way attractive.

So I am always carefully rationing my impulses, which are a girl's and therefore ardent, but which feel shameful to the degree that I am led around by them, even though, in retrospect, they are completely innocent and age appropriate. One day A Group of Us are lying on the sun in the grass while discussing Saul Bellow's *Mr. Sammler's Planet* and I'm noticing the sunbaked look of the side of this particular professor's very tanned and sturdy neck. He is lying on his side, chin in hand, head propped on his elbow, and I understand how easy it would be to scoot just a little ways this way so my girl's body lay parallel to his, and for me to pull his weight, which I knew to be willing, down onto me.

He is married, of course, but he has paid particularly kind attention to me and let me know I am somehow curious to him: He has noticed, perhaps, my spinnaker at full sail or the glints off the polished, high-up, clanging riggings, or has seen or sensed all those particular gaps and lacks and emptinesses that always make a well-meaning, slightly parental person such as my professor want to offer me sympathy and solace, which are of almost no possible use to me.

He asks which character I identify with in Bellow's novel, meaning am I reading along with the story of the old man behind his eyes—the old man is intelligent and crabby and in every way a perfect crustily misogynistic, Chicago Jewish, Bellow-ish character—or am I more in league with the slightly distasteful hippie girl to whom Sammler (or, more likely, Bellow) finds himself uncomfortably attracted?

Mr. Sammler, of course, I say, but am shocked by the question. I add, He's the protagonist—it's so totally *his planet*.

Did my professor ask me this because he took me for some vacant hippie chick who doesn't wash her underpants? My current version of myself is that I am more like a girl Will Shakespeare. I think Shakespeare would have totally *got me* and my drodgy getup, which is why it seems that he speaks directly *to me* across the ages, it being Shakespeare who teaches us you don't have to *be* a blackamoor to *be* Othello.

My great-looking professor invites us to his house and we meet his wife, named Nona, and they are very happily married, so I don't lie back on the grass and ask him to put his weight on me, which I sometimes do, often with some usually pretty random and unlikely man whom I actually have not even the slightest intention of honestly fucking.

I want to feel the weight of an actual man, though I am probably not yet old enough to deal with the gravity of what that might mean. It's a conceit of girls and women that we can somehow *handle* a man by keeping our most true self hidden from him. We speak from this hidden place in order to control him, thinking we can either reason with him or beguile him. They are not the same as we are, my mother said. We think our being attractive to these men makes them stupider than we are, which makes us feel omnipotent. It's this dangerous arrogance that can get us into trouble.

What a less Calder-like and better-integrated girl might have done is more likely fall in love with the slender boy who'd then thicken alongside of her, so she'd end up at an older age lying with the person who goes with her.

And I am anyway outgrowing boys, and I am so honestly sick of the cult of California. I want someone East of Here—someone less sunny, more doomed? I want someone who went to a decent college or university, as everyone in my family has all down the line, until we got to my own particularly, urchinish generation.

I am being very patchily educated, since I am doing it myself and am barely competent. I wasn't an early reader—more an early watcher, an eavesdropper, the habitual overhearer. I wasn't even a reader of books;

I was more the reader of the titles of things, the spines on my parents' bookshelves, for instance, where I'd spell out *The Gathering Storm* and *Look Homeward, Angel.*

And I am beginning to understand that these words are only dust, pinpricks of ancient light on the most all-encompassing star chart; that the title of every book is only a single atomic particle in the whole huge and cosmic swirl that is all written human history, and that is as universal and ongoing as one vastly expanding pearl.

ᴔᴔᴔ

When I leave college, my professor with the beautiful neck says to me, You won't just get married, Jane, and vanish down the rabbit hole? You'll let us hear from you?

Hear from me? I think. *I am still just this hidden girl who has nothing original to say, and he is asking me to become the hero of my own story?*

He is asking me to go and *do something,* but in order to do this I'd have to stop letting my life be all about my parents, which is anyway an impossible assignment.

I'd have to stop being a girl, which is all I've ever been; I'd have to set out alone on a galactic journey that would separate me from everyone. Become that singular event that results when a bit of dust caroms across the night sky, he is saying to this person who feels as weightless as an electron. He is asking me to become the grain of sand inside the shell of the oyster that will allow experience to adhere to me.

Which is a terrible assignment for me, as I feel I've *already* been sentenced to a lifetime of loneliness. I'd need to become the subject of the sentence, rather than its direct object, and I'd need to abandon the only identity I've ever known: In the case of orphans, as it is with girls, it is our lack that most easily defines us.

In order to become the hero of my own story, I feel, I need to find a better-muscled and more self-confident vocabulary, need to dress like a different person, buy some shoes, a couple of good outfits. I need to break up with the projectionist, who is bad not only for my soul but for every other part of me as well.

Who, when I tell him, thinks it is for all the societal reasons: that I want to now go off and find some suitable person who is actually better than he is, someone who has a good job, a nice car, some view of a reasonable future.

From high up in the armature, I watch and I decide I'll let him think this. I believe it is a kindness not to say what I really think, which is that I simply can't continue to have sex with a man whose writing sucks as bad as his.

He is so furious that he throws his big bunch of keys down onto the hood of his own car. They scratch the paint, bounce over the front of the car, then clatter down a storm drain.

Fuck! he yells. Now see what you made me do!

This is in the alley across from the theater's entry. That night it is crowded with moviegoers and bar patrons who catch my eye in passing, all of us thinking, What an *alcoholic* way to act.

⦿

Will and I are each working our own way through school, and it is still possible for a girl as poor as I am to live alone in an amazing apartment. A studio in my building in Hayes Valley rents for $75 a month. Mine is one huge unfurnished room with a great view and a walk-in closet so large I even consider—since I have so few clothes—putting my bed in there.

This is on Market at Hermann, a couple of blocks from the San Francisco Zen Center. My seventh-floor windows sit in a bay that looks

out over the streetcar tracks. A couple of miles away, beer is being perpetually poured into a frothing glass on top of a building at the foot of Potrero
Hill. Ribbons of pale yellow and gold and white are formed into streams
of liquid and bubbles by thousands of small, blinking incandescent bulbs.
It is the sign on the roof of the Hamm's Building at Second and Howard.

My building has an elevator and is well maintained: 1930s art
nouveau, all black-and-white tiles and polished brass detailing. It has a
grand foyer with a locked front door and someone always at the desk.
It's full of gay guys, some very newly, very raucously OUT. AIDS is
already happening, but no one knows this yet, so boys and young men
and older men are all still frolicking in the bathhouses. This is pre–
Harvey Milk, a really sweet guy with a bitchy boyfriend, who's not yet
been elected to anything and still just has the camera shop.

There is militancy about the gay men in the Castro and in my building, a new tribalism, I think, that has them dressing amazingly alike—it
is the peacoat time, the era of the Greek fisherman's cap.

For the first time I hear someone refer to heterosexuals—or it may
be all women—as *breeders*. I am a breeder, I think, have always been a
breeder, which is why, as I was surviving my own childhood, I needed
to guard my body.

Breeder. The word is repulsive.

I get a new job, a day job, so I don't have to get to and from work at
night using public transportation. I needed to leave the theater because
I was robbed in the ticket booth. One night after the first show started,
a guy who'd hidden in the bathroom followed me into my little cubicle.
He said he had a gun, but I didn't for a second believe him.

He didn't really much scare me. He was a tiny white dude, actually
diminutive, and his head was shaved in the manner of Synanon.

Sorry, man, he told me, even as the robbery was going on, but I'm a
junkie, you know? To which I said, Sure, sure, I completely get it. I was

busy emptying the till into the paper bag he was holding out to me. This robber was so small he looked like a little boy on Halloween, trick-or-treating for candy.

My new day job is right down the street at Ninth and Market—it is even at a company that sort of pertains to me. I am answering phones at Scrimshaw Press, which has a best-selling picture book called *Handmade Houses*.

This feels like the end of my hippie days, the first moments of my attaining purchase in the Middle Classes. I am so busy leaving poverty and risk behind, moving my body on toward its next adventure in—I hope—much more prosperous surroundings and a better wardrobe, that I am honestly surprised to let myself into my locked apartment after work one evening and find the dumped projectionist.

Oh, fuck, I think. My heart contracts. The door, which is heavy because this is an old-fashioned building, just then closes behind me.

He is sitting on my couch. On the little table in front of him are a bottle and a glass. He's been drinking in the dark, as this sort of self-pitying person always likes to do—my glass, my ice, his whiskey.

Hey, I say. Fancy finding you here . . . ?

My voice is fake, flat, nonchalant. I need to hide from both of us the enormity of what he's done: This man has *broken into my apartment*. Sane people don't act like this. I need to pretend he is a different kind of person, a more well-balanced one. I need him not to know I am physically afraid of him.

You didn't return my phone calls, he said.

Sorry, I say. Meant to. Don't really know how to work that thing.

I gesture at the big answering machine next to my phone on my desk in the bay window. These home telephone-recording devices are new, but I've used one before, when I made the message that told the start times of the movies at the theater. I would then call myself from home to find out when I needed to go to work, would hear my own soft voice so earnestly saying the times, saying the titles of films—*lays ON-fawn d' pair-a-dee*—as a phrase of music, as sounds learned, to disguise the fact that I don't know languages.

I honestly meant to, I tell him; then I say his name, say it carefully, as if I am talking to an animal.

How did you get in? I ask him.

Some faggot in a Greek fisherman's cap, he says.

Oh, that would *vastly* narrow the field, I think but don't say.

What I say is: No, not in the building; I meant—and I only mouth the words—how did you get *in here*? and I point at the floor.

Used this, he says, and he shows me a credit card, which can be stuck into a doorjamb beside the lock and slid along to work the sloping edge of the bolt back into its chamber. This works only in older buildings like mine, whose doorknobs and locks were manufactured in other, more innocent times.

And you're here because . . . ?

Because I need to confront you about some of the things you said, he tells me. Some things said, others left unsaid.

Right, I say. *Confront me?* I think. *Said and unsaid?* I am just some grad student who sold tickets where he works with whom he had a dalliance.

Still sitting on the couch, he hunches forward to tip the bottle, which is empty, over the glass, which—except for the ice—is also empty.

I advance a few steps into the room, my bag still slung over my shoulder, still holding my mail in my hand. I am terrified of him but need for him not to know this. I need him to think this could still be resolved without consequence, that no one has to be angry, that no part of this is hopeless.

I, as usual, play both parts: I am myself being robbed, even as I am simultaneously the Synanon junkie who is robbing me—a form of mind meld known as *painful empathy*. I became good at it by growing up in a crazy family.

Because I've just moved in and have been fixing things—painting and hanging pictures—my tools are out, lying along the top of a bookcase above which I've hung a print of Mark Rothko's *Black Over Red*, which I had framed. The three-shelf bookcase is waist-high and still empty—I have painted it the exact red that's in the Rothko.

I arranged these two objects—the framed print and the red bookcase—to look like two spatial pieces that match or rhyme. I like that kind of thing, a visual joke or resonance, with the one object being mundane and the other transcendent, the one standing out, planted in a physical room, the other falling back and away into timelessness.

My tools—including a hammer and nails and the fasteners for picture hanging—lie atop the bookshelf. These are close enough to the projectionist that if he turns only slightly, his eyes will fall on the hammer and screwdriver. I worry that if he sees the tools lying like weapons in a story, it might occur to him to use them.

I am still naïve, a vegetarian, and I thought we'd evolved to a moment in our species' history that says war is pointless, that violence between a man and a woman isn't necessary. We can have sex *as equals*, a girl can think, can talk to one another *as equals*, so I am in shock that someone could break into my apartment and sit here exuding a threat to me.

As bad as anyone in my own family ever acted, we didn't do *this* kind of thing. I keep thinking it isn't even possible for me to know a man like this. He's educated, even if he—okay—only went to the same kinds of shitty public universities I myself attended. I can't believe that a man would become so desperate that he'd resort to violence.

Really? I keep thinking. *People actually behave like this?*

My childhood hasn't actually prepared me for further disasters and has not taught me you are in fact powerless over people, places, the current of the river, the large events of history. Rather, I imagine I can, by way of my total understanding, control not only that robber but also this projectionist. I still imagine myself as someone so far-seeing that I am like a character in James, controlling everyone with my acuity.

But he is drunk, labile, seething, and his anger is far past rationality. The light from the streetlamps plays upon his facial planes, hardened, masklike, the skin around his mouth pale, the pupils of his eyes so hugely dilated they look concave. It is rage that blinds someone, makes his eyes go as dead as that.

And I know this look. It means this person who has loved me in the past can no longer see me when he looks at me, and has now locked on to something in the shadows behind me, so he's looking past me to his own more base and elemental lack.

Lack, cast large, is projection.

You're a nothing, he tells me.

I shrug, bite my lip. He can go ahead and think that if he needs to.

She kicked me out, he says. We're in a trial separation.

Jeeez, I say. Well, that's too bad.

She knows, he says. I told her.

Told her?

About us.

And I think, But there *is* no us! It is his inability to use the proper pronoun and the proper tense that makes me really begin to worry about his sanity.

Hey! I say, suddenly energetic. Not to change the subject, and we will talk about all this, but would you like something to eat? I'm starving, and you look like you could maybe eat something. We for sure need to talk about all this, but let's eat something first. And my brother's in town—you remember I mentioned him? The older one who's in the PhD program in sociology at the University of Texas? He just flew in from Austin and he's coming over in a little while; let's just give him a call at his hotel . . . ?

My brother isn't really in town, of course, but I suddenly need to hold the heavy black earpiece of the Bakelite phone in my hand, to enjoy the weight of it. I take a step toward my desk, where the phone sits, and my hand reaches out, but before it makes contact the projectionist comes at me.

He doesn't actually hit me, more wrestles me across the room, and there is, as there always is, a discrepancy between people whose body masses are not balanced and whose levels of rage and desperation are not matched, one also lacking the other's upper body strength.

Girls and women can't be expected to fight these fights, because we so rarely can win them. Being a sister among brothers and boy cousins taught me this. Female athletes respect this: We can swim our fastest and not ever beat the faster man.

He shoves me back onto my bed, holds my upper arms so tightly they'll be visibly bruised. I am astonished. No one has ever treated me like this.

He knocks me back, falls on top of me, holds me there with the power of his insistence. Pushes our clothes out of the way. It happens. It continues happening.

When he is done, he collapses and weeps on top of me. Like the junkie, he is instantly sorry for what he's done.

Men? my mother used to say in her fake French accent. They are such *BAY-bees*.

We are each only partly undressed. He is still lying atop my body, weeping for himself, weeping over his disappointment in himself, over his maybe ruined marriage, but mostly for the generally shitty way his life is turning out.

I am thinking about his nine-year-old, what a father would feel knowing someone has treated his daughter like this, if his girl or I ever had one.

Light falls through the three tall windows beyond my desk that look out over Market Street, where far below the streetcars are still running. The only light in the apartment remains the one I flipped on in the entryway. I am breathing carefully, am staring at the Rothko, in which the image of one swath of color floats above another. I use it to calm myself. I've already joined the only church I'll ever belong to, which is art, which has the power to redeem us from the complete chaos of our confused and sordid lives. I'd heard that red was called a fugitive pigment for the way light tends to fade it. I want to not turn out to be fugitive pigment.

The surface of the framed print catches the light from the window. In the reflection, the sign on the Hamm's Building keeps pouring beer endlessly.

My head is turned. I keep my eyes fixed on the Rothko. I don't look at the hammer that is lying right beneath it. It is my hammer, so I know exactly what its weight feels like in my hand.

I am perfectly prepared to kill him.

The projectionist falls into a deep sleep, breathing noisily. He is still lying half on top of me. He is a big man, tall and overweight, and I am afraid to move because I think it might awaken him. On the nightstand there stands the kind of illuminated clock that isn't actually digital but works mechanically. Time is spelled out on thin, yellow plastic flaps that flip over in columns that hang on a horizontal axis, the numbers printed in black Helvetica. A card flips every minute, then every ten, then—on the other side of the dot-dot that makes the colon—every hour. Time is the river into which you cannot step twice. The flaps flipping over and hitting the ones they are replacing make a small, satisfying smack.

Time passes as it always passes, a lesson I learned in childhood.

It is ten, then eleven, then twelve. The streetcars stop. He wakes. He's sobered up enough to look around anxiously for the authority who'd confirm he is in trouble.

He lied earlier, he confesses. He didn't actually tell his wife about us, because he didn't want to hurt her.

Anger sizzles along the surface of my skin like it is giving off electricity.

That's nice, I say.

When he leaves, I call Will in Texas and tell him what happened.

Jesus, shit! he says. Where do they even *get* these people? What's his name?

Henry James, I say. Number Ten G.I.

Name and phone number, Will says. I need to call Mr. Henry James and read him the riot act. Someone *will be speaking* with Mr. James. This *will be happening* first thing in the morning, when Number Ten G.I. is still suffering from the whiskey flu.

This manner of speaking in the future progressive is a technique my brother has perfected working his way through college as a psych tech—you calm a mental patient by convincing him you have complete control of the narrative. A crazy person has no use for options and can be settled down by hearing what's what and what is going to be definitively happening. The future is not the process for the crazy person, as it remains for the rest of us. Rather, it's this tableau that is already fixed.

Either you'll be doing this for me *now*, as my brother would instruct the mental patient, or you will be doing it for me in a little while.

I tell my brother his name, say we can't call the police, that I've already done enough to mess up the lives of the projectionist's wife and daughter, who now have to continue to put up with him.

Later that day, Will phones me back. Jesus, what an asshole. You gotta promise you're gonna do better next time.

Couldn't probably do much worse.

You didn't see that coming?

No idea. I just didn't believe anyone would actually act like that, at least not someone so pretentious and Jamesian and *antique*. What'd you say to him?

Told him who I was, that I knew what he'd done and where he lives, works, where his wife works, where his kid goes to school. Told him I have a shotgun. Said I have a shotgun, described my shotgun, said I'd trained in the Army as a marksman, that I'd already killed someone, which isn't actually true, but he doesn't need to know that.

Said it'd disturb me *not at all* to have to kill again, my brother says.

So Mr. Henry James puffs up and says I can't threaten him. I said, *Wellllll*, actually, I obviously *caaaannnn* threaten you because I *aaaammmm* threatening you. Said I'd kill him if he ever so much as spoke to my sister again, said I am, and I quote, *A very angry person*, that this derives from our shitty childhood, so forth. Said killing him would actually give me a great deal of pleasure. Told him I participate in a voucher program with a certain airline, that I have tons of these $25 vouchers that I've saved for free flights, that I'd be more than happy to redeem all of them to come out there and shoot him, that it'd cost me nothing more than the cost of a cab from the airport. I told him his address—I talked the operator into giving it to me; she used the reverse directory. Told him I could read a map, that I was looking at his cross street, right there a couple blocks off the park in the Richmond district. Told him it would take me seven hours to get there.

Before was when a girl might still hitchhike, might stand on a street corner with her friends, wearing miniskirts or hiphuggers, faces hidden behind long cascades of hair, eyes shy but hips tipped forward into the future, where, they sense, they will be using their bodies to bring them toward infinite possibility.

Before was when we were still young and hadn't coalesced, were still simply pieces of who we'd turn out to be. We believed we were weightless, had almost no idea of the power our bodies had, and so would still have sex for the most slight and silly reasons, not in the name of love but out of these *ideas* we came up with, from a certain political stance that said a girl got to do what a boy might do. Or we'd screw, say, out of friendliness or a philosophical commitment to international brotherhood or some hyperarticulated bullshit for the sake, say, of gender equality.

Manners and mores still exist in the *before* as cultural artifacts of a girlhood like mine, a time when my brother could still go to the airport and board a plane to fly west from Texas while carrying a loaded shotgun, when a girl didn't have the experience to know that *sex* and *violence* might mean SEX AND VIOLENCE!

That was *before*, which was a more innocent time.

14

Take Me With You

CAROLE AND I ARE sitting in front of a fire in the wood-burning stove in the main room of her house, wrapping gifts for Our People, which is what my mother called girls and women. These are the beautiful things Carole has owned that she now needs to give away. Before we wrap each gift we discuss who it ought to belong to, as if there's an element of spiritual ownership that pre-exists in these items, things she's made and artifacts of her travels and friendships.

She is giving my daughter a dried rose, for instance, brought by a friend of Carole's from Paris, this flower preserved by some miraculous French process. Something Americans will never master, she says, and I agree, Americans don't care enough about beauty to have made a cult of it, like the French have, with all their *produits chemiques*. There's probably something wrong with it, she says. Probably nuclear, I agree, they're so *into* nuclear. The Japanese, too, she adds, they're nothing if not part of the cult of beauty.

Have you heard, she adds, that there's this swirling island of crap— plastic bags and Q-tips—that's half as big as Texas and is just out there floating about in the Pacific Ocean, just outside various shipping lanes? Carole looks up at me, gamine, shock of black hair, grinning broadly, amused by the way the human animal acts like such a global toddler, dropping its junk here and there.

The flower she's wrapping looks fragile but isn't and all its colors seem to have been preserved though it's been pushed to the side of what it was, like it's a three-dimensional photograph.

This friend, the one who gave her the flower, divorced her husband, Carole tells me. Then instead of hunkering down in some house on a piece of land and holding on for dear life, she went to Paris to spend her money on ephemera. This rose, she says. Great food, learning to speak the language.

All of which will die with her, Carole adds, her face animated with humor.

Carole is one of the few people I know who can manage to physically smile even as she is speaking—nothing she's endured has caused her to lose her sunny countenance. Like my husband, Carole is one of those lucky people who are simply gifted at happiness.

We nod in our small conspiracy, acknowledging the horror that actually *spending money* would strike in our two very similar California families, all these staunch, upright Republicans, these oh so determinedly *middle class* individuals, so tidy and thrifty and modest.

The sameness of our two families makes us like sisters. It also preserves a certain class/caste fiction that has Carole and me more *well-born* in our husbands' minds, these manly guys who like to claim more hardscrabble, less elegant early existences. Each has, according to their somewhat elaborated fictions, created himself—before they *married up* when they married us.

Gary once came home from the dentist in Nevada City, smiling to show Carole that he'd had one of his eyeteeth capped in gold, and Jack, who'd gone to town with him, had evidently done nothing to dissuade him and had probably even aided and abetted, which is why Carole turned to me and said, It's what we get for marrying crackers.[+]

What we get for marrying these two particular crackers is to be sitting together wrapping presents in the warmth of our now long and loving friendship, which began in our husbands' lives and work—they've now been together as poet-and-publisher for more than forty years—and has grown as we have come to know one another deeply.

Oh, well, Jane, she tells me now. I supposed we've led *original* lives?

Our original lives have the two of us spending this dark day in the shelter of the beautiful house that was built by hand with Japanese woodworking tools on a huge piece of undeveloped land. The land is in the watershed of the south fork of the Yuba River in the foothills of Sierra Nevada mountains. We're in Gold Country, high in the range whose backbone lies along the California-Nevada border.

It's tax day, and it's pouring a cold and drenching April rain. Jack and Gary have taken our dogs and gone into town to make what Jack will later tell me is two and a half hours out of twenty minutes' errands.

[+] *Gary Snyder writes:* When I was a poor graduate student at Berkeley studying Chinese, I was admitted as a patient into the UC Dental College. I needed to get my teeth fixed before I went to Japan to study Buddhism, so I'd bicycle to the Oakland ferry, take my bike across to Market Street, and ride up to the Med School, over the course of many months. When they asked me what sort of work I wanted done, I asked, What's best? They said gold because it flexes. So I said let's do gold. They were delighted because all the students had to do a certain amount of gold work to graduate and there were fewer and fewer people who wanted it. So I got a lot of gold work done at a great bargain. This was the 1950s, and many of the dental students who worked on me were Japanese American, who had spent some of their youthful years in the camps.

My new dentist agreed that since I already had so much gold, we might as well match it up. Contemporary dentists will always ask me, Where and why did you get all that gold work? and I tell them, and they nod. Nobody today, they say, could afford all that.

Though these are Carole's last days on earth, the house looks the same and has not been transformed into a hospital, little reference to her illness is even made in the common rooms aside from the notes she's first calligraphed and then posted as reminders to herself in the places your eyes automatically fall, opposite the toilet, for instance.

On five-by-seven note cards, Carole has written: TIRED? IN EXCRU-CIATING PAIN? I HAVE A GREAT IDEA, CAROLE! WHY NOT *PUSH YOUR BUTTON?*

The button is on the pump that's been permanently affixed to her belly under her shirt and will, when pressed, deliver the most powerful of opiates straight to her gut. The sound it makes is a click, a mechanical gulp, then a pronounced *whoosh*. This soft rhythmic sucking, followed by an expelling sound, along with the pounding of the rain and the crackle of the fire, in which a log rolls down every once in a while with a thump, make the only music we are listening to, as this house is off the grid.

I'm here to stay with her while Gary and Jack are gone. It's been weeks since Gary's been to town—he no longer leaves her alone, as attending to Carole's dying has become the one main thing each of them is doing.

◊◊◊

Carole has been sick for so long it's become her vocation. Like any job that comes along and appears to pick you and at which you feel yourself to be a natural, Carole does this with what seems like grace and ease. What's hidden in the notion of vocation is the sense of true unmitigated agony, that each of us must so often wish to have anything but *this* job, which is too inhumanly hard.

Carole objects when she's heard her relationship with this cancer characterized as being *a battle*. It has none of the drama of warfare, she says, it's more an isometric exercise of mutual resistance, as if she and this cancer each have the rather simple need to occupy the same space, which happens to be Carole's own physical person. Less a battle, she says, more like sitting next to some huge bullying life form in the bleachers at a sold-out football game where you need to be constantly vigilant that Its Largeness doesn't take more space than it's already claimed.

It's forced her to concentrate, Jack feels, has purified her, has made her so much what she already essentially was, that is, direct and honest, generous and fun.

Let's face it, Jane, she said recently to me, dying is one of those okay now, let's-just-cut-the-crap experiences.

Carole's other vocation is what she might describe as *homemaker*. She's *made her home* here on this land as a subsequent wife to this big-deal man, entering fully formed into his large and famous life already well-populated by various literary and political celebrities. To do this she needed to take her place, one that had been very thoroughly occupied by the wife who came before. Carole accomplished this in the way she does everything: with style and wit and patience.

The place is called Kitkitdizze. It's in part of what was once a land cooperative founded in 1968 after Gary came back from living in a Buddhist monastery in Japan. This was during the back-to-the-land movement of the era of the Vietnam War that saw groups of people trying to implement change as part of a social matrix by moving together into the back country. They were artists or writers, teachers, crafts persons of various kinds, builders and designers, marijuana growers, those on a spiritual quest, those seeking to implement a new political paradigm. Unlike many of these intentional communities, this one became viable and has lasted for what is now three generations. These people think of themselves as those living On the Ridge. Grown children will go away, marry, have children, and then miraculously return.

Community is what these back country types turned out to be all about. This wasn't some sentimental notion that folks ought to be neighborly. Rather the rigors of life out here demanded that people work together toward common goals. This deep interconnectedness has nothing do with that strange American solipsism that produces an isolate like Ted Kaczynski, who was trying to live off the grid even as he perfected the mail bombs he was launching back into the society he was at war with.

When Gary and his family and friends moved to the San Juan Ridge, they invented a different kind of grid that was constantly being expanded and altered. These people vote and are elected to boards and committees, essentially redefining the society to which they've become an active part, just as the 77 million have become the power we once thought we needed to overthrow.

Nevada City, when they came, was another played-out gold mining town—a poor, mostly forgotten place, with its couple of stoplights. It was not only not a city, it was a barely economically viable village that was then peopled largely by under- and marginally employed rednecks, laboring in the dying industries of mining and forestry. Who were hardly welcoming to these longhairs, Beat poets and visionaries with their Buddhist chanting and their swimming naked in the river.

Nevada City lies about four hours northeast of San Francisco and has been made recently prosperous by tourism and by the wealthy tech-ish Bay Area types who're able to telecommute from a place like this, which works for their get-away houses. But Kitkitdizze is even more remote, lying another forty minutes out of town north and east along a gravel road you meet by taking the turnoff at the mailboxes into one of the more barren landscapes you're likely to see. These are the Malakoff Diggings that resulted from the high-tech hydraulic strip mining that was begun in the 1850s and used high-pressure hoses to wash alluvial gold from the ground.

The gravel road in through the Diggings to Kitkitdizze is kept open in winter snows and in floods and guarded from fire during the summer cooperatively by those who live along it in widespread outposts that include the Ring of Bone zendo and the Ananda sitting group. You bump along this road scraping the undercarriage of the ridiculous minivan you have recently come to own, this because you've returned to California to find yourself having acquired multiple grandchildren, including infant twins, all these children requiring car seats that must be rigorously tethered and affixed. You drive this silly low-slung soccer-mom-ish car through yet another muddy clearing to find an expanse of the great broad blue Georgia O'Keeffe once described as the color the sky will once again be when all mankind's destruction is done.

That was yesterday afternoon, before this monumental storm rolled in.

But it is possible in a place like Kitkitdizze with its great wealth of silence and modest, human-scaled industry to believe people can live what we once called *intentionally*, that folks can dig a pond and clear it naturally over time, can get their electrical power from solar panels, can exist like this for decades in a kind of active, working equilibrium, with periodic upgrades to running water and propane, to electrical illumination, to email, to an indoor flushing toilet. Writing. Living within the seasons, growing fruits and vegetables. Painting. Playing piano. Making things by hand.

The most important thing they've made is this *homestead*, whose lesson is that it still might be possible for humankind to mend its ways. The solidity of this home is instructive, as Jack and I have spent the past decade living first in Berkeley, then in the East, then home to Berkeley again.

Jack and I usually come up once or twice a year. Until this last winter, during which Carole's been too sick for guests, we would usually
sleep on tatami mats in the main house or out in the barn that they've
converted to a workroom and study. We like to haul our bedding out
to the deck there in the summertime to sleep under the stars. At 3,700
feet it's high and arid, and there are remarkably few bugs here on a
summer's night. The night skies, here without the haze of moisture, are
crystalline. No humidity, no bugs, these woods lack the hum and whirr
of cicadas, also the great flocks of songbirds we were used to in the
hardwood forests of the East.

The dryness of California's summers have always startled the new im-
migrants, often refugees from the hotter, wetter places. The dry weather
has a certain effect on the Western imagination and children growing up—
such kids as Gary and Carole, Jack and I—who were taught to believe in
the healthful purity of our air and our water. Nature has seemed the most
basic Western god, all else being such citified obvious human elaboration.

To sleep outside at Kitkitdizze under a night sky so thickly blanket-
ed with tiny brittle pinpoints that seem to flicker and bounce, is to regain
a childlike perspective. These are the same stars you knew in childhood
and they exist in the same numbers, are stable and unchanged, and you
realize we've done nothing that can diminish that, something we tend to
forget back in the city where you're sealed under the glaze of the light-
smeared dome of human time.

𝄢

Sometimes Jack and I will stay at Bedrock, the little cabin that's a five-
minute walk through the woods from Gary and Carole's. Bedrock was
built by Allen Ginsberg, but Gary and Carole have owned it since Allen's
death in 1997.

Jack tells the tale of one of the last times he saw Allen. He and Allen and Gary were all staying at the same upscale hotel in SoHo—all were in New York for a meeting of the American Academy of Arts and Letters, where someone else in their circle was being inducted.

The Academy sent a car to their hotel to call for them. These two old beats hopped into the stretch limo in their black tie, accompanied by Jack, who after moving east had become strangely expert in formal wear, the tux? the morning suit? My husband is the same man born, according to Jack himself, in culturally impoverished circumstances in a home where no books were read or paintings hung or music played that wasn't his dad and his uncles on a peddle steel guitar, and who, in his longhair days, was regularly banned from certain brass plaque restaurants in Washington and New York where he'd go to eat with his committee of the National Endowment of the Arts, and it *was* specifically Jack, according to Jack, who was being refused service.

The *maître d'* just *didn't care* who Jack was or who he knew, and he was refused service because he dressed in boots and jeans and wore a buckknife on his belt and had the hair and beard of a wild man and it mattered not one whit to this restaurant's management that it was Jack, in fact, who'd been the one to bring the meeting to this fabulous place of exceptional dining, in that it was Jack who was the chairman of the literature panel, a committee he'd come to head before he turned thirty-two.

But time moves on and in one direction only and people grow and age and change and this night in New York found all three former iconoclasts being embraced by the Eastern establishment of literary society that once soundly rejected them, so here they came, all dressed alike in their penguin suits. Once seated in the limo, Jack told me, Allen slipped off his shoes so he could run his stocking feet over the plush of the car's thick rug, then sat back with his arms outstretched along the top of the back seat and sang out:

O it's *fine* to be a poet in America!

∭

KJ, Carole's daughter, who she brought to the Ridge when she married Gary, is a year older than my daughter, Eva. When they were still in elementary school we would ship Eva off to Carole and Gary's when our kids were still small enough that we could just simply tell them where they would spend their vacation time and with whom. Carole and I thought of this as an importation of interesting playmates, an activity especially vital to KJ since she lived so far outside town.

When Jack and I were living in Berkeley, before we moved East, Carole and I would arrange to meet halfway between our houses to pick a girl up or drop one off. It was in the aisles of the Tower Records in Sacramento that Carole once remarked, Well, this one is so entirely your kid, Jane, in that she can totally keep her part of the narrative going.

The Ridge has always been a place KJ loved and her big sister, Mika, didn't. Mika hated the dust, the dry look of the place, hated having to do her laundry in the wash house, the isolation from her friends in town. It was all hard. I imagined she saw every piece of life as physically arduous as it might have seemed to the original pioneers.

Mika resisted even the hues and tints of where the Ridge sat on the color wheel, she told me, its sparrow browns and nuthatch rusts, the drab brush that was sage and oak and manzanita. She went away to boarding school, then to Colby College, and found Maine to be so visually alive as to seem like somewhere put together after the invention of Technicolor, with birds whose names were bluebird, cardinal, the scarlet tanager. A *green* place, she said, and she didn't mind that winters were so cold her eyelashes froze as she left her dorm on a bright blue day with her face wet from the shower. She was born in California, she didn't know any better than to go out into the cloudless day not understanding that it could be freezing, and she didn't mind the Nor'easters or the ice storms that knocked down trees.

It just breaks my mom's heart, she told me, but the weather here speaks to me and what it says is I was *meant* to live in New England.

KJ and Eva are our younger ones, the daughters Gary and Jack never had. Our younger ones have always seemed to share an affinity with these two men, and why not, Carole and I would ask, when it is these men who've made their mothers happy?

∞

We're in Carole's house on this rainy day, one of the last she will spend on earth, and she's busy being resistant as ever to anyone's waiting on her. She's not letting me be the caretaker, a job at which I happen to excel. When our fire needs another log, it's Carole who gets up on her spindly legs and hobbles over to the woodpile.

Let me, I say.

Why should I? she asks. I *like* doing it, Jane. I *like* the feeling of actually being able to perform this one small simple task. Work is a *benefit* in the cost/benefit ratio, remember? she says, to quote our friend Wendell Berry.

We're drinking tea, eating chocolate thumbprint cookies. Sugar and chocolate have been hard for Carole to metabolize in the past, but what she can and cannot metabolize seems to no longer be the issue.

We've been talking about our parents and our siblings, our children and our husbands. I'm reporting amusingly about the horrific new car

Jack and I just bought, the frog green minivan with the seven seatbelts that's come equipped with something ominously titled The Crumple Zone, as if this car is wearing the kind of crinoline slip Carole and I might have once worn to Cotillion in the Bad Old Days of our more upmarket Republican youth.

This car shrieks so piteously, I'm telling her, that it gives you the piercing little ice-pick headache just above your eye. And it cries out for *no discernable reason* whenever you're backing up, screaming like it's in total sympathy for whatever you are just about to hit, even though it hallucinates and shrieks when there's *nothing there*, so you go ahead and begin to ignore the warning and begin to idly wonder how to disable it, this being its own distraction.

I hate that car, I say, plus which when Eva saw me in it, she laughed at me. Mom, she said, do you realize you're driving a *minivan*? My daughter is now living in Vermont, where she's a senior in college.

Carole's knitting, I'm sewing. We've been talking about the pure mindless meditative pleasure that derives from making crafts and how this is so completely different from the agony that goes into art.

My theory of the earth, I say, is that I was probably born a little too well adjusted to become a writer. She grins at this. No really, I say, Stuff Happens, and this is what I have. I didn't want to be a writer any more than you wanted to be sick.

Face it, I say. Art's its own particular agony and derives from whatever horrible depths and if I were given the choice I'd *so much* rather have my dead dad back and my dead mom back and I want Geo too, who's lost to the street, and to not have all this interesting material.

You know Gary's a snob about art?

Me too, I say.

Me too, she agrees.

Few do it well. I say, *No one knows why.*

I'm misquoting Lew Welch, as Carole well knows. Lew Welch, Beat poet, Gary and Philip Whalen's roommate at Reed, friend of Jack Kerouac's, who walked away from this house one day in 1971 and completely vanished from the earth. He was drunk, was in despair, was carrying a loaded gun. Friends looked for him for weeks but in woods like these a person's bones will be carried away by animals.

What Lew Welch meant was how hard it is to write a single good and original line, let alone the whole poem that line will need to stand in. You write one good poem, then you always need to go back, settle in, put your queer shoulder to the wheel to try to write *another* one.

And now I'm telling Carole about the time Jack and I were at a poetry reading given by _____ (and here you may insert the name of whichever crappy, second-rate poet who just now especially irks you and were it not for my CIA great-uncle who one day showed up with an interventionist plan this could very easily be mine) when Jack took out one of the note cards he keeps in his breast pocket and wrote something that he then passed to me.

His note read: *It was knowing I was destined to be a poet almost exactly this good that made me lay down my pen forever.*

Good for him, Carole says. Most people just frankly aren't any good at art—I'm not. Isn't the same in crafts, where you can learn to DO something, given a little dexterity and being willing to work at it. Knitting's been enough for me or playing the piano or painting canvasses no one else then needs to bother looking at.

Jack says the world needs more people like him, I say, more contented members of the audience.

I'm an expert opera-goer, she says. I am *really* good at listening to opera. I *love* disappearing into something as huge and beautiful as that, she adds.

I wish I could hear that well, I say, but I can't. Big music makes me feel stuff I just don't necessarily *want* to feel.

Not me, she says. The huge stuff is exactly what I want to be feeling.

The huge stuff, I admit, often makes me want to go take a pill to take the edge off. You know, the least little push of joy . . . ?

Carole smiles. She is surely the most intellectually confident woman friend I've ever had but I realize I've never heard her play piano, never seen a single canvass. I begin to say something lame and conciliatory about her never having been intellectually overshadowed by Gary, though he is one of the honestly original thinkers of the twentieth century, then remember I have no need to reassure her.

Crafts matter, she's saying, in the day-to-day. Work matters, anything that you make that's tangible, even if it's only this fire or maybe dinner. She grins at me. Or these chocolate thumbprint cookies. She picks one up and waves it in the air, like she's singing OutKast's *Hey yaaa, hey yaaa, shake it like a Polaroid pic-chur* . . .

God, how I love this woman.

And it's because she's so self-confident that she's never needed to spend a lot of time and energy being jealous about Gary being out there in his Big Life.

I'm reminded of the conversation she and Gary had before they were married, them both agreeing that theirs would be a monogamous relationship, his then coming back into the house from the barn a couple of hours later to ask her, But how are we defining monogamy again?

And how, as she was telling me this, tears were raining down she was laughing so helplessly.

◊◊◊

What she and I got for marrying the men we did was to sometimes need to wade through throngs of wife-dismissing girls at this or that writers' conference. One day, Carole and I arrived simultaneously at one of these—she'd had Eva on the Ridge with KJ and our two families were going to meet here, at Squaw Valley, to share a huge bizarre off-season ski chalet. It was equipped with a home theater system with hundreds of cable channels and a bank of swiveling captain's chairs, with drink holders, all this as shelter for a conference that maybe ironically was titled: "The Art of the Wild." We'd usually agree to do these things because they offered what seemed like a paid vacation where our kids could bring extra friends and tag along with us to this blissful outdoor place to swim and bike and ride horseback.

Carole was already dying of the rare and very specific cancer that she'd share the bench with over the course of the next fifteen years. Her sister, Mary Ann Koda Kimble, who was the first woman to head the department of pharmaceutical medicine at UCSF, had managed to get all kinds of expert opinion. Carole herself had a graduate degree in medicine from UC Davis, where she trained as a physician's assistant. Everyone knew the stats, which provided a clear picture of the rather grim prognosis, one that only further clarified Carole's wish to spend her time in a meaningful way.

On this one bright summer's day in the parking lot at Squaw, we had arrived just in time to see our husbands emerging from a building across the way—both completely surrounded by would-be poets and writers, all of whom needed whatever they guessed our husbands might have to offer them: time, attention, access.

These were young, long-limbed girls wearing shorts and halter tops. In my day as a would-be novelist during grad school, I would have positioned in my superior watchful way in the wings and merely *observed* a scene such as this. It simply would never have crossed my mind to yap up and be all eagerly participant. I was what one of my cousins calls the PIBs, or People In Black, a costume that let me imagine myself to be too cool for enthusiasm, a sophisticate. The PIBs wore clothes from the thrift store. We drank wine, smoked cigarettes. We spelled it Amerika. We hung out in coffeehouses named things like The Esoteric.

These girls, by contrast, were tanned, kempt, and enthusiastically engaged in the soul-sucking activity known as *networking,* something one friend of ours who works in Hollywood refers to as "sleeping one's way to the middle." This was the new variety girl—she looked clean, vegetarian, as lightweight as her lingerie. And here were Carole and I, arriving encumbered with all this shit: our kids, our complicated lives, her health, our middle age.

She and I watched the scene for a moment before she turned to me. Know what, Jane? she asked. I have an idea, if you're up for it. How about this? I leave KJ with you and Eva so they can have the week we planned and I go home? She asked this grinning brightly, as if this was truly an inspiration.

And she didn't mean home to the ridiculous 5,000 square foot off-season ski lodge that we'd walk around in asking, where do they even GET these people and how do they imagine they're going to HEAT this thing? Carole meant she'd take her dog, get in her car, and drive the two hours back to Kitkitdizze.

Tell Gary, okay? she said before she closed the door. She motioned toward the throng preventing our two husbands from even noticing.

Tell him I'm sorry but I just can't come up with *that kind* of energy.

∞

Carole and I had in common our being part of the subsequent marriages to the men who were full stride in their important careers, also the complications of the kids and dogs and travel, all the travail of the coming-and-going lives we led, the sidekick nature of our existences, also our being *Californian* in such a deep and thorough way that only happens over the span of generations that it was somehow in our souls.

Carole's and my families were also remarkably similar: educated, successful, Republican. The main differences between her family and mine were occupational and geographic, hers being rice and almond growers in the San Joaquin Valley while mine were merchants, landowners, in Los Angeles, church-going Episcopalians, WASPs, the class of people who had easy-to-pronounce white people's names who went to breakfast meetings and were elected president of Rotary.

Carole's parents were Japanese American of the Nisei generation—those that were born and educated here. My family was traditionally educated at Cal, where both my parents and grandparents had met. Her father went to Davis and both her parents spoke completely unaccented and idiomatic English.

In California racism was almost always subtle and genteel, everything accomplished by inflection or what was just never said. But then people came along who would say flat out what they were thinking and so we learn that it is only by listening to those who aren't in the dominant culture that we can learn how to talk about race.

Carole once told me the story of her making a new friend in elementary school, Jon'esquia. The word to describe Jon'esquia at that time would have been *Negro* or *colored girl*. Jon'esquia, who was named, she said, after her father—or maybe the word for a certain star in Swahili—had invited Carole to play at her house after school, and they walked home together. When her mother opened the door to them, she was frankly astonished. You friends with *her?* she asked Jon'esquia. *That skinny little yellow thang?*

〇〇〇

It was 1997 and Jack and I were living in the East when Carole found Dr. Paul Sugarbaker at Washington Hospital Center through research done by her sister Mary Ann and her colleagues at UCSF. It was then that Carole began her calm and insistent campaign to get accepted as his patient.

Carole's cancer had been variously diagnosed as that of the several organs its masses had first enshrouded then engulfed so by the time Dr. Sugarbaker agreed to take a look at her films, she had already had five different major surgeries.

Jack and I were back in Washington, D.C., where we'd moved when he was asked to come there to found a literary press. We still saw Gary often but Carole wasn't traveling much and I hadn't seen her in so long I was nervous as I drove out to Dulles to get her.

I was *scared* and I am someone who—while haunted by nebulous fears—is hardly ever frightened by anything that appears here in the physical world.

She and I had agreed to meet at baggage claim.

Here we are, she said. She had begun to refer to the disease as her traveling companion—in time she would start calling it Vesuvius. Carole looked smaller and thinner but in no way diminished.

Wanna see? she asked, then pulled up her shirt. She pointed at the bulges that showed through the skin of her belly. There, she said, and there. Carole, who was watching my face, saw that I was neither horrified nor shocked. Instead I was *interested,* as she would have been had our positions been reversed.

Each of us simply prefers the precise language of science and accurate diagnosis to the eliding words that allow the thing-ness of something to remain both unuttered and ever mysterious.

It actually feels soft, she said as she placed my hand on the skin where one mass bulged. Which is why they call it *jelly belly*, she said. Cute name, no? For something so basically gross? She was smiling, also being professional, the physician's assistant—for which she'd trained, acting to calm my apprehensions.

And it was that the tumors were made of cells that produced mucus in the way of healthy perineal cells but in such obvious overabundance, as a natural process that's somehow gone wildly wrong, and that they behaved like *this* and could be expected to do just *this* and not some other thing, that they were caused by *this particular cancer*, whose name is pseudomyxoma peritonei, or PMP, that gave both Carole and me, if not hope, then at least an intellectual understanding of exactly what there was that needed to be reckoned with. Carole and I are simply like this: we prefer hard knowledge in the cold light of day to being left to our own wild and dark imaginings.

���

Carole knew she needed to qualify for the Sugarbaker procedure, and knew that because of the more than several surgeries, she did not look like the best of candidates, at least on paper. She'd started out weighing only a hundred pounds and each of the operations further compromised her digestive system. She now needed to struggle to keep her weight up.

The cancer is a peritoneal carcinoma, one of the skin of the abdomen—it goes anywhere and everywhere in the gut. Its repeated incursions had taken, so far, her appendix and her reproductive organs, as well as some length of her large intestine. Still she needed to show up at this meeting looking like someone who was going to not only survive the radical procedure—it is truly terrible to describe—but come down on the right side of the hospital's ledger, showing that no one had wasted his time and effort.

What is now known as the Sugarbaker Procedure demands an excision of every affected organ that a person can live without, then radically debulking the masses, then bathing the entire gut in a heated chemical bath meant to kill all the skin cells this chemotherapy can find. It sounded like medieval torture that took, if all went well, at least fourteen hours.

She had a late morning consultation with Dr. Sugarbaker scheduled for the day after I got her at Dulles. We left the house early to go to my gym where she intended to run on the treadmill. Carole, who was thin but not frail, wanted to arrive at that meeting looking pumped up and vital. She asked me to come along to meet him, to sit in with them and take notes.

We got on side-by-side treadmills. She began to run while I—as was my habit—put my book in its holder and tilted the treadmill to a very steep incline that produced the slow trudge uphill. I was, just then, some ways into a new translation of *The Inferno* that had internal rhyme and sprung rhyme and off-rhyme which were supposed to somewhat approximate in English the sound of Dante's terzarima. I like to walk and to read aloud. The gym, with the noise of its machines and everyone else wearing earbuds, is a great place to not be heard. I like to read a poem out loud under my breath in order to help myself hear it better. Moving while you are reading allows the language to enter your brain in a deeper way, or at least differently, lodging it in a more physical three-dimensional place.

I don't understand the brain science of how this happens and only know that it was a personal discovery of mine when I was in high school and was trying to memorize verb declensions in Spanish and found out I simply learned better when I walked in circles in my room while saying the words aloud.

So I was reading out loud to myself on the treadmill at my gym when I noticed that the skinny little yellow thing—who was also, by the way, dying—running along on the treadmill next to me had started laughing.

What? I said.

Nice pace, Jane, Carole told me. She was winded, gasping, which seemed to be getting in the way of her laughing.

Mind your own business, I said. I'm reading. I'm hearing the terzarima, if you need to know, which—in Italian—is rumored to *sound like rain.*

She was laughing so hard by then she'd stopped her treadmill and was having trouble speaking. *Like rain!* she asked.

Anyway, I never run, I told her. I'm saving my knees.

Saving your knees? Carole, now doubled over, whooping helplessly with laughter.

Saving them? she asked when she could speak again. May I ask for exactly *what?*

⚆⚆⚆

There was a map of the U.S. on the wall of Dr. Sugarbaker's office that had roundheaded glass pins in different colors stuck in it. There were fifteen or twenty pins sitting close to one another in California's still largely agricultural San Joaquin Valley. Many of the pins were right around Modesto, the closest large town to where Carole grew up in her family's rice farm in Dos Palos.

That's a cluster? I asked Dr. Sugarbaker.

A cluster, he agreed.

He turned to Carole. And many of my patients are your age and the majority are women though we don't yet have any good idea why that would be. PMP is perhaps most often positively diagnosed early when a mass is detected on the ovaries so it may be that it's still being more often missed in men.

Carole grew up twenty miles from the Kesterson National Wildlife Refuge, where over a period of time in the mid-1980s birds were being born horribly deformed. I remember the shock and dismay on the faces of the wildlife managers in the refuge during that time who came on television to talk about the ecological disaster that was transpiring before their eyes. The wetlands of the Pacific flyway had become a place where species, instead of finding rest and food, were being poisoned with heavy metals, including selenium—some were threatened with extinction. And it wasn't simple—toxins from the agricultural runoff from the flooding of the rice fields was involved.

Our future is all about water, I remember one of the wildlife managers saying. He was holding a chick in his hand that had hatched with two heads. There were holes where the beaks should be.

This kind of death will not stop in a single generation, he said. This is global, he was telling the television camera. This is the sort of death that will go *on and on.*

I was a new mother and had only then begun to live in what I'd started to think of as ecological dread.

This is about the watershed? I asked Dr. Sugarbaker.

Watershed is what Gary calls one's own geographical address, it's the ridge of high land dividing areas drained by different river systems, a drainage basin, a parting of the waters. A watershed is all the land onto which rain and snow falls that feeds a certain river system or any other body of water.

Watershed is also the poem with which Gary often signs an email:

Kitkitdizze
  north of the South Yuba River
    near the headwaters of Blind Shady Creek
  in the trees at the high end of a bunchgrass meadow

Watershed, Dr. Sugarbaker said, might be one really good way to put it.

∞

Carole had brought her most recent films in a big manila envelope. Sugarbaker got them out and snapped them up on the light box on the wall behind his desk.

In Carole's films the tumors read bright white. I had no experience in reading x-rays but was having no trouble noticing that the masses were both numerous and huge.

Well, these aren't the *worst* films I've ever seen, Dr. Sugarbaker told her.

But pretty bad, huh? Carole asked.

Pretty bad, he agreed.

Carole already knew this—Mary Anne had helped her read the films before she came so even the worst news was never really news to her and Mary Ann was such a tough minded medical professional Carole once said to me about her: You know, Jane, my sister would make a really good *man.*

Carole sat forward, soberly. She was focused and completely serious.

I have a thirteen-year-old daughter, she told him. My older girl's eighteen and is going off to college—Mika will be okay. But KJ's adopted, so I have this small moral problem, you see? in that I need to finish my commitment to raising her?

Dr. Sugarbaker nodded.

I need five years, she told him.

Five years? he asked, and after the merest pause he nodded: Okay, Carole, you're on.

〇〇〇

We are sitting on cushions on the tatami at the low table in front of the fire. Their electricity comes off solar panels and a generator so the lighting is always low, but this is one of the darkest afternoons I can remember, an ambiance that feels like an almost throttled daylight.

The sensation, Carole is telling me on the last afternoon we will ever spend together on this earth, is that she's completely entrapped by a nausea so grave she's unable to escape it even in her deepest sleep.

There's the constant nausea, also the extreme cramping in her gut, cramps that are as excruciating as contractions in transition during natural childbirth. Transition is the place in labor where the baby's head comes charging down the birth canal and the pain from one contraction begins to blend into the pain from the next so you finally suffer the one long unrelieved agony that doesn't end until the baby's out, which is what makes you really want to push.

Transition is up there at nine or ten in an ER room's Descriptive Pain Scale—it's the kind of pain that you honestly feel you may die of, though she and I are Western and we tend to be stoic about physical pain. The morphine in Carole's power pack doesn't make the pain go away, instead it *abstracts* her from the sense that she is the one who is feeling it.

I remind Carole of the phone conversation we were having even as we were all witnessing Bush stealing the 2000 election. I was upset, was acting exercised, was cradling the phone as we spoke, talking coast-to-coast and was all the while anxiously cracking hazelnuts with the grip of a pair of kitchen scissors held upside down when one nut slipped.

Oops, I said.

What's wrong?

I seemed to have cut off the tip of my finger.

Hang up, Jane, she said. You're going to have to go to the hospital.

Did you go? she asks me now.

Oh you know, not being sensible, I wrapped it in about a thousand band-aids and when it began to throb I took a Motrin and a sleeping pill and Eva came home after school and was furious, just furious—she's a First Responder, you know, trained in first aid since she's a lifeguard. But I did once drive myself to the ER.

Yeah? Carole asks.

I was stung by a hornet on my finger, which actually hurt like hell. Slow news day at Sibley Hospital, evidently, so I got the undivided attention of just about everyone around, and a bed and a nap and an IV of morphine and Benadryl.

This feels completely *ridiculous*, comparing our levels of pain—my wasp sting, her terminal cancer?

Good for you, Carole says cheerfully.

Jack wouldn't take me. Said I was overreacting.

That's because of Kathleen, she says.

Kathleen was Jack's mother. She was Southern. She was said to *enjoy poor health.*

Gary used to be like that, Carole says, but man, did he get over it.

Because of Lois, I say.

Gary's mother Lois lived to be ninety-eight. Lois attributed her long life to her habit of drinking a pint of half & half every morning. Lois, with her half & half, was proof to Carole and me of the fact of God's

Justice, in that there really is no rhyme or reason to any of this, so all any of us can ever do is to do the best we can.

Gary bought Lois a house in Grass Valley, even hired help, but Lois accused every one of them of stealing from her and fired them. Gary arranged for her to have Meals on Wheels, and for a social worker to come by to look in on her.

Once when Gary was in Washington staying with us—this was yet another time Carole was in the hospital—the social services called him to say Lois had been arrested.

Why? he asked.

Mrs. Hennessey seems to have a hole in her bedroom floor, they said. It's about four feet in diameter that you can see through to the basement, so her house is no longer safe, was the reply.

How'd that get there? Gary asked.

We have no idea. And your mother will not say.

So she's been arrested? Gary asked.

She has been arrested, the social worker said, because the house was red tagged and your mother refused to leave. We asked the police to come out in the hope that they might impress upon her our deep concern about the situation's seriousness, which is when your mother became abusive.

What she actually said to the sheriff, Gary told us later, was: Oh, you think you're so smart with your uniform and your testicles.

I miss Lois, Carole says now, though that's completely perverse.

Me too, I miss her, I say, and I've never even met her.

And now the firelight's flickering across one side of her face, making her cheekbones look pronounced, Carole now weighs less than seventy pounds. The wasting has now taken all the collagen from her face and it's collagen that does the padding. I keep being almost overwhelmed by an odd need, that feels very primitive and atavistic, to get my hands on her, to somehow minister to her physical person, though Carole won't let me DO anything more for her than get up and go boil more tea water.

Would you like me to wash your hair? I ask.

KJ just did it, she says. Why, does it look really terrible? KJ comes over every Monday and we have dinner and she gives me a shampoo. We eat in bed and watch a movie and I always fall asleep.

KJ, who was thirteen when Carole first met Paul Sugarbaker, is now twenty-two and is living on her own in Grass Valley.

I say: And that is the *exact* reason a woman needs a daughter or a sister or at least one special friend. One of Our People who knows something about hair *products*. Jack's good to great at most of it but he doesn't get *products*, what they are, which ones you need for shine or curl or volume.

I probably need more product, Carole says. Maybe a little mousse?

And she jumps up and we both go together into the bathroom where she whooshes foam into the palm of her hand, then combs through her hair with her fingers. Her hair has hardly grayed, is still thick and is still almost that entirely Asian black that looks almost blue aside from a few bright strands of silver.

She's sticking her hair up punkishly, when she catches me watching her in the mirror. There, she says, so now I look *even more* like Jiminy Cricket.

෴

She is finishing knitting a little doggy cap for the two-and-a-half-year-old who lives with his parents in the Japanese house Dick Baker, then abbot of San Francisco Zen Center, had brought by freighter from Japan and reassembled on his land on the Ridge.

I'm sewing silky binding on a crib blanket. I try to make one of these for each of the new babies who comes along these days, adding a rich gloss to the new fleece ones parents these days like. The soft edge like this encourages thumb sucking, I say, but who honestly gives a shit? I believe in bottles and pacifiers and thumb sucking, anything that lets you grow up at the proper pace so you don't have to go out and practice chemical warfare.

Besides, it's pretty, Carole says, and everybody needs a little beauty.

I was a thumb sucker, I tell her, and I believe in having nigh-nighs and baby dolls and your own oinky blanket, anything that helps get you from this place to wherever.

We all need something, she agrees, to get us to the next place along this *long and difficult* migratory road.

She shrugs. The pain of this, for me, is now becoming almost unbearable.

We're both quiet for a moment.

I brought my mother home from the hospital to take care of when she was dying of cancer. She was supposed to die any minute but when she got to my house ensconced in her hospital bed in a back room that had a great view of the redwoods and the rose garden, she perked up and lived for another seven weeks. Taking care of her was the hardest thing I have ever done, it was also the most important thing, since it taught me how brave I am and how natural and normal bravery is, that it's something we're actually born to.

I suddenly want to tell Carole that watching my mother die was just like watching someone grow up, and it was delicate and even beautiful. It was like she was growing up except that my mother was growing down and she was being born but she was going in the other direction, born into that poem of Wendell Berry's where he describes

314

the world as being "birthwet and shining, as even/the sun at noon had never made it shine."

None of which I can gracefully say, under the circumstances, without sounding mawkish and sentimental.

∭

It's always been her idea that we need to fill our kids with lore. We need, she says, to equip particularly our daughters with the items of housekeeping that they will one day need, and these are the realistic stories of what men and women are and how our people came to be here and these need to be things like whatever items might have once gone into a girl's hope chest: her own sewing kit, a teapot.

And I've brought my own daughter's special teapot up to the Ridge for us to use so Eva will have this material object into which I can somehow place the story of this day, so her teapot will, I think, somehow contain a part of the memory of Carole, this implement, its usage. She and I are drinking the Chinese Silver Needle tea I bought at Teance on Fourth Street in Berkeley, a tea so heavenly and light it tastes like extremely expensive nothing.

Our conversation, never linear, now roams more than usual in the way of poems or dreams and it is this that Gary says is the proof that the mind is a wild system, in that we can never know what the next thing is that we are going to think, as the mind, like art, will always follows its own unpredictable logic.

Carole is losing her memory, she's told me, also her remarkable assuredness in language. This halting, stumbling, hunting around looking for a term is simply more than she's signed on for, and throughout the afternoon her pump heaves and clicks and wheezes and she is, as always, uncomplaining. The Japanese call this kind of physical bravery *gaman*—it's associated with the values of the Samurai or war-rior class, from which her family is descended, or at least—and she almost twinkled when she told me this—according to some people's *version* of things.

〇〇〇

Carole has given our granddaughter a packet of beautifully painted rice candy from Japan.

I don't want Hazel to eat it, I tell Carole.

Why? Carole asks.

She needs to save it, I say, I want her to have it for the future when she gets to some big event, when I can explain what it means.

Save it? Carole asks and I hear myself, out there beyond the break-line, waiting, always saving it, *like my knees or this story.*

This is all there is, Jane, Carole says, and each of us nods. We need to buck up now, she says, and go out and spend the principle.

And *buck up* is, I realize, exactly the kind of thing my mother might have said.

We're wrapping the last of the gifts and Carole's huge and inspiring love is now being concentrated down into each of the notes she's writing with her Mont Blanc meisterstuck, this note-writing being a process that started out hard and has now become arduous.

Every part of it is difficult, she says. All the people coming over or else studiously *not* coming over, since they've already said their goodbyes.

Because Carole was supposed to have died last summer and she quit eating entirely and was sent home from the doctor with palliative care, which is when the cancer was finally starved into remission. Vesuvius jumped ship, but it was then way too late.

Everyone on the Ridge knew she was dying. Then one day she appeared among them, there in town with Gary, standing in line for the penguin movie.

What are *you* doing here? they asked.

Bored, Carole said. I got bored. Dying's *boring,* okay? same old *boring* thing day after day.

That was hard, she says now, and it's hard that I won't become a grandmother, that I'll miss knowing Mika's children and KJ's and that I'm going to miss growing old with Gary, who is honestly one of the most remarkable men. And I'm going to miss training Emmy to sit and stay with this clicker method I've been learning.

Miss my friends, she adds. She glances up, smiles at me cheerfully.

And I ask if there isn't one little teeny sentimental part of her that thinks there could be some dark bar somewhere in the cosmos paneled in mahogany where her dad, who died when she was twelve, and my dad and Jack's mom and mine, Gary's too, are all drinking colorful Boat Drinks and congratulating one another on their clever and amusing children? Bragging on us, as the crackers would say.

Nope, she says. I mean it isn't actually very *likely,* when you think of it. I mean, how old is everybody, and whose *version* of heaven is this, anyway, and why would *Lois* have to be there? *Lois?* who might conceivably amuse your mom but she would simply *horrify* my father, who was above all *decorous* man.

My dad too, I tell her. Really dedicated to preserving his dignity.

Something Lois, Carole says, never actually heard of.

⬮⬮⬮

Carole is one of the best readers I've ever known. She is keenly and justly critical and has always seemed to know exactly what I'm hoping for in my writing so I gave her the manuscript to my second novel during one of her long stays in the hospital when the book was still a work in progress.

Have you ever had anal sex? Carole asked. Since she was in recovery from her Sugarbaker I was slightly shocked that she'd ask, under the circumstances.

Well, um, sure, I said.

I know why Alec and Anna do it, Carole said—she was talking about the characters in my second book, whose sexuality I'd set out to write about graphically from both a man's and a woman's point of view, because this seemed like work that hadn't been done well by most of the writers I admire.

It's because they're so crazy about each other they want to do *everything*.

I nodded.

And Carole says, Gary and I were like that.

👀

The dogs romp in, with Emmy leading, wagging her pompom dog tail—our men are home from town. Emmy's a standard poodle in the variety known as *apricot*, this being one tick off the color more commonly known as *pink* and seems, in her styling and coloring, the most unlikely dog for this old and weathered Beat to have, whose dress is more woodsman-homesteader. But KJ has allergies so this family has always needed to own dogs with hair instead of fur.

Carole's given all these gifts for me to carry away, but nothing for me to keep. I am wrapping Eva's teapot and each of the four cups the four of us have used to drink from and the needy atavistic feeling that's washed over me in waves all afternoon begins to come surging back.

Because our fathers died when we were children, Carole and I are each well acquainted with death—neither of us has ever been afraid to call it that but this in no way spares me the shock of this here and now actually being true.

I look at her and think: *She's dying* and this makes me want something. I want to eat Hazel's candy or to belong to some old religion where they give you a sacred wafer or a sip of ecclesiastical wine, or I want a whole great lot of crappy liquor to swill or anything I can ingest and carry away in my own stomach and therefore take away, in my physical person, a grasping, desperate feeling that's both base and primitive.

And it's this neediness, I know, that makes even the most loving relatives act so insane when someone dies and money and property are involved. It's as if we are all overtaken by this same archaic hunger, like we need to *take things in,* like eaters of carrion. The three dimensional objects are translated into a different more age-old language and the things stop being whatever they were and are transubstantiated into the currency of memory by which the mysterious transaction is being performed.

And art figures in here too.

But the agreement is even more complex than our loved one simply being present in the object, as Carole will forever reside in the teacups we've been using to drink from today. It isn't only that we, the living, will go on remembering them—it's that our dead, through what they've given us, seem to promise to continue to cluster around us and hold us to this place that we have shared.

My hands are aching with grief and need and, as always, it's the same loss, my father or my mother or a house or place I loved, and I suddenly want my own mother back and I want my father to have lived to be proud of me and I want Carole to have given me something, even as I understand that if she had it would only have made us cry.

Kitkitdizze is one of the truly beautiful houses, Japanese in style, both elegant and simple. Its main rooms are built around star-shaped tree limbs, Carole and I are standing under the skylight in the center of this house where the light is very quickly leeching upward and away from us, escaping through the roof toward the more ancient light that lies outside our own atmosphere.

As I hold her to me, I whisper, My mother died the day after her birthday in the back bedroom of my house. The last words she said were *Take me with you.*

You do, she says, you will, and as she and I hold one another she adds, Know what, Jane? You *will* see me again, I know it now.

000

And in truth I've gone for years saying goodbye to her, over and over again, each time believing I was seeing Carole for the very last time. She's been so frail a cold might have killed her, and she and I lived for a decade not only a continent apart from one another but then far off at the end of a long dirt road.

So we would say goodbye and I'd privately weep and cry out and I'd drive out to our barn in the country and wail aloud to the heavens, the sound I was making drowned out by my vacuum. The barn sat a hundred yards from a horse barn and in the dead of winter, as this was, the floor was dark with the bodies of freeze dried flies.

I'd cry and vac and go with my current dog to a place on that land where I discovered that it was possible to see and hear not one single thing that had been made by the hand of man, even in looking upward for the space of time that stood between this moment and the next plane flying over.

I'd listen to the animated dark, in which I have always been at home, and get myself in hand and know my friend Carole to be a better, braver person than I could ever be, more heroic and more peaceful and that this display of psychic agony was somehow beneath her dignity, as this loss wasn't my loss, this grief, my own particular grief, and that remonstration of this kind really helps me not at all.

And I'd need to then accommodate to the knowledge that she would no longer be here as my friend on this our shared plane of time and that, more than likely, I'd never lay eyes on her again, then she'll just oddly turn up, alive, right there standing in the movie line.

⁂

The last year Jack and I were living in the East, we came home to Berkeley for the holidays and—as usual—were staying at the Golden Bear Motel at Cedar on San Pablo Avenue. The Golden Bear's everyone's favorite fleabag motel—everyone who was ever young in Berkeley has a Golden Bear story, some interlude that's either colorfully sordid or almost tragic, having to do with low-rent romance and the way we're all so adept at ruining blissful marital happiness, so no one actually really *minds* staying at the Golden Bear where the whores will sometimes fight loudly with their pimps in the room right upstairs from where your little family is conducting its out-of-town holiday rituals, then these same whores will stomp outside to smoke and sit in their cars in the parking lot, scheduling dates on their cell phones even as they re-do their elaborate makeup in their car's rearview mirror.

Prostitution isn't actually legal in Berkeley but our cops no longer arrest even the streetwalkers, who are considered to be participating in

what everyone around here imagines is a victimless crime and if you
don't like it, *you can always go live someplace else.*

We always stayed at the Golden Bear because it's cheap and clean
and takes dogs and has a great Japanese restaurant called Genki in its
parking lot and is right across San Pablo from Café Fanny, where you
can get the most amazing poached egg on toast on, maybe, earth.

Isn't that Emmy? I asked, pointing at the large poodle that had just
come rocking around the corner of a building. She was prancing lightly
on her pink puffs like she's a circus dog and this is a dog so honestly
pink she might put you in mind of an alcoholic's nightmare.

Synder's dog? Jack asked, just as Gary came rounding the corner,
looking as he does these days, his half-Japanese to three-parts-wizened-
elf, wide-brimmed felt Australian outback hat and gold tooth gleaming.
Synder is what Jack often calls him after a long-ago typo.

Hi ho, Jack and Jane, he said. *Thought* we might be running into
you here.

He and Carole, who'd been at Mary Ann's for Christmas, had just
put Mika and Tom on their plane for Maine in Oakland, but Carole
was too torn down from the all the busy-ness of the holidays to drive the
four hours from Berkeley back up to the Ridge.

Carole was also, as it turned out, too tired to sit in a restaurant,
so Jack and Gary went to eat at Genki while she and I hung out in the
bathroom of their room. She was soaking in the tub, reading *The New
Yorker* magazine, adding hot water constantly, as a hot soak was one of
the few things that calmed the cramping in her gut.

Bye, I told her that time. I'll call you soon.

And if I'm not answering, she said, just leave me one of your long *to
longish* messages, all right, and don't worry that it's long, I'll listen to it
a little bit at a time, so just feel free to go on and on.

000

Carole's here, I feel her here with me. I can hear her and see her, particularly her face, which is, as always, lit up by the intensity with which she smiles. She's right here, standing in front of me as she did on that last day as she shows me the painting she's recently done.

And I am completely amazed, as it's completely unlike anything I imagined Carole would ever do. I thought she was spending her time doing impressionistic watercolors, seascapes, doing what Eva used to call *painting her mind.*

But this isn't that at all. What it is is exactly like a Wayne Thiebaud, who worked for Disney in his youth, so this is like one of his jokes within a joke. Her oil is like his gumball machines or the dialed out lipsticks, but Carole's is a series of five of the various brightly painted fire hydrants of Nevada City, each different, each carefully and very jauntily, rendered as if from life.

I didn't know you could paint, Carole, I say. I mean really *paint* paint—this is completely wonderful.

Nah, she says, it's so derivative. I'm not a painter, Jane. I'm not original.

But, Carole, this is all *any* of us is ever doing. All any of us is ever doing is looking hard and trying to listen really carefully, then seeing if we can get it down?

I'm just so embarrassed, she says, which is why I hang them in the bedroom.

But it's *good*, it's funny, it's wonderful. Wayne Thiebaud would *love* this painting, by the way. His paintings are meant to be cheerful, you know. It has to do with animation.

Our kids are original, she says. We did that, didn't we?

And they aren't even ours any more, have you noticed? In that now we get out of their way and let them go become the heroes in their own stories.

And we've had interesting times? she says. And now you get to go and write something and tell this one little piece of it.

And of course this was exactly what she meant, that she was giving me this part to tell, that she thought I was up to the work of writing what has often just felt much too hard, so I stay there waiting, out there beyond the breakline, imagining I still have all the time in the world.

She's given this to me to tell: how we need to remember how physically she smiled and how physically she laughed and how on the day she and Gary met—this was at the zendo at the Ring of Bone—they rocked forward at the same instant laughing so hard they literally bumped heads.

15

Random Incident

THE FIRST TIME Jack and I were hit by a car in a crosswalk, we'd just left the community theater after hearing Thich Nhat Hanh. It was nine-thirty or ten at night, we were surrounded by hundreds of Buddhists moving along according to some no doubt widely known law of physics that governs disbursal of crowds, the arc of carsplash or outfly of particles from the explosion marking the inception of the universe.

This was in Berkeley where our Buddhists are diverse and maybe more representative of what I think of as My America, so the shaven-headed ones were men and women, young and old, white and black and Asian. Robed Buddhists don't really walk, rather seem to float almost imperceptibly along, wearing saffron or crimson or their dark brown everydays, their bald heads gleaming dully.

And it was a foggy night so our town's dim yellowish anti-crime lights cast this preternatural glow as droves of Buddhists crossed the park and floated down the streets along this grid of organized randomness. They moved quietly in and out of shadows in sets of twos and threes.

And though Jack is a Buddhist he doesn't walk around dressed like one. He was wearing clothes from the office, a crisp white dress shirt with a Robert Palmer collar, slacks, sport coat. His tie was Italian, one I'd recently bought for him.

As we were walking back to our car Jack was explaining the difference between the Greater and the Lesser Vehicles, this being doctrine intrinsic to the larger understanding of Buddhism. I was not intently listening to what Jack was saying, rather I was aware of the voice with which he was saying it. His voice is deep and bass and comforting, a voice for the radio, as a French friend of mine once said, a voice you enter as you do music, as you'd enter a peaceful room.

I wasn't listening to whatever he was saying about the tenets of Buddhism because I really don't care about Buddhism. I know American Buddhism likes to pretend it isn't *really* a religion involving anything as distasteful as Some Embarrassing Deity, but it actually is a rigorous system of well-organized historical belief that requires actual study, practice, discipline. And I've never been adequately gulled by all the Buddhistic stuff that surrounds us, what's for sale in the yoga aisle of Whole Foods, for instance, made of 100 percent unbleached cotton and no animal cruelty. It's marketed to make you feel slightly better about your same old rampant consumerism but I know even as I'm purchasing it that this is just more physical stuff, that it's just me standing at the check-out paying for things I'll have only until I lose track of them, that my buying things in no way constitutes a holy act.

Spiritual devotion is simply one of those aspects of human endeavor—like Late Capitalism or the single-minded accumulation of huge amounts of anything—that's simply lost on me. I just can't *get* and *stay* interested enough long enough to pay attention to why you do whatever y'all folks all've agreed to do—bow, ring bells, genuflect—not even when a person I know to be a good man, and thorough, is saying something no doubt brilliant that is also interesting.

I therefore scuttle along at the side of listening, having to settle for sights, sounds, and smells—color of robes, incense, sound of plainsong, of chants or matins. I have to settle for my admiration for the variety of head shapes in the species *homo sapiens*.

And I'm polite about Buddhism, trying not to mock its stupider aspects to our countless Buddhist friends just as I try to be respectful of the devout High Church Episcopalians in my own family and the largely secular Judaism of the family into which I was once married, as I'm most recently respectful of Muslims, who are surely our most persecuted religious minority. I don't want my own looking askance at religious practice to fellow travel with persecution so I try to make my face look benign and above all *accepting* whenever I catch the eye of some woman who's veiled her face from me for complicated and archaic reasons I can't hope to understand.

Buddhists may just have a better attitude toward whole grain breads, toward locally grown organic fruits and vegetables, but it's only in Berkeley that *shopping* would begin to take on this pent-up aspect that makes people act like they're experiencing a sacrament.

And honestly? I am someone who compulsively chews great wads of Trident sugarless bubble gum when I'm writing—this in lieu of the mafia-truckload of cigarettes I'd prefer to be inhaling or the seven gallons of wine or the as-much-hashish-as-the-world-contains I'd actually like to be consuming and so remain this gum-chewing wiseacre who can't keep this tiny voice from mentally piping up to mimic, mock, and scorn whenever I get stuck in some pious situation.

Listening to Thich Nhat Hanh, for instance?

Thich Nhat Hanh, quite honestly, reminds me of just another one of these soul-saving televangelists spouting platitudes in barely comprehensible baby talk and I don't care that he's short and round and cheerful or that he's Vietnamese and what all we did to the Vietnamese. Thich Nhat Hanh has always struck me as a type of Chauncey Gardner, another of those really clever simpletons.

◌◌◌

The car that hit us that night actually didn't hit me, since Jack saw it turning the corner in the fog and was able to push me out of the way. It was a big light-colored American car, heavy, solid bodied, grand, an Impala or whathaveyou, the kind of car that sailed forth as if out of our extravagant youth, given to this girl, no doubt, by her more-our-age uncle. A car that might have achieved Classic Status, might have earned the Grandfather Exemption that kept it from having to be smogged each year by the State of California.

An Impala driven by an angel of perfect Berkeley girl with gorgeous middle class dreads and some interesting ethnic mix—Jewish/ African-American/Korean and/or Haitian? A junior at Cal majoring in I can't remember, working nights at the Y where she'd just ended her shift as a trainer in the women's gym. She'd just started her car and was pulling away from the curb, just turning the corner onto Oxford and was reaching forward to rub a clear place in her fogged-up windshield with her bare fingers so she saw us at the *exact* moment we saw her.

So the entire event had this almost known-beforehand quality, slow motion and underwater that partook of *recognition*. It's what's so comforting about fairytales, that all the charmed pieces are magically numbered, all the parts fit together and are already somehow known to us, that her car was one we understood from our California youth, that it was going slowly, that Jack was knocked down slowly, that she immediately stopped and got out to render aid, that we were instantly surrounded by all these really comforting Buddhists.

The cops and ambulance immediately appeared and were articulate and highly educated. In Berkeley you can almost always trust people to know how to act in these situations, as this is part of our deeply shared social compact, an agreement as to how we must courteously occupy our town's Neutral Middle Distance, at least in moments of grave emergency.

Jack had done something instinctive, I'd noticed, which was to reach out when he hit the ground in order to pick his wallet up from where it flew. That what he believed to be his wallet was not actually his wallet, but one of those flatish but still fully three-dimensional reflectors used to mark the crosswalk, seemed immaterial. It's the kind of mistake you'd make if you were Jack and had just been hit by a car. He tried to lift his wallet, and couldn't understand why he couldn't until I explained that it wasn't *really* his wallet but was actually this wallet-shaped object, this piece of glowing goldish orange reflective plastic securely affixed to the street.

Jack is the kind of a person who simply gets proactive in a crisis and tries to immediately set things right by packing and organizing while I—in extremity—begin to cast off, to care even less than I ordinarily do about all these *objects* we're required to lug around. I wished I cared more about physical things but my relationship to even the necessary items has always been both transitory and tentative.

Sure, I'll like something even overmuch for a little while, I'll become *really* attached to it. People may find it strange that I wear the same clothes day after day for weeks, or at least some version of the exact same clothes, then abruptly change to another outfit, but remember this is what a toddler will do if left to his or her own devices. Both the toddler and I feel simply most *ourselves* in our bathing suit or this certain pair of shorts for a time, as we're moving along toward the next developmental milestone, which will come with its own sandals or shirt that becomes the object of our next passionate attachment.

That it's Jack—the Buddhist in our household—who must maintain our material possessions probably approximates someone's definition of irony. What I seem to care about deeply are the tools: that my pen allows the right milli-micronic amount of the right color of archival pigment to flow onto the right weight of really expensive paper.

◊◊◊

When Jack got hit that night, he steadied himself, got his real wallet out, offered his real ID and insurance information to whomsoever, checked the time on his pocket watch, then informed the ambulance guys he wasn't going with them. Not only that, he wasn't going to the hospital, period, that I wasn't taking him, either—he announced this in his deep authoritative voice-for-the-theater voice.

And the folks involved began to get right away that they were not going to change this man's mind. Jack's supremely confident, also a brilliant negotiator who's both calm and patient. He waits, I've seen him waiting. He waits as a carp might wait, half hidden beneath the lily pads down in the murk. He waits knowing he can and will outwait you. Jack's calm. He knows he's going to get his way, if not now, then in a little while.

Folks forget he's waiting then there's this quick deft flash of brilliance that has expended no angry energy.

It was pointless trying to make him go to the hospital, so the ambulance guys gave up, as did the cops—what were they going to do, *arrest him?* Hold him for seventy-two hours under the California Statute called the 5150, this being the period of observation in a hospital designed to determine whether you're a threat to yourself or others? His judgment might not have been *all* that sound, as he did formulate the argument that it was he, of the two of us, who was obviously best equipped to drive our own car home.

And I can no longer remember who won that one but when we got home I called John, Jack's doctor, who is a friend of ours. John said to take his temperature, which was scarily low. Jack was in shock, John said, as well as probably all methed up, as John put it, on an extra dose of Emergency Adrenalin. John told me to tell Jack he had to take pills or else go to the hospital—John knows Jack hates taking pills. John said Jack was to take a horsetab of Ibuprofen, also a sleeping pill. If he did *exactly* as John said, Jack could stay home, sleep in his own bed, and John would see him in the morning. John's the kind of doctor we used to have, this sweet, smart, practical man who one day ran screaming from private practice, which is when Jack and I were consigned to Soviet Medicine.

Jack was—John assured me—going to be fine.

And Jack was fine, aside from the headlamp-shaped bruise on the side of his upper leg that turned a lurid and melodramatic purple, then shades of brown and sickly yellow that eventually melted greenishly down his leg from thigh to knee to calf to foot where it somehow evaporated back into the dust-unto-dust, demonstrating that even the injured tissue in a bruise is a *physical object* and thus susceptible to gravity.

The girl's insurance paid for several months' worth of excellent massages billed as physical therapy and everyone acted exactly as they're supposed to act, in that Green Green Grass of Home that marks the circular kind of storytelling you find in fairytales: the girl was charmed and her car was charmed and we were charmed and no one took anyone to court or needed to hire a lawyer and no one was ever even angry at anybody. Our Berkeley, This Peaceable Kingdom, where everything can be amicably resolved.

And soon enough the accident faded and changed and became a dinner party story in which Jack was hit by a beautiful girl in a white Impala as we walked in a floating world where robed Buddhists moved through the fog like koi.

∞

Jack's reaching out to calmly retrieve the reflector is what immediately occurs to him. Jack wants to pack things up, catalog, alphabetize, set things right, hence his need to quickly knock back a shot or two of Emergency Adrenaline.

My own psyche's different: in any kind of traumatic situation I get really quiet and very, very logical. I abandon any interest in any object that can be replaced, I begin to immediately fictionalize. The story I start writing is often this rhapsodic Third Person Rural thing I began as a young girl reading about places I'd never been.

This necessity of mine to fix on *what might be* reminds me of the global positioning system of our dog, Wayne Thiebaud, who cannot relax on a car ride because he has the profound physical need to remain alert and attentive as he watches out the back window in order to memorize the exact route by which we've come.

I've never met a dog like this before, one who enjoys a car ride but only so he can observe the journey in *vigilant retrospect*. I think it has to do with Wayne Thiebaud's relationship to yearning or The Past—but that's just me again writing my own version of the Green Green Grass of Wales or Wyoming, my thinking he's studying our path so—if we ever do get lost—he can lead Jack and me home.

I read *The Incredible Journey*, I know his species operates by way of extrasensory breadcrumbs but I so sometimes wish the dog could just *relax*. He doesn't sit, will not lie down. When we drove 3,000 miles along

Route 80 moving home from the East two years ago, our dog acted like an interstate trucker on whites: he didn't eat, didn't drink, didn't nap, but stood the entire time, positioned for balance on his long thin well-muscled legs. He's quite a feminine dog, almost delicate, and while balletic, hasn't the heft and meat you'd expect from the dog version of Mikhail Baryshnikov.

Thiebaud is part greyhound—and we don't call him Wayne, very obviously, because of the serial killer connotations—and resembles a ballerina on point, all black except for his dipped-in-white-satin-finish toe-shoes. Ours is an almost too-tall dog to stand in an ordinary car so he has to lower his head to look back like a sight hound. He'd probably prefer better animal transport, horse or cattle trailer with a half door so he could commune with folks in the car traveling behind us.

The How Green Was My Valley thing harkens back to a converted barn we kept in West Virginia—this is where Jack and I rescued Wayne Thiebaud from the Morgan County Animal Shelter where our dog was poised standing on the chicken wire fence, waiting for us as if he was sure we'd come. Thiebaud and I are just *really* attentive in this way, we just have to memorize every particle contained within every mica-like bit embedded in the surface of the roadbed.

It's our job.

∞

So when Jack and I were hit by a car in a crosswalk a second time and I began to immediately write my Green Green Grass of Wherever even as I flew, it's because no one in his or her right mind would want to experience the actual reality to which I—who did not lose consciousness—was suddenly really carefully attending.

The car presented as a quiet moving wall of metal, it hadn't braked, slowed, honked, swerved, hadn't acknowledged Jack and me in this incident, which is known in legal/medical circles as the Vehicle vs. Pedestrian.

We were about ten paces into the crosswalk at seven o'clock on a clear, cloudless summer's evening when the car plowed directly into us. The car was going between 25 and 30 MPH, it weighed—these are statistics gathered later—2,373 pounds.

It came quietly, out of nowhere, which did feel sinister. What remains most odd about the incident is that it hit both Jack and me completely silently. They say hearing is the last sense to go. It occurred to me that this might be what it was like to die.

〰〰

Jack and I were not actually mowed down by this car as we were mowed upward, were actually scooped up and launched by the force of impact, his body flying away one direction, mine another. We flew—and here comes my Green Green thing—like the myriad winged insects that fly out in every shimmering direction before my older brother's riding mower as he trundles up and down the wide lawn of his river-viewing hillside.

My older brother is the last surviving non-psychotic member of my natal family and so is the person I've known longest on this earth who still might recognize me if we met on the street, and it was Will who recently reminded me that our mother deemed me *conventional,* which I've always found to be her most crushing and effective put-down.

Anyone knowing the first thing about the childhood my brothers and I endured might appreciate the work it's been for me to achieve anything like *conventionality.* To be able to get up in the morning and make one's bed? To own an outfit or two whose parts go together intentionally even if it may look to others like something tattered and cast off, like something that someone with an interventionist spirit—my husband, say, or daughter—will sometimes confiscate from the floor of my closet which serves as my costume shop and walk this bedraggled item down the hall toward the trash saying, That'll be about enough of *that*?

That I own silverware? my own full complement of nesting measuring cups?

That I *got* to eat dinner at the House of Curry on Solano Avenue with my husband on the night of July 30, that I *got* to be mildly annoyed with him as he was in one of his pasha moods, in which he'll order Indian food expansively from all the several columns and categories as if participant in some banquet though there is no possible way two people can eat all this? Nor will we be carrying these fragrant parcels home because Jack will not eat leftovers, which he calls *dead* or *penicillin.*

That I had the luxury of being vexed by his needing always to have New Food? And because he imagines he needs to always eat some kind of organized legitimate *dinner*?

That we got to walk out into that perfect evening in which the sky was an arc of azure, that we got to step into the crosswalk at Curtis and Solano being completely untroubled by any thought more complex than our need to get Wayne Thiebaud out of our car so he could pee against a tree, and did our dog need another walk and would I like to go for a coffee and a gelato?

Shall we try Scoops on Fourth Street? he'd asked to which I was about to say, We'd be fools not to.

That Will and I get to be conventional? That my older brother *gets* to have a wife and daughter, *gets* to live in a renovated farmhouse on a hillside overlooking the Mohawk River, that he *gets* to have a PhD and a wide sloping lawn to mow?

〇〇〇

As I flew one way and Jack another, I remember thinking *And now they've hit us with a car?* then wondering who this *they* is, since I don't actually believe I have any organized enemies. I don't even believe in the construct known as Enemies or The Terrorists or even A Terrorist or why this Terrorist would take any interest in me.

What I know to be the real enemy of any and all of us is plain cold indifference.

So I then became *affronted* by being hit by this car, believing who-ever driving it to be insensitive, thoughtless, rude.

The car had come down Solano following a gradual slope from the hills westward toward the bay. Jack had been walking on the uphill side and had turned to face me as we tackled the gelato question, so he was struck first and harder. I heard nothing, but saw him fly off backwards as if he'd been summarily plucked away. He simply disappeared from my field of vision. So had the car that kept going without ever slowing and I knew immediately, given my hyper-vigillence, that no matter how terrible whatever was happening to me was, what was happening to Jack was likely worse.

I hit the street on one shoulder and upper arm and back, then my head hit immediately, then hit again as I bounced to the other side. The compression of my chest knocked the wind from my lungs. I heard the pained sound as my breath was expelled. I hadn't lost consciousness but I could neither take a breath nor speak.

I'd been struck in my left leg, both above and below the knee, but that leg didn't particularly hurt and was even oddly numb. My toes stung. What hurt most was my chest, my head.

My sunglasses had vanished as had my shoes and I remembered happening to *want* those shoes. My clothes—a skirt and shirt and my year-round all-purpose undergarment which does happen to be a certain lap-swimmer's bathing suit—were in disarray. But that my shoes were gone really hurt my feelings, as they'd been part of my everyday summer uniform for as long as I can remember.

These were wooden thong sandals, fabricated in India, I believe, and I liked their height and weight and the precise clip of footsteps taken in these sandals, which made me sound self-confident. Their leather straps were embossed with a very faint pattern in beige and rust and rose, a subtle pattern of flowers and you'd actually have to look closely to decide these were flowers, which is important as I'm not the kind of person who'd ordinarily go about with an obvious floral pattern on the leather straps of her wooden thongs.

And I, who can barely be bothered to manage my own possessions, only had these sandals because Jack had once brought them home to me, and this is the kind of man I was married to on that summer's evening: someone who would buy shoes for a woman while away on a business trip, shoes that not only fit her but in every way *suited* her.

Nor am I the only woman for whom Jack had a history of successfully buying shoes. He once bought a pair of shoes for every woman in his office, and I can imagine exactly how this came to be: he first noticed a pair of shoes too perfectly Trish for Trish to not own them and as he was making his way toward the register holding the box, he noticed the display that held the perfect Heather ones and right over there were Keltie's.

In, no doubt, one of his pasha moods.

And when our daughter was younger and more unsure he'd take her shopping for clothes, and when she couldn't decide between the two colors of a certain dress, he'd make a little gathering motion with his fingers to tell the clerk to go ahead and wrap one of each.

Doesn't it ever bother you that he orders for you in a restaurant? a friend once asked.

No, I said. Saves me from having to read the menu.

But this *is* the twenty-first century, she said. Have you honestly never heard of the concept called *feminism?* Or is there some *clinical* reason you can't read the menu?

I can read the menu, I told her, witheringly. I just don't particularly *want* to. There're just too many words on a menu and all these B heads and A heads and lists and asides and parenthetical comments and oh my god the illustrations? I get way too involved in the grammar and punctuation. And the hyphens! I added. Home-made? Fresh-squeezed?

She glared at me.

Okay, I said, I admit it, it's actually the adjectives, you have to have noticed how food adjectives go all lurid and purple—juicy? creamy? succulent? I mean, Jesus Christ! It verges on *pornography.*

But she was not amused as she was one of those friends you have who basically don't really *like* you. She disapproved of me. She considered my whole existence a form of gender treason.

Look at it this way, I said. There are so many good things to read that are not a menu.

Have you honestly never ordered something of your *own free will?* she all but yelled.

I can, I said. I totally can if I absolutely have to.

But she knew I was being less than honest, as this was a way-too-elaborate excuse and the truth is usually a simple thing. The truth is plain. It is also something I just didn't happen to want to tell her: Jack didn't order for *me.* Rather he liked to thoughtfully compose the meal he was ordering for *the two of us.*

〇〇〇

This man—who in a pasha mood might buy a young girl the same dress in alternate colors—lay some ways down the street from me across the entire intersection. I knew where he was because I could see where the other crowd was gathering.

As soon as my body came to rest and my head hit once and then again and I was still alert and counting, I understood that I would live. I was conscious, even supersonically conscious, so I quickly realized certain distressing things.

I knew, for instance, that Jack had flown way too far away for this to have its usual storybook ending. I also felt he'd used up some of his Green Grass of Whatever in the incident with the girl in the white Impala, that that in and of itself had required an expenditure of luck.

Jack's always said he is a lucky man. He credits this to chance, he doesn't believe he's earned it. He never, ever, calls it karma, though he is one of those few people who might actually have a glimmering of what the term *karma* might actually mean.

I do not know what karma is, and I will never know, and I therefore never say the word, never allude to my positive or negative parking karma and also try not to make those gacky pseudo-metaphysical statements that always sound self-congratulatory, at base, about how stuff goes around then comes around to substantially reward you, or how you pay something forward, or my least favorite of all, which is Everything Happens for a Reason.

No, I'd say aloud if I were less spiritually tolerant, it actually does not. Encountered any twelve-year-old sex workers in the Philippines? Met an AIDS orphan lately? Been to the circus recently, seen what they've done to the Zulus?

And the term *mantra*? That one's mantra is not whatever trite, cliché-ridden crap one's always habitually saying, as in Amy Winehouse's

"No-No-No" had become my mantra that summer! when no, actually, it isn't, and no, actually, it hadn't.

I recently heard the term *mantra* bizarrely pronounced like the first syllable in the phrase *manhole cover*.

And I get agitated by having these perfectly good terms admitted to the American language only to have them immediately wasted. They're tamed and the first thing we know is they come looping back at us, *baa*-ing and hysterical, as shorn of meaning as sheep on their way to slaughter.

If I had a "mantra," which I do not, it might be *Remember the circus Zulus*, which isn't a mantra but a motto. It might be saying to anyone who insists all of this is well planned out for one's own personal American benefit, Oh, won't you please shut up?

௦௦௦

I'd flown X number of yards, been deposited by an arc of so-and-so many feet from the point of impact that's marked on the Factual Diagram as A. Jack and I are given to describe any unknown numeric quantity as Carry the Nine, after the name of a rock band that doesn't exist but might.

The distance flown by each of the bodies of the trauma couple became an issue later for legal reasons, since the car hit us while we were in an occupied crosswalk but had knocked us way the hell out of this crosswalk, which was then no longer occupied. Among the jobs and duties of the Responding Officer was to pace off distances, chalk the accident, and then map it, all measurements simplified these days in that they're marked with that laser measuring device invented by real estate brokers and called the Lidar.

Had I walked, rolled, inched, or crawled any distance, or was the place I lay in the middle of the intersection at Curtis and Solano more or less the true and accurate placement of where my body had come to rest? This was being asked over my head. In the diagram, my body is named B.

Oh she totally landed right there, Witness One said. I work over there. I had the outside tables so I completely saw it.

In the small town world that is My Berkeley, Witness One turns out to be the friend of a friend of our daughter's, working at Fonda that night, which is the tapas place on that corner.

And there were other confident witnesses, stepping up as competent First Responders, delegating responsibility, identifying themselves aloud by their individual skills, an M.D. in Internal Medicine who quickly checked my vitals. Because I was having trouble breathing, he put his head down on my chest.

Winded, I whispered as his head lay there. He checked my pulse, my pupils, gave my hand a squeeze, then ran down the street toward Jack.

And a social worker—Witness Number Three in the Factual Statement, who announced herself an MSW with clinical experience—said she'd stay by me as others moved the crowd back. Witness Number Three had the kind of gray hair I want, really straight and shiny and silverish. As she reached over me, some strands brushed my arm. She'd just washed her hair and it was still slightly damp.

What hurts? she asked.

Head, I said. Chest, I added. I happen to know the names of the 206 bones in the human body, or I did until I *got hit by a car!*

Sternum, I whispered.

Chest injury, she reported to the cop who came over to us. Leg, shoulder, head.

Toes, I whispered helpfully.

Heart condition? he asked. He was talking over his squawking shoulder to my First Responder. It was immediately apparent that she'd act as my advocate.

Do you have a heart condition? she asked me.

Winded, I said.

She's just winded, she told the cop.

He asked the State of Consciousness questions, but in the pro forma way that meant he wasn't interested in the answers, only that I continued to put the effort into answering. Name? Age? Date? Time of day? He seemed clipped, rushed.

My husband? I asked.

Witness Number Three leaned closer to hear what I was mouthing, then sat up.

She's asking about her husband, she said to the officer. But he'd turned to other items of business, talking to witnesses who were volunteering information on road conditions, lack of skid marks, angle of the sun, how fast the car was going. He had a clipboard.

He turned back to me to ask more questions. Can you hear me? Date? Never mind. Day of week? Can you hear the siren?

My husband, I breathed. Is he conscious?

The cop didn't answer and the social worker couldn't know, but still she said to me, He's fine, he's like you, he's sitting up and talking, and since I was neither fine nor sitting up and talking, I knew she meant well but was lying. Had I been able to speak I'd have told her that in order to be believed you just need to lie less enthusiastically, less grandly.

You're doing a really good job of staying calm, said Witness Three.

Same ambulance, I told her.

I was talking to Witness Three because the cop was multitasking, doing traffic stuff, crowd control, and intermittently asking the same

State of Consciousness questions to stay in touch with me: Name, Date (which I never know anyway), Time of Day (which I can usually make a pretty good stab at), Name of the Asshole President.

She's asking for them to go in the same ambulance, said the woman with the silver hair.

Day of week? the cop evaded.

〰

We needed to ride in the same ambulance because I knew Jack would be more gravely hurt than I and I was worried that if we were triaged separately, I'd never see him again.

I began then to notice other things, that Witness Three had never let go of my hand and that there was another woman now at my feet dangling my own car keys, that she was showing me an opened cell phone, that she was talking past the cops and the just-arriving EMTs.

She was speaking right to me:

I'm going to go get your dog from your car and take him home with me. I've called your daughter. You're going to Highland Hospital. She's on her way already. She'll meet you there.

Wait a minute, I thought. *Do I somehow know you?* And then, *Highland? Why not Alta Bates? I understand Alta Bates. Alta Bates is where I was born. My children were born there too, and Alta Bates is closer.*

Same ambulance, I whispered.

Same ambulance? the woman above me asked the cop again.

Berkeley's here, he was telling someone. Does Berkeley want this? Where's Albany? We're a block from the line. Does Albany want it?

I hear Albany, someone said, they're on the way.

It's Albany's, but Berkeley can easily take it.

Either way—we're one block in.

Can they go in the same ambulance? the social worker said again.

Albany's here, someone said. Albany's got it if they want it.

Same ambulance? the cop above us yelled to someone.

Need to ask down there.

There were four ambulances by then, I'd heard them converge, two each from either town.

Albany's got it. They can do it in one, someone came back to say. We have to load her first so he's first out when we get there.

Got it.

Okay, one ambulance, he said to me. Then the EMTs were there in numbers.

Now we're going to move you, do you understand? You're not to move. We're going to do it for you. This is a neck brace, and this is a backboard, and we're going to roll you onto it, all right? Okay, now on my one-two-*three*.

The social worker was pulling my clothes down, smoothing them. There, she said, you look presentable. She still held one hand. I tried to smile at her.

First out when we get there meant Jack was still alive.

⚉

Jack's theory of the universe doesn't revolve around karma. Rather he believes all this to be an interesting Time/Space occurrence, this three-ring circus, and that it's my own particular circle where the more fun participants tend to congregate, the clowns and kids and animals.

He believes that if there's anyone vaguely madcap or slightly psycho-logically tipped or marginal they'll gravitate my way, this according to some kind of Family-Share Plan or Affinity Grouping or Team Building

Exercise. Maybe it's that I'm used to these types from my childhood and therefore tolerant of them?

My version is that I've just always been pretty good at telling exactly where the story stops being the How Green Was My Valley and begins to turn grim. It's when you get that sinking feeling.

Take the time my friend Diane and I took our kids to the Ringling Bros. and Barnum & Bailey Circus. We'd just paid some astonishing amount of money for this event, way upwards of one or maybe two hundred dollars and had then begun to automatically buy all the kinds of crap kids at circuses need to have, the thirty dollar light saber, for instance, that was done as a bush warrior sword thing because the theme that year was "Africa," but even as we climbed the steps to our seats, these wands had begun to flicker and go dim.

This sucks, Mom, Noah said. What am I supposed to *do* with this?

Got me, Noah, I said. Trade it for the Day-Glo num-chucks?

And as we found our seats each of our children had been equipped with a $7.50 pre-made multicolored sno-cone whose ice was already hard, dry, and stale, and Leah had begun to fuss because she didn't *want* her flavors mixed but mixed was the only way a circus sno-cone came.

I don't want this, Leah said. What I want is a cherry Slurpee from 7-11.

The circus parade was starting—it was all on a Zulu theme. Zebras, elephants, showgirls dressed as Zulus atop elephants, followed by more parading animals, giraffes, giant cats in cages.

And then came scores of Zulu warriors. These were actual *Zulus* in regalia, dusty, barefoot, defeated, all of them up-and-downing listlessly in time to the *om-pa-pa*-ing music, raising and lowering their own bush warrior swords that resembled actual artifacts.

Diane, I said under my breath, those are *Zulus*.

Yup, she said.

Real Zulus, I whispered urgently.

I know, Diane said.

Leah was fussing, Noah'd thrown his light saber thing away. Diane and I were staring straight ahead trying to ignore the two of them.

Is it just me, I said, or do the Zulus seem suicidal?

We waited a minute, then another minute. Leah was still discussing sno-cone vs. Slurpee, Aaron telling her to be quiet because no one was actually listening.

Diane, I asked. Do you think we're going to be able to *do* this?

We waited. A moment or two ticked by.

It was Diane who broke it to the kids: Okay, that's it. Well, *that* was another fun childhood experience. Okay, let's pack it up. Check under your seats. We can get a fifty-dollar cotton candy on our way out and maybe a hundred-dollar hot dog.

BUT WE JUST GOT HERE! our kids started screaming. AND THE CIRCUS HASN'T EVEN STARTED!

Right, Diane said. We're leaving and not one minute too soon.

∭

The circus atmosphere of the storytelling inevitably begins to give way, for me, to the realm of the Harsher Brighter Realities, whereby light begins to leak in under the edge of the tent and the tragic faces of the suicidal Zulus are seen etched in dust and the showgirls dressed as Zulus look like sex workers kidnapped young and sold into slavery and they all seem to be afflicted with leper sores and this wasn't probably *exactly* the theme circus management was looking for.

Real life simply does intrude and when it does I simply notice it: I was being rolled onto the backboard where they strap your arms to your sides and your forehead and thighs to the board, and then your knees and ankles, but the board itself is slender so these extra parts of you seem to fall off on either side unbecomingly, like they accidentally issued you the child's size.

I was on the backboard, my head and neck in braces being hoisted *on-my-three* by several burly firemen, when I saw this woman standing at my feet, looking down at me with a certain intensity. What began immediately to worry me was that she was wringing her hands in a Lady Macbethish way and that her hands were covered in what looked like blood.

I also knew immediately that it was she who'd hit us, and as the driver of the car, it made no sense that she'd be way bloodier than I was, but there you go. She seemed to be what you'd call Older, also a little out of register, in that she wasn't immediately explicable in the way of the sturdy solid EMTs or the take-charge cop and the MD in Internal Medicine or my own personal MSW with the freshly washed silver hair.

This woman was older, for one thing, but she was wearing disturbing hair items, these being these really infantile barrettes, way too spangled and pink to go with her age or race or caste or class or even *species*. These were poodle barrettes, the ones you'd buy for your twelve-year-old at Claire's as a consolation after explaining why today was *not* the day she'd be getting her ears pierced.

And I immediately did not like her, as I was getting possibly karmically involved vibes from her, that she and I were there because Everything Happened for a Reason. According to this version, this would need to *mean* something. According to my usual version of life, there is coincidence, and she and I had simply arrived at this one place and time in this large and often sullen universe and it was there that the paths of our Lines of Action had intersected, which did not mean we were symbolically linked.

But the way she was looking at me made me feel like I was being asked to participate in a Ray Carver story in which she and I were going to furnish one another with some cheap and crappy redemption. She seemed right on the verge of wanting to keen, moan, cry out, loudly remonstrate, and while you do get to largely do whatever you want in this life and say whatever idiotic thing, no one has to listen to it and life actually is *not* a stage. Right that moment was not the time for her to discharge her anxieties, in that Jack and I had problems of our own.

And no one else, I noticed, was being very nice to her, either, not the EMTs nor my personal MSW, who was tidying me up, as if she were an emissary from my Grandmother Vandenburgh who was always telling me to Stand Up Straight, for Gawdssake, and to please, Jane, get your clothes on right!

And the Mental State cop was now speaking to her in his talking-to-a-mental-patient voice, saying, I'm going to need for you to step away, Ma'am. I need for you to go back to where we've asked you to sit. You cannot be here. Do you understand me? Do you need someone to help you get back over there?

But she ignored him so her yearning blue-eyed look was the last thing I saw as I was loaded into the back of the ambulance.

They ratcheted my gurney up and rolled it over to the ambulance, where they slid it in in that really well-engineered, very thought-out way so its legs collapse automatically, folding up like an insect's. Then they moved me way far over to the left facing the back door and began securing the gurney to the frame with belts and loops and flanges, like the LATCH system on kids' car seats. I was shoved right up against the wall, which made it tight, so the EMT who was attending me was hunched and crowded. It was obviously awkward for him as he got oxygen going through a feed and then tried to find my best vein for the IV.

We were crowding against the side to make room for Jack—this space that would remind you of an elevator—and there his gurney was in the open doorway, then it was slid in head first, then ratcheted up to stand at the same height as mine, and here lay my husband, with one arm and shoulder wrong, his glasses gone, forehead open and blood all over his face.

There you are, he said.

Our heads and necks were strapped down and braced, making it hard to turn, but he reached out with one hand as I reached out with mine.

〇〇〇

Does everybody else already know they cut your clothes off in the ambulance? They cut off all your clothes, and you can't negotiate, you can't save your two hundred fifty dollar Christmas shirt by arguing that Jack bought it for you at By Hand on Shattuck right by Chez Panisse, that you've hardly worn it because you still have these few pounds to lose, you can't save your Eileen Fisher skirt that, okay, wasn't all that expensive since you bought it at the outlet store. Or your best everyday bathing suit or your Brown Jesus T-shirt from the Chicano art show at the de Young, sponsored by Cheech Marin.

Jack later said he found the experience of having his clothes cut off *invigorating,* but I have no idea why. It may be because he managed to save his boots.

The EMT was struggling with my IV, a complicated process involving precise needle-piercing-vein in an ambulance that's rocking back and forth, cornering, and starting and stopping because it's on the freeway.

The EMT said the worst was when they had to work on motorcycle riders who have the most gory accidents, gaping wounds, compound fractures, friction burns, loss of vast amounts of blood, and these guys may be way more than half dead but still rouse themselves to beg the ambulance guys to please not cut off their leathers. This is not only because the jackets and pants are so expensive but because a biker doesn't really feel like a true biker unless he's in his colors.

It was that kind of institutional resistance that my husband was up against as he undertook his Save-the-Boots campaign.

His legs and feet were fine, Jack said. If the EMT could just slip these boots off—they were soft, easy to get off—Jack would wiggle his toes to show him. He'd just got these boots, Jack said, which had been handmade for him by a bootmaker named Armando in So-and-So Forth, Texas, for which Jack's feet needed to be measured in something like seventeen places, including width of individual heel and height of right and left instep, all this accomplished by mail order and by intricate phone messages and you don't even pay for the boots until they're done and fitting perfectly. This is the same bootmaker used by Sean Penn and Peter Coyote and Willie Nelson, Jack said, and he'd begun mentioning other famous people, I noticed, that Jack either did or didn't know—Robin Williams, Boz Scaggs—who either did or didn't own boots handmade by Armando.

Jack wanted just two things, well, three: his boots, his cashmere socks, and the medal around his neck. If his EMT could just slip the boots off—great!—and the socks, then unhook the chain and drop the metal down into one boot and put the socks in after it, everything would be safe and Jack would know where to find it later.

The medal Jack wears is a St. Anthony, patron saint of lost things.

⚭

The EMTs explain Shock Trauma to you as the ambulance is arriving, that it may seem chaotic but that's because there will be a lot of people working frantically on you at once to do one simple thing, which is save your life. There are teams who have specific jobs, each in one area of expertise, and they'll be talking over you and won't waste a lot of time explaining things to you.

Jack was going in first. I'd be right behind him. We'd be in the same place. As soon as we got in there, we'd be given something for the pain.

Right, I remember thinking. *Oh, I well imagine, probably a Tic-Tac sized Tylenol with codeine.* What you want in a situation like this is something Heavy Duty. I've had babies naturally and that's right up there at the top of the pain scale. This is misery of a different order. It's simply hard to explain how it feels to hurt so much in so many places.

Shock Trauma seemed to me to be a jolly place, reminded me actually of the cocktail party atmosphere that attended the birth of my first child where all these relaxed people are going about their business calmly, their business being helping you, meanwhile they are talking over your body because you're this project of theirs that they're cheerfully working together on. It feels like it's the afternoon before the prom, they're decorating the gym, and *you're* the gym.

The person in our family who was no doubt suffering the most was our daughter, Eva, who'd arrived at the hospital before we had and had been shown, with her boyfriend, Tyler, to a grim silent private family waiting room, where she was handed a box of Kleenex.

Someone recently receiving terrible news in that waiting room, Eva told us later, had kicked a hole in the wall so fresh the plaster was still lying there.

The only information she had was from the woman on the cell phone, the passerby who'd inexplicably dangled my car keys at me. She called Eva to say we'd been hurt and to tell her where we were going, that she had our dog at her house. She had dogs too and Thiebaud was fine.

Your mother's fully conscious, she said to Eva.

What about Jack? Eva asked.

Well, the woman hedged, maybe not so much. Maybe not fully?

But it was Jack—while semi-conscious or maybe slightly *un*—who had put together the plan. He'd rolled over and asked this woman, one of the first on the scene, to get his cell phone from the pocket of his jeans, saying our daughter would be the first number on Recently Dialed. Then, if she could find his wife's car keys from the big blue bag that read Moon Books—it'd be around there somewhere—and use the transponder on the key ring to unlock our car? Our car was right across the street, Jack said, pointing with his good hand, showing her where Thiebaud was standing watching the entire thing. If she called our daughter, she would come and get him.

Jack had performed these management skills while lapsing in and out of consciousness. I've seen this capacity before. Once, when we were living in the East and he'd just had oral surgery, the nurse followed him out into the waiting room to reiterate the instructions. She also handed me a sheet titled "Aftercare."

He's not to smoke, she said to me. He's on a powerful pain med, no driving, no heavy machinery. He needs to get into bed. The most important decision he gets to make today is which movie he'd like to watch. We've discussed this.

She turned to him. No deal making today, remember? No signing contracts.

This was on K Street in Washington, D.C., where the most politically powerful folks in the world might stagger out of the oral surgeon's and head off, all drugged and omnipotent and woozy, to go make policy.

Jack and I rode down on the elevator, went out to stand on the sidewalk while we waited for the parking valet to bring our car. We were standing in the sun. Jack immediately lit a cigarette.

I can drive, he told me.

Of course you *can* drive, I said, but you sure as hell *aren't going to.*

But you could swing me by the office?

Why would you want to swing by the office?

He paused, considered. He smoked. I can make executive decisions, he told me.

000

Our own Trauma crew chief was a spirited young woman named Dr. Kwan, who had a four-inch ponytail sticking horizontally out the back of her scrub cap. It was her really jaunty attitude that completely cheered me up.

You guys, she said, as she was working over me, shaking her head as if to say *tsk, tsk, tsk.* You pedestrians. You just never win these things.

It was like we were discussing Cal vs. Stanford.

We kinda won, I said. Her car's totaled, for instance.

What was it?

I didn't see it. Someone said some off-brand VW—a Golf or Rabbit? Someone said it looked like she'd hit a deer, then someone else said, Or *two* deer.

You guys did not win this one, Dr. Kwan said. Your husband's elbow and shoulder and face took out her windshield.

But we're not totaled, I said. At least not totally totaled, and her car's not going anyplace anytime very soon.

I really liked her. Her attitude was completely reassuring. I was also cheered that Jack and I were each being given massive amounts of IV Fentanol, a powerful narcotic painkiller and muscle relaxant that doesn't knock you out. You're not supposed to be knocked out if you have a head injury—you need to be as alert as possible in order to tell

Shock Trauma what's currently hurting to help them find whatever secret thing might be quietly killing you.

In Shock Trauma they do that one thing really well: save your life. They don't nurse, don't bandage, don't do wound care, don't cast or stitch, but none of this mattered to me because both Jack and I were alive and fully conscious and on Fentanol.

I had something bad going on in my sternum and on the right side of my abdomen but was jolly because Jack—with his face and head and shoulder and arm all obviously messed up—was just on the other side of some machines and monitors.

After a while they let Eva and Tyler come right into Trauma, a true kindness because Eva really needed to lay eyes on us and see that it was still just me with my hair all which way and hear Jack talking about holding a dead pencil in the dead hand of his dead arm, which turned into Bob Dole's commercial on erectile disfunction.

It just doesn't do any good for people to reassure you that so and so's okay. You don't know what *okay* is, don't even know what the definition of "still alive" might be, or what it means when someone's lapsing in and out of consciousness.

And Eva is our youngest child, the youngest of the four we brought to our marriage, and our only girl, and it was she who needed then to call our three older boys, leaving the terrifying message on all their various voice mails so it was she they were calling back.

The great thing about Fentanol is that it's amazingly effective, and it really needs to be because when you're hit by a car, you manage to hurt almost everywhere. They know this, they're really sympathetic, but they still have to do all these things to you involving manipulating parts of you that may be broken.

Pain of this kind almost immediately becomes abstraction. I'd also already begun my fictionalizing wherein we'd each miraculously bounced and *against all odds* had landed with no broken bones! No internal injuries! A version which, while comforting, didn't happen to be true.

∞

It was CT scans and X-rays and more Fentanol, and no water or anything to drink, and we'd been moved and were waiting in a large bright room commanded by a huge nurse named Hazel, who drank a Mountain Dew right in front of Jack while humming "Getting to Know You" from *The King and I*. When Jack said he too was thirsty, Hazel told him that was how it was and how it was gonna be.

What is this? he asked her. Some kind of Big Nurse type torture?

There's one main difference between us, she said. I happen to work here, and you? You're in the hospital because *you got hit by a car*.

Jack was NPO because they didn't know yet whether he'd need surgery.

I wasn't going to need surgery, I knew. I was completely confident of this and I told Sean, our oldest, when he and his wife, Heida, arrived, that I intended to go home.

Why? he asked. If you stay in here, there's someone to take care of you. There's also that. Sean nodded at the IV pole that held the drip that held the Fentanol.

Yeah, but they don't really take care of you, I said. We're in Observation, where they're observing us. We're not really being treated. *Treated* isn't really what Shock Trauma does. Then you're in Observation, where you're observed. First there's Shock Trauma, I said, where you're not really treated . . .

Right, Sean said. Then comes Observation?

Where you're observed, I agreed.

He and Heida were eyeing one another like, You're getting this?

And where you also are not treated, I went on.

There was one nurse-ish person who might have been cleaning Jack's face and washing the blood out of his hair except that she had her book open and was sitting in the exact center of the room monitoring the monitors. She was also obviously studying for an exam. She once brought me a bedpan. I hated to ask her, hating to interrupt her studies.

Everyone was waiting to get the results of tests, waiting to take MRIs or CT scans or X-rays and then waiting for these to be read. Meanwhile we were observed by Hazel, who called Jack "31" and me "34."

Where's 31? someone would ask.

Out in radiology, Hazel would say. He'll be back in a little while.

Or, Where's 31? We need to get some sutures in.

Then 31 would be back parked across the room diagonally from me, negotiating with Hazel for ice chips. Hazel wasn't gonna budge. He'd settle for a wet washcloth. He wanted to wipe his face, which she guessed was okay as long as he didn't suck on it.

There was the usual workplace banter about who stole someone's *People* magazine. I know, I said. This actually is the kind of triviality I am extremely good at.

You do?

Female, I said. I'm almost certain it was definitely female.

Blonde? she asked. About this tall?

Can't remember, I said. I seem to have lost the detail.

Why should you remember? she asked. You just got *hit by a car!*

And there was some strange form of twenty-four-hour clock that might have been running backwards and then a woman was rolled in on a gurney who was simply drunk and homeless and she was put in a corner with blankets over her and a curtain pulled around her to sleep and nothing was ever said about her again so you thought she might not have even been an official patient.

And 31 was over there trying to get someone to help him clean himself up, and Hazel, who didn't seem to like either of us at first and wouldn't let our kids stay with us because there were too many of them and we talked too much and what did we think this was some kind of fun-type family reunion? eventually warmed to us, especially Jack who gets his way, if not now then in a little while.

When iced tea appeared in the form of a whole plastic pitcher from the cafeteria, it meant 31 was not having surgery, at least not that evening, night, or whatever day this now might be. Jack told Hazel that we were naming our first grandchild after her.

And at two or three in the morning, the cops began arriving with the 5150s, folks in restraints being admitted against their will. First came Beverly, who was white and blonde and had an expensive haircut, whose husband had variously beaten her or thrown her down the stairs and practiced such mental cruelty as to call the cops over some slight disagreement so, as of that moment, she was having nothing more to do with him.

She had what my mother-in-law would call *airs*.

Are you a *Registered* Nurse? she asked Hazel. What's your full name? Write it down for me. I want your badge number. I demand to see my own *physician*. No? Well, when will I be seen by a *medical doctor?*

Could happen, Hazel said, looking at the backwards clock, maybe five-six hours from now?

But I need my *medications*, Beverly said.

And what *medications* might these be? Hazel asked.

The ones my husband flushed down the toilet, Beverly said, then began to enumerate what all she'd been taking, and Hazel listened for a while then drifted off to do something else. She sent an aid to write the list. Beverly knew the PDR by heart, which drug, what shape, which strength, how often, which tint or color, cap or tab, brand or generic. The aid was still writing fifteen minutes later.

She said she takes belladonna, Jack told me later. Do they still even *have* belladonna? What's belladonna good for?

Then, almost immediately on the heels of Beverly came Dante, who'd been 5150ed by his mother. Dante was a twenty-one-year-old African American youth brought in by cops in restraints and whose mother was not his mother but, in fact, a demon, and Dante had been called forth pre-birth from the better place at the right hand of Jesus and was only here to testify in order to save his brother.

Dante didn't want meds. Dante wanted a cigarette.

Hazel wanted him to *take this*, which was an antipsychotic medication that would dissolve upon his tongue.

Don't want it, eh? Dante asked. Don't wanna be all tired out, eh?

That one won't make you sleepy, Beverly called out. That's actually a pretty good one.

Don't want it, Dante said. Need to be my own man, eh? Need to keep my wits about me, think own thoughts, eh? With my own mind?

Your mind's a shithole, Beverly called from my side of the room, and if I were you I'd take as much as you can of *everything* they offer.

Beverly, Hazel said. You are not being *helpful*.

Hazel then leaned over and spoke to Jack, who was washing his face with his washcloth and enjoying his iced tea, also observing the Observation Room like it was about to become our favorite program on HBO.

It's gonna get jiggy in here now, Hazel told him. Then she went to get an orderly so she could move Jack's bed from next to Dante to the space next to mine. Hazel pulled the curtains around the two of us, saying, Okay, we're gonna designate this area The Honeymoon Suite.

Or we could go home? I said.

No you actually can't, she said. You're not ambulatory.

But we *could* be, Jack said.

You can't go home, she said. You have to have your ADLs.

I knew that one. The ADLs, I told Jack, are the Activities of Daily Living.

Dr. Kwan came in some while later.

Guys, I know you want to go home, and here's what I think, she said. Here's what I don't like. Usually when someone's hit by a car and they just wanna go home and crawl into their own bed, it's okay because there's this *other person* to take care of them. In your case your other person was *also* hit by a car.

But we have all these kids, I said, who're grown and who totally *owe* us.

Your call, Dr. Kwan said. She was looking at 31. It was 31 who was more gravely injured. We all knew 31 could *make* an executive decision, but we really needed for this to be the right one.

൜

We had no clothes that hadn't been cut off then stuffed down into white plastic hospital sacks so they gave us paper surgical booties, scrub pants, green paper modesty drapes, hospital gowns, which we wore tied back to front and front to back. We had to dress ourselves to demonstrate that we could perform the ADLs—getting dressed, getting ourselves to the toilet, using the toilet, getting back from the toilet. We were unhooked from the Fentanol so each little movement became an increasing agony.

Hazel approved of none of this. We were not assisted. We needed to prove we could walk out of there so there were no helpful wheelchairs. Hazel had her arms folded across her chest, still skeptically observing.

Eva and Tyler had gone out to bring the car around to the ER entrance.

Jack and I were set to do this. We started out. We got to the doorway, turned right, began to make our way down the crowded hallway by people lying on gurneys waiting for whatever was their next step. A man with his shirt open and blood spurting came dashing past us toward the Trauma Center, as if whoever shot him was still chasing him.

These gowns are really *green*, Jack observed. We look *wrapped*, we look like *Christmas presents*.

Our paper clothes were making this *shush-shush* sound.

Hazel watched us walk, and then she came quickly along to bring us another white plastic bag of our cut-up clothes. She also needed to add her own two cents—I thought it'd be another little scolding, but what she said was this:

You two really are about the cutest trauma couple we've had here in a good long while.

We still needed to make our way along this very well-lit hall and out through an over-populated waiting room to the door where the kids and Eva's car were waiting.

Highland is in East Oakland and its ER was packed that night with people displaying every kind and degree of human misery, but as we walked, folks stopped, looked up, openly gaped at us: the battered, still-bloodied trauma couple still improbably dressed in their hospital clothes, holding hands and, inch-by-inch, escaping.

16
The Gates

THE BEGINNING, as Aristotle tells us, falls *exactly* where its ending starts, so you'd think we'd all somehow be better prepared for it, or at least understand which elements we might expect an ending to contain.

In fact, an ending often comes upon you so unexpectedly as to hold almost nothing but the shock: to realize we really *are* mortal, that the last days are *always* upon us, and to be, therefore, joyful because, bam! there you go, being suddenly mowed down by a ridiculous car being driven by a woman wearing poodle barrettes whose husband has died—as we later discover—and who has either no kids or none who have been by recently to notice she's become a Rescuer, and to deal with it by at least taking away her car keys. The ignominy? To be hit by *a Golf!* about which the reporting office will write, This car was *full* of dogs! But that isn't the ending of this story, because it hasn't happened yet. The ending of the story I am currently engaged with falls somewhat earlier along its narrative arc and is—as things often are—out of chronological order.

It is February of 2005. Jack and I are living in Washington. Our boys are all in the West. Eva's away at college but is coming down by train from Vermont to meet us in New York. This for a four-day weekend in Manhattan that has been very meticulously planned.

The planning for the event, in the larger sense, has been intricate and has transpired over a quarter century. The project artists, Jeanne-Claude and Christo, began working on *The Gates* in 1979, the year before my son, Noah, was born. They always knew *The Gates* had to go up in February, as Jeanne-Claude said, as this is when the foliage in the park appears most dead, its trees most lifeless.

They needed the wet-black to buff to the gray leafless trees so nothing would interfere with their palette, none of that hazy greenish blur of promising early spring. It's always Jeanne-Claude talking, Jeanne-Claude who is explaining these things in that clipped, really annoyed French-seeming way of hers, while Christo is bent over his drawing table, hair in his face, continuing to sketch or paint or draw.

〰

The Ending starts, you realize, when the story you've envisioned suddenly *contains* you, and you and Jack see yourselves as part of the processional that is old and moving and universal, only you're walking along behind the rest of the group. We are walking behind them when I notice that the colors of their clothes—and, by extension, ours—are being used as part of the pattern of brushstroke and smear. Because it's the dead of winter and we are all in dark colors, bundled up on our first cold morning here, and the trunks of trees—as Jeanne-Claude has decreed—are naked bark, pale or darkish browns, with only a thin gray etch of branch or twig.

The Ending has started. It is always surprising to realize it contains what you have not necessarily put into it, which is to say, these matters of chance and coincidence, these meetings in Time and Space that seem to speak of Larger Factors being at work and play.

The date is February 24, two days before the one I've dreaded since I was ten years old, for what is now, so far, five-sixths of my life.

And it has snowed the night before, so the fields and meadows around us are immaculate, an absolutely brilliant white. The two women a few paces in front of us are of almost identical height, the younger one so young she's probably only recently begun to call herself a woman, the other elderly but erect. Their heads are leaning into each other, talking as they walk together beneath one of the gates. One points upward with her black gloved hand and the other sees and nods, and they both turn to make sure we're seeing what they're seeing.

Because these women belong to me: They are my aunt and my daughter, and it's been my aunt's idea to make this trip, to spend four days in New York staying at an excellent hotel that's close enough to the park to get to without a cab ride, which is why we chose the Warwick. She set this trip in motion months before, saying she'd fly into Washington from Salt Lake City, where she lives, one of the staunch Episcopalians who live like an almost hidden sect within the dominant culture, which might remind you of a cult. Salt Lake is where she finished raising her children, divorced my uncle, and embarked on her own career.

She flew into Washington so she could take the train to New York with Jack and me. She loves trains. It was the sound of trains, she told me, that made her feel connected to the world when she was growing up in California, in that you could at least get on a train and end up somewhere.

She's left it to Jack to make the arrangements, as she understands him to be someone at home in the world. Her only requirements are that we have a suite with a common area, that her room have its own bath, and that we get tickets to a couple of Broadway shows. She left the dates to him, as he's the one with the busy schedule.

And this: She wished to walk in Central Park *twice*.

My aunt's arm is resting in the bend of my daughter's elbow, so Jack and I, behind them, take turns pushing the hotel wheelchair. My aunt walks perfectly well, if slowly, but she's had trouble with her balance recently, so, though she doesn't *need* this wheelchair, we bring it along in case. Using it would humiliate her, but *that* humiliation would be preferable to her worrying over slowing down the rest of us.

My aunt, my daughter, all of us are moving against the shimmering blur of orange of the gates in watery reflection. Snowmelt sends wet sheets satining across the path. There are 7503 gates along twenty-three miles of walkways. The sun is so bright now that the new snow is audibly melting, which is why it's flowing from underneath.

They walk carefully, my aunt, who is in her mid-eighties, aided by the springform cane she uses not for support—as she's careful to say—but for stability, and my daughter, who's patient, attentive and kind, though she had no grandmother to teach her this.

The trees are etched like pen scratches. The gates, which are made of a heavy woven fabric, flap in their rigging like flags. People walking by—and the paths are crowded—are respectful, but there is nothing somber about any of it. We are simply all part of the same processional: the light, the dark, the bright or somber, whatever's needed for this sense of pageantry.

My aunt and my daughter are passing beneath one of the gates, which catches a gust of wind, catches, seems to heavily undulate. Three robed monks pass them coming toward us, their robes a somewhat darker but more washed and duller saffron. My aunt turns to make sure we too are missing no part of the spectacle.

Jack? my aunt says as she turns to him. Look, she mouths, I think those are *actual Buddhists.*

∞

Late afternoon, back in our suite, I reading aloud from a pamphlet called "Factual Errors" to anyone who will listen. Actually, no one is listening, as Jack's in our bedroom on a business call and my aunt's in her own room, resting before dinner.

My only audience is Eva and Lou. Lou is my aunt's oldest grandson, so these two are the children of first cousins, which makes them either second cousins or maybe thirds, or maybe they're once removed, or maybe Lou's my own second cousin? My aunt can do this, what I think of as deep and institutional memory that used to serve some sort of function but that's now completely outmoded. It has to do with *one's lineage*, about which no one, anymore *cares.*

I'm reading aloud, but Lou and Eva, who know each other only slightly, are having their own conversation. They're about the same age and in the same year in school. She's in theater at Castleton, which is a small state college near Rutland, and she's telling him why she loves it. Lou's at Bard and he's telling her why he hates it.

No really, this is interesting. Listen to this, I instruct them, it's almost even *philosophically* important. Listen, I tell them, and begin to read out, This statement contains six factual errors.

And you might want to take notes I say—a quiz may be given, look. You'll want to receive full credit.

No, Eva says.

No, what?

I won't participate, Eva says. She says to Lou, We don't have to participate; my mom just gets like this, you know? And you don't have to play along. It's just more of her fun and games.

You do so have to participate, I say.

Can't make us, Eva says.

I can too, I say. Do you want to, for instance, eat? And Jack's hired a car to take us to the theater. Do you want to ride with us? Or maybe you'd like to try your luck getting a cab.

I rock getting a cab in Manhattan, Eva says to Lou. I so totally can get a cab, any time of night or day—she snaps her fingers—like that.

I know how to take the subway, Lou says.

We can totally rock the subway, she says.

No, I say, I'm the grown-up and I say you're going to participate. Okay, here's the statement that has six factual errors. I read: Christo wrapped some islands in Florida off the coast of Miami in Key Biscayne in pink plastic.

I don't think we had a unit on this yet, my daughter says. Sorry, Ma, she adds; then she yawns, stretches, opens *O* magazine, puts it in front of her face, and starts elaborately turning the pages. My daughter belongs, as she likes to say, to the Church of Oprah.

But I still have *Lou's* attention, I notice. Six factual errors, I say, which are . . . ?

Just ignore her, Eva says from behind her magazine.

That Jeanne-Claude isn't mentioned? Lou asks.

That's one.

That they didn't use pink plastic?

Bingo, I say.

That none of this ever happened? he asks. I mean, what's the empirical evidence? Could have been Photoshopped.

Exactly, I say. It's all right here. That's what this whole little book-let is—*what never happened*—and it's really excruciatingly detailed. Jeanne-Claude lists them. Factual Error Number One is that, and I quote: Jeanne-Claude and Christo never wrapped *any* islands, they *surrounded* the islands. Most journalists do not understand the difference between *wrapping* and *surrounding,* even though they *do* know that England, for instance, while *surrounded* by water it is not *wrapped* in water . . .

Eva is looking over the top of her magazine.

Did you hear it? I ask them. How, in trying *to correct* the factual errors, someone will *always* go ahead and introduce some new ones?

Lou asks, Is it that *England,* strictly speaking, isn't actually *an island,* that it's a geopolitical unit?

Totally!

And that *actually,* he goes on, it's part of the British Isles, which would also include Ireland and Northern Ireland and Wales and Scotland, and that one's called Great Britain and the other is called Ireland?

But *Jeanne-Claude* couldn't be expected to know that, Eva says, since *Jeanne-Claude* is French and the only thing the French know about the English is how much the French detest them.

If no one likes the English, my aunt says, as she emerges from her room, it's their own damn fault. Why, hello, Lou, happy to see you've made it.

No one likes the English, Jack says, as he enters from our room, which feels—because this is a perfect weekend and everyone knows their comedic lines—like stage right. Because, like us, he goes on, they wouldn't stay home and tend to their own business, and so they became imperialists.

My aunt is holding a plastic see-through bladder with a red-tipped spout that seems to be filled with about a quart of urine. Is it time for drinks? she asks, and she walks over and plops whatever this sack is down on the sideboard where I've put the barware.

She and I share a horror at the cost of room service, which may be congenital. While each of us is perfectly happy staying at a nice hotel, we aren't going to be paying a hundred dollars for a couple of cheeseburgers. She won't order from room service at all, while I do it the first night only, ordering all kinds of things, tea and desserts and cheese platters, in order to get the setups, the cups and saucers, creamer and utensils, which I then wash myself and hide from the housekeepers.

Drinks? my aunt says again. Lou, you go get ice. Jack, will you do the honors? Jack is staring at the bladder that my aunt seems to be holding out to him.

Don't tell me you're a wine snob, she says to him. This is a perfectly adequate pinot grigio. You take it out of the box, you see? It costs $14.99 at Target and packs quite wonderfully.

◊◊◊

We have tickets to *Twelve Angry Men*, which the five of us see and is excellent. We come and go in a white stretch limo with colored disco lights and a hip-hop soundtrack that my aunt finds hilarious. We also have tickets for *Rent*, which Jack doesn't want to go to because he has business to do and this is a matinee and, while he's an opera lover, he simply cannot stand musical comedy.

It isn't a comedy, I say. It's actually a musical tragedy. It's actually *La Bohème* set downtown and done in modern garb.

Don't *want to*, Jack says, making his mouth very small. *Please* don't make me.

Why? I say.

Because it has music, story, lyrics. I *hate* that kind of thing. I always hate the *La Bohème* kind of thing set downtown and redone in modern garb by someone not as good as Puccini.

His mouth is very tiny: Please, please don't make me. So he doesn't go and so misses the spectacle of the final act, during which I sit between my aunt and my daughter and we three hold hands, our faces awash, as we weep uncontrollable tears.

〰

Do you think he was actually gay? I ask my aunt. She and I are alone in the room. I mean, *gay* gay.

The kids are out. It's our last evening in New York.

She sips her wine, which she drinks from a stemless wine glass.

Your mother thought not, she finally says.

But what do *you* think? I ask.

My aunt, even in old age, is very beautiful, and her not actually realizing this about herself is a piece of what seems now like her almost exaggerated dignity. My mother's dignity looked somewhat wounded, while my aunt's is oddly triumphant. And her looks, her coloring, the structure of her face, so closely echo those of the face of the man I can almost not remember and whose death date is today, a fact that neither of us, for whatever reason, now mentions.

And my aunt—to whom I've become close over the past decade or so—has previously confessed her theory that if she's been silent at times, it is because she is naturally left-handed but—as was the custom then—her teachers made her write with her right. Her late career was in working with developmentally handicapped children, some of whom lay along the autism scale, all of whom were delayed. She believes—as

I do—in the verities of brain science, believes that we now might have known more about what went wrong with Geo and might have been able to do more to help him. She believes that her sense of physical clumsiness lies along the same neural pathways that make her feel verbally maladroit. She simply becomes tongue-tied, she has told me, when feeling what she calls *emotional*.

My mother used the term *emotional* in exactly this same way, as in, Let's not become *all emotional*, as if this were beneath us.

Your father, my aunt says. She stops, she sips. She drinks her wine with ice in it.

People were drawn to him, she says. Oh, I never really understood how these things worked. I wasn't like that, in that people, you know, always wanted to . . . Her voice trails off.

He was charismatic? I ask.

She nods immediately. Like you.

Like me? I think. I am *dumbfounded*. In this part of my family, *no one* ever, for any kind of reason, would offer anyone else a *compliment*.

But she goes on: And it was all kinds of people who loved Johnny, who wanted to be with him, or maybe just wanted to listen to his stories. He was a marvelous storyteller. She stops. I don't know about *gay* gay, she says.

Maybe *gay* gay, I ask, but not *gay* gay gay?

My aunt smiles. Or maybe, she says, he was what we called an *opportunist*.

⚭

Her God, her church, has been—as she's explained to me—her absolute salvation. After Lizzie left for college and my aunt divorced my uncle, she volunteered to work with handicapped children, eventually becoming the assistant director of the center. Then she had another late career that involved going with the church into impoverished Africa; these were the first of the tiny enterprise ventures that gave women of certain villages microloans to start their own home-based industries, a model that has proved so astonishingly successful that its inventor has won the Nobel Prize in economics.

I love my aunt—the dry style of her humor and the sound of her voice, whose cadences rise and fall with the rhythms of the Book of Common Prayer that she forced into my hands when I didn't want it there, that she made me read aloud while I stood next to her in church, and whose language I didn't understand until I was old enough to read Shakespeare.

We do not, of course, know each other very well. I more or less vanished from her life when I left for college, when she was still astonishingly young, a fact that was completely obscured not just from me, but from all of us: She was barely older than a girl—only in her thirties—and suddenly raising seven children.

So now we are almost like new people to each other, and I know she reads my work and admires it, even if she doesn't altogether approve of it.

I'll publish something, and no matter how far off and obscure the journal, someone will find it and—unhelpfully—send it off to her, and I'll get the call from Graham, my oldest cousin, who lives in Hawaii and who is appointed in these instances to deal with me.

Mother read your piece, he says.

So I guess I need to call her? I ask, and it's *exactly* like hearing your name being said over the PA, ordering you to the principal's office because you are in trouble.

I phone her, hem and haw, stumble around about how I'm sorry for angering her, and she cuts me off.

I was not *angry*, she says. I was depressed for *three days!*

〇〇〇

The second time we walk in the park, the two are passing beneath a gate. Beyond them are the leafless trees, the unimaginable white of the snowfields. The gates above them shimmer and flap; they are the color of saffron that lies directly opposite, on the color wheel, the pure blue of the bluest sky you can imagine. This is *azure* and the whole thing feels like a dream or a scene from a movie or a symphony, when you know the thing is almost over and you're going to finally, finally, get to *get out* of here, which shows in the perfectly restful yet upbeat way the parts have begun to come together and this whole vexing experience that is Art is finally ending and we're about to be released from its spell.

When I walk with my aunt, I have to remember to relax and let her hold on to me, rather than to cling to her.

The Ending has already started in that *The Gates* are coming down tomorrow, so they will no longer exist. They are something made to be unmade. We are here together on this day, in celebration of what the Buddhists call impermanence.

The night before, looking at the catalog, I'd asked Jack, Gateless Gates? That's *mu,* isn't it? *Way will open.* That's Buddhist, right? *Way will open,* right? The Gateless Gates?

Mu's a koan, he said, not looking up. *Mu* means *no.*

Mu means *no*? I ask.

It's really complicated, he said.

I thought it meant *Way will open,* I said. I'm always telling people that that's what *mu* means.

Way will open? he asks. *Way will open* isn't something Buddhists say.

〇〇〇

My aunt, if she spoke of these things, which she does not, would call it grace, and it is by grace that we are given this last day in which we will walk in Central Park under a dome of heaven that is this pulsing burning blue.

The color of the sky this day is why we have need of the word *cerulean*.

And this color stands—with the light of my aunt's High Church God behind it—exactly opposite the color saffron, which seems to belong on the metaphysical color wheel where we go to find all the many tints and hues and variations that are in no way satisfied by our saying *orange*, and that seem to belong to my Buddhist husband. These people are something I can never be, which is actual practitioners of faith.

And there is new snow on the ground and the snowmelt leaks across the walkways so they are gleaming, turning silver and mirrorlike, and all this casts the sunlight upward, and there is suddenly light so loud that it seems to drown out shadows, and it is light that lies everywhere and we are alive in it, and almost breathless in our awe of it, and this is what is meant, I know, by the hymn that sings, Light, Oh Light Abounding.

I have been so afraid. I have been so afraid, but I am older now and I am not alone, and it's not that I'm no longer afraid, but that the fear now comes intermittently.

The Gates, which took twenty-four years to erect, are here now for only this moment. It is February 27. The ending is happening, The End is now, and it is final, so we can't even say to one another, by way of solace, Next year in Jerusalem.

I am walking with my aunt. Lou has gone back to school. Jack is behind us, pushing the wheelchair, which, because the day's turned warm, is now heaped with our bags and jackets and then with Eva, who has plopped herself down in it, yelling for Jack to push her. Jack pushes her for a while, then dumps her into a snow bank on purpose, and now she's screaming and throwing snow chunks at him, and her cheeks are aflame with cold and her burnished curly hair is flying, and she picks up to heave what looks like lightweight snow brick, but this flies apart as she hurls it, and we are all dusted with infinite particles of what feels like both beauty and timelessness.

Then she gets up, forms a hard real snowball, and lobs a good one that connects. She screams with laughter and comes around us to crouch down, laughing as she's yelling, Save me! save me! save me! using the bodies of her mother and her really quite aged great-aunt as cover from a snowball counterattack.

Like this, dear, my aunt says to me, as she slips her hand from mine and rearranges our arms, changing hers so it lies lightly on top of mine.

Her skin is delicate, her bones are frail—I keep forgetting it. Dear, she says, you tend to hold my hand too tightly.

She always does that, Eva says. My mom has a grip like a vice.

I do? I ask.

You do, she says, and my aunt nods. Eva adds, You act like everyone's made of helium.

God, I'm sorry! I say. I am *so sorry*. I honestly had *no idea*.

And that is what I'm saying, but what I'm thinking is: *Dear? My aunt called me dear, that she said the word so fondly.*

Acknowledgments

WITH SO MUCH LOVE for my big brother, Hank Vandenburgh, and for my cousins, Douglas Godfrey, Peter Godfrey, Gordon Godfrey, and Carolyn Godfrey Roll.

And profound thanks to those other family members, friends and colleagues who've helped me over the many years it took to write this book: Susan Bobst, Trish Hoard, Alice Powers, Brian Powers, Heida Shoemaker, Jan Wurm, and Eva Zimmerman.

And with particular gratitude to Laura Mazer, whose editing has been an inspired gift to this project.

And to Jack Shoemaker, who does actually know what the word "penultimate" means and means it when he says it.

"Take Me With You" is dedicated to the memory of Carole Lynn Koda, 1947–2006.

For George:
Where there is injury, pardon,
Where there is doubt, faith.

About the Author

JANE VANDENBURGH is the author of two novels, *Failure to Zigzag* and *The Physics of Sunset*. Her fiction and essays have been published in the *New York Times, Boston Globe, Los Angeles Times, Wall Street Journal, Threepenny Review,* and other publications. She lives in Point Richmond, California. Visit her at www.janevandenburgh.com.